AFTER THE END OF HISTORY

AFTER THE END OF HISTORY

American Fiction in the 1990s

Samuel Cohen

◆

University of Iowa Press | Iowa City

University of Iowa Press, Iowa City 52242
Copyright © 2009 by the University of Iowa Press
www.uiowapress.org
Printed in the United States of America

Design by April Leidig-Higgins

The University of Iowa Press is a member of Green
Press Initiative and is committed to preserving
natural resources.

Printed on acid-free paper

Library of Congress Cataloging-in-Publication Data
Cohen, Samuel S.
After the end of history: American fiction in the
1990s/by Samuel Cohen.
p.   cm.
Includes bibliographical references and index.
ISBN-13: 978-1-58729-815-8 (cloth)
ISBN-10: 1-58729-815-5 (cloth)
1. American fiction—20th century—History and
criticism.   2. Literature and history—United
States—History—20th century.   I. Title.
PS379.C58   2009
813'.5409—dc22
2009006881

To Kristin

CONTENTS

CONTENTS

ACKNOWLEDGMENTS

The history of *After the End of History* is the history of all the help I've been given over the years. The people who have taught me, supported me, and responded to my work are responsible for anything of value in this book. Any faults in it are mine alone.

The Ph.D. program in English at the Graduate Center of the City University of New York gave me the opportunity to learn from and with an outstanding group of scholars and friends: Luke Menand, who still teaches me something every time I read him; Morris Dickstein, Nancy K. Miller, and John Brenkman; and Tom Cerasulo, who has been and remains a reliably rigorous first reader and a great friend.

The English department of the University of Missouri has given me a professional home, leave time to work on the book, and the company of an energizing community of scholars: my senior colleagues, too numerous to mention, who welcomed me and have helped me in ways big and small; Elizabeth Chang, Joanna Hearne, and Donna Strickland, who have read and reread every word of this book (except these) and without whom it would be immeasurably poorer; and Andy Hoberek, who has been supportive of me as a colleague, fellow contemporary Americanist, and friend. I am also especially eager to thank my students for inviting me to deliver part of what is now my final chapter to the department, for challenging me every day, and for Friday morning basketball.

For giving me support and feedback for my work over the years, I have to thank Jack Vernon, John Krafft, Derek Parker Royal, Tim Bewes, Peter Ginna, Evan Brier, Laura Tanenbaum, Daniel Listoe, Michael LeMahieu, John Conley, Michael Pietsch, and especially Khachig Tölölyan.

I owe a lot to Lee Zimmerman and everyone at *Twentieth-*

Century Literature. I am especially indebted to James Berger for his tireless work as the reader of three drafts of my first published article, for his own eye-opening work on Pynchon and on post-apocalypse and for the example he has provided me as a critic and a mentor. An earlier version of my chapter on Pynchon appeared in 48.3 (Fall 2002), a portion of my chapter on Eugenides and Lethem appeared in 53.3 (Fall 2007), and a very small bit of my Morrison chapter appeared in 51.1 (Spring 2005); I am grateful for permission to include revised versions of this material here. I am also grateful to Lynette Felber and *Clio* for their support; a portion of my chapter on O'Brien and Didion appeared in 36.2 (Spring 2007), and I thank them for allowing a revised version to appear here. I also want to thank Steve Scipione, Karen Henry, Joan Feinberg, Amy Gershman, and everyone at Bedford/St. Martin's for their patience when textbooks went (temporarily) unwritten while this book was completed.

I am pleased as all get-out to thank Joe Parsons and everyone at the University of Iowa Press, including Charlotte Wright, Holly Carver, Jim McCoy, Allison Thomas, Karen Copp, my relentless copyeditor, who wishes to go unnamed so I can take all the credit, and the irrepressible John Kerpan, as well as my anonymous readers, who read my work with more care than it always deserved. I want to especially acknowledge the hard work Joe has put into the care and feeding of this new book and its author, both of whom needed it. I hope the book lives up to what he saw in it.

Finally, for their love and support, I want to thank all of my families, especially my parents, Phyllis Romm and Richard Cohen, who taught me to love books and to get angry at newspapers. Most of all, I want to thank my boys, Ben and Henry, for putting up with me and this book, and Kristin, for everything.

INTRODUCTION

The End of History

"I miss it," he says, "the cold war. It gave you
a reason to get up in the morning."
John Updike, *Rabbit at Rest*

We now seem to be less appalled by our knowledge of the Bomb
than we were in the sixties. Perhaps we have simply grown ac-
customed to the idea; or perhaps the end of the Cold War has
eased minds all too ready to welcome such remission. Whether
we are right to feel so complacent is quite another matter.
Frank Kermode, new epilogue to 2000
edition of *The Sense of an Ending*

Is it the end of history?
Thomas Pynchon, *Gravity's Rainbow*

I
n or about September 11, 2001, human character did not change. American character probably did not fundamentally change either. However, the intentional crashing of four commercial airlines—two into the twin towers of New York's World Trade Center, one into the Pentagon, and another, probably destined for the White House, in a field in western Pennsylvania —altered more than daily life. The events of that day were taken by countless cultural commentators to constitute a significant historical moment, in particular the end of an era. As the close of the millennium occasioned retrospective evaluations of the century just ended, many of the responses to the events of September 11 took the form of postmortems on the recent past, most often on the 1990s.

After the End of History looks back on the period whose end is marked by September 11 and reads the historical fiction of that period in the light of the event that marks its beginning—the end of the Cold War. This book argues that the historical turn evident across American culture in the 1990s took particular shape in an explosion of historical novels, many by major figures in American fiction, and that these novels are not only evidence of a general trend toward looking back but also reactions to the triumphalist reception of the end of the Cold War. Against the hailing of the end of history inspired by the Cold War's end, these novels—Thomas Pynchon's *Mason & Dixon* (1997), Philip Roth's *American Pastoral* (1997), Toni Morrison's *Paradise* (1997), Tim O'Brien's *In the Lake of the Woods* (1994), Joan Didion's *The Last Thing He Wanted* (1996), and Don DeLillo's *Underworld* (1997)—construct their own histories, exploring the national past to investigate the process whereby what happened has become history. In other words, these novels don't just do history: they reflect historically on the making of historical narrative, examining how the times in which we live shape the way we understand the past. In doing so, they confirm Linda Hutcheon's late 1980s insight into the particular character of certain contemporary historical novels, which she called "historiographic metafiction" (ix); they also, I will suggest, say something about Hutcheon's conclusions regarding the ability of these fictions to approach truth in their accounts of past events. The appearance of these novels challenges a variety of arguments that the 1990s saw the "end of history"—not just Francis Fukuyama's on the end of ideological struggle, but also Fredric Jameson's on the impossibility of postmodern historical understanding, as well as Walter Benn Michaels's on the replacement of historicism with identitarianism. In looking at the ways in which the national past has been and continues to be narrated, these novels reconnect the past to the present and—as I argue in my final chapter, which reads two post-9/11 novels, Jeffrey Eugenides's *Middlesex* (2002) and Jonathan Lethem's *The Fortress of Solitude* (2003)—also connect the past to a future whose tenuousness places it at the center of the contemporary American historical imagination.

When seen as bracketed on one side by the end of the Cold War and on the other by the terrorist attack and subsequently declared "war on terrorism"—by the fall of the Wall and the fall of the Towers—the 1990s begins to look like an interwar decade. While the Cold War went out with a kind of whimper, it did so only after decades of violence around the world and the long-felt threat of attack on America itself and a ratcheting back up of bipolar rhetoric under Reagan. The fall of the Wall in 1989 and the dissolution of the Soviet Union in 1991, then, signaled the end to a time of great actual violence in the world and great potential violence to America. The Gulf War, while it caused great destruction in Iraq, was, in fact if not in perception, about oil, not ideological struggle, and it took place half a world away. There was no felt threat of harm to American soil as during the Cold War. While fear of the bomb was not in the latter decades of the Cold War what it had been in the 1950s and 1960s, in the days of "duck and cover" and the Cuban missile crisis, there was still great anxiety in the 1980s over the arms race and tensions between the superpowers (as events in Nicaragua showed) as well as over who else had the bomb or was trying to get it. The years after the Cold War did not provide sources for the same level of anxiety.

This difference between the levels of anxiety in Cold War and post–Cold War America explains what was perhaps one of the greatest shocks of September 11—not its suddenness, or even its scale, but its location. As John Lewis Gaddis wrote,

> Except for Pearl Harbor and a few isolated pinpricks like Japanese attempts to start forest fires with incendiary bombs in the Pacific Northwest in 1944 and 1945, or the Mexican guerrilla leader Pancho Villa's raid on Columbus, N.M., in 1916, the United States has suffered no foreign attack on its soil since British troops captured Washington and burned the White House and the Capitol in 1814. ("Setting Right")

And the single-day death toll of the attacks was one of the three largest ever in America, with Antietam and Pearl Harbor, and the largest so overwhelmingly civilian. These were no isolated pinpricks. And they did not take place on a field of battle or a military installation, widening the anxiety; as Gaddis put it in "Setting Right," "Everybody has airplanes, and everything that lies below them must now be considered a potential target."

One result of September 11, then, was the return of the kind of fear and resulting rhetoric that characterized the Cold War.[1] Much of the rhetoric produced in immediate response to the attacks and in the buildup to the war in Afghanistan echoed the language of the Cold War: facing an "evil enemy," it was said, America had to defend "its way of life" in a "war between civilizations" (or, in a telling variation, a war between civilization and the absence thereof). These attitudes, or at least their public expression, had not disappeared from American life since the end of the Cold War, but their expression intensified with the return of the kind of fear felt in America during the Cold War. This fear could be seen in the drop in air travel, in the stock market, in personal spending. It could be seen in the reluctance of private citizens to open their mail for fear of anthrax. Rather than the almost old-fashioned-seeming fear of a nuclear holocaust, the American imagination was teeming instead with threats of jet fuel–filled flying bombs, poisoned letters, and any number of as yet unimagined acts of terrorism. The Arab and Muslim worlds were demonized, leading to acts of verbal and physical violence against Americans of Arab descent and those mistaken for them, widespread government investigation based on ethnicity, and generally a return to the fear-filled yet comfortingly familiar world of us-versus-them. In Marilyn Young's words, "The world that seemed to crumble with the Berlin Wall in 1989 reappeared, a little dusty. Good and Evil, Us and Them, Enemies Everywhere" (12).[2]

This return tells us as much about the post–Cold War 1990s in America as it tells us about America after 9/11. It allows us to see the 1990s as a time between wars, between times characterized by the fear of threat to America, and as a result, as a moment during which it became perhaps more possible for some to recognize and examine the binary orientation such fear encourages and the resulting narrative constructions of the past such orientation makes possible. At least three of these writers—Pynchon, Roth, and Morrison—may have been especially able to look back into history because of the correspondence between the place they were in their lives and careers and the national retrospective moment. These authors were at a point in their lives and work that encouraged retrospection, and so the nation's post–Cold War moment of retrospection coincided with their own. But just as important as the fact that they reached their sixties in the 1990s is the fact that they reached their thirties in the 1960s. Born in the 1930s, before World War II, they lived through the Cold War and were made, artistically and ideologically, by the 1960s, the time at the center of the Cold War and so of the second half of the twentieth century, the moment that the nation looked back on, argued about, and reevaluated in the 1990s. What they and others saw when they looked back was that the issues of the Cold War and 1960s were not unique to the time but were related to issues threaded through all of American history. They saw that the persistence of thinking characterized by difference, division, and exclusion throughout that history was matched only by the continuing reliance on particular narratives to comprehend that history, narratives shaped by ideas of the pastoral, of paradise, and of utopia.

From the beginning of the decade, the importance of the past to the 1990s was clear. This influence could be seen during a ceremony held in Pearl Harbor on December 7, 1991, the fiftieth anniversary of the Japanese attack, when President George Bush put the end of the Cold War into what he saw as its proper context: "Now we stand triumphant," he said, "for a third time this century, this time in the wake of the cold war. As in 1919 and 1945, we face no enemy menacing our security" (Engelhardt, "Victors" 214). The dissolution of the Soviet Union, for Bush, became part of the ongoing story of America's success, notable not just for the resulting absence of threat to America but for the triumph of America.[3] The triumphalist school of American history, emphasizing American victory from the Indian wars on (and eliding moments, such as Vietnam, that prove difficult to incorporate into the narrative), could without difficulty declare the fall of the Wall and the breakup of the USSR a victory for capitalism, democracy, and the American way of life. Two years earlier, as the beginning of the end of the Cold War was already under way, Francis Fukuyama had declared the end of history in a widely discussed article. Fukuyama's claim was not that all international conflict was forever in the past, but rather that, as the champion of a victorious ideology, America too had won: the idea was that "the last systemic rival to Western liberalism, Marxism-Leninism, was dead as a mobilizing ideology. The 'triumph of the West' was complete" (Mills 27).

Contributing to this felt sense of triumph was the soothing of the nuclear anxiety that was so central to the Cold War experience. Nuclear anxiety was not only a phenomenon of the "hot" Cold War. Although it had cooled in the 1970s, the years before the fall of the Berlin Wall and the breakup of the Soviet Union saw its resurgence. There was, Cold War historian Paul Boyer writes, a wave of heightened nuclear fear that gripped the nation during President Ronald Reagan's first term. The nuclear-weapons freeze campaign . . . emerged as the political manifestation of this fear. At the same time, a tidal wave of movies, television programs, rock songs, and science-fiction stories bore witness to the public's renewed obsession with the specter of nuclear holocaust. (*Fallout* xv)

The resurrection of the Soviet threat enacted by Reagan's 1983 "evil empire" speech occasioned the return of nuclear fear. That anxiety did not magically disappear in 1991, as the continued appearance in the 1990s of nuclear disaster scenarios in film, fiction, and video games attests (Boyer and Idsvoog). Nonetheless, it is inarguable that it significantly lessened as a result of the Cold War's end.[4] The fact that so many began to reexamine the past after the end of the Cold War supports the notion that anxiety about the present had decreased. As Boyer wrote in 1998, "As the Cold War recedes further into the past, the moment is opportune for those who lived through all or part of that stressful time to begin seriously the process of historical assessment—not just of the diplomacy of the Cold War, but of its social and cultural ramifications as well" (*Fallout* xi).

While the end of the Cold War meant for some an end to bipolar conflict (and with it the threat of nuclear annihilation) and perhaps the beginning of investigation into its meaning, for others it was a signal to step up the offensive on other fronts. In a 1993 interview, Irving Kristol said, "There is no 'after the Cold War' for me. So far from having ended, my cold war has increased in intensity, as sector after sector of American life has been ruthlessly corrupted by the liberal ethos. . . . Now that the other 'Cold War' is over, the real cold war has begun" (qtd. in Sherry 107). Pat Buchanan described this conflict in his speech to the 1992 Republican convention: "It is about who we are. It is about what we believe. It is about what we stand for as Americans. There is a religious war going on in our country for the soul of America. It is a cultural war, as critical to the kind of nation we will one day be as was the Cold War itself." For Kristol and Buchanan and many others on the right, the end of the Cold War proper was cause for greater vigilance in the war between those who saw themselves as defenders of America's traditional values and those they saw threatening them. As Todd Gitlin puts it:

> The collapse of Communism left America with an enemy crisis. The 1991 Gulf War did, it is true, produce a righteous mobilization, but the yellow-beribboned uproar in behalf of the Desert Storm troops, intense as it was, came and went within months. . . . America the centrifugal was left to itself (or its selves). We fell, and what we fell into was the culture wars. (80)

The end of the Cold War intensified the already begun culture wars. Both had their roots deep in America's past, in narratives born long before either of them. As became clear by the mid-1990s, Kristol's cold war was very much about the American past: as in 1919 and 1945, it held, America was triumphant against an external enemy, but an internal enemy remained, and it threatened America's understanding of itself.

This importance of the past to the 1990s was crystallized in the controversy that arose from another fiftieth anniversary, that of the bombing of Hiroshima. In honor of this anniversary, the Smithsonian Institution planned a 1995 exhibit of the Enola Gay. The original plans for the National Air and Space Museum's showing of the plane that dropped the bomb included material concerning the resulting devastation as well as the fear created by the use of the bomb. Veterans' groups were outraged and began a campaign to pressure the Smithsonian to make its exhibit less critical of the bombing. Patrick Buchanan weighed in on the scholarship behind the exhibit, which he viewed as less than patriotic: "In all this, friends, there is something less benign than the timidity of academics desperate to be seen as politically correct. What is under way is a sleepless campaign to inculcate in American youth a revulsion toward America's past" (qtd. in Boyer, *Fallout* 248). This campaign, for Buchanan, was not first against the state or a set of values, but rather against the past. The unquestioning pride Americans should take in all of America's history, Buchanan was saying, was absent from the hearts of these academics, and in its place was something sinister. Aggressive protection of the past was a way to protect America, for the present and in the future, from any doubts about America's rightness, its justification in using violence, and its continued triumph.

From the anniversaries of Pearl Harbor and Hiroshima, from the end of the Cold War and the fiftieth anniversary of the last World War, from the end of the century and the millennium, the 1990s took on a markedly retrospective quality. Paul Boyer refers specifically to "the retrospective moment of 1995" (*Fallout* xviii), but culture throughout the 1990s exhibited a fascination with history. This turn back to the past could be seen in the rise of the historical documentary, in particular those of Ken Burns, starting with *Civil War* in 1990 through *Baseball* in 1994 to *Jazz* in 2000, which collectively served to institutionalize not only the movement of camera over sepia-toned archival photograph but also the historical inclination of the age. This inclination also could be seen in the popularity of the History Channel, which was launched in 1995, and the A&E series *Biography*, which first aired as a weekly series in 1987 but expanded to five nights a week in 1994; in the number of presidential histories in print and on television; and in the concomitant ubiquity of historians Doris Kearns Goodwin and Michael Beschloss. It could be seen in the attention to World War II in particular in these media, in the growth of historian Stephen Ambrose's work into a cottage industry, in war films such as *Saving Private Ryan* (1998), *The Thin Red Line* (1998), and *Pearl Harbor* (2001). It could be seen in CNN's twenty-four part history of the Cold War, which was proposed by Ted Turner in 1994 and aired in 1998 (CNN). It could be seen in the almost archivally faithful borrowings from past decades in popular music, such as those of Bob Dylan's son, Jakob, whose band, the Wallflowers, recreated the sound of his father's 1970s work with the Band, in decade-specific situation comedies like *That Seventies Show* (1998), and in the miniseries dramatization of the 1960s called, sensibly, *The Sixties* (1999).

While much of the historical attention in the 1990s was paid to the 1940s, due in some part to the various fiftieth anniversaries and in larger part to the sense that the era they inaugurated was now over, and to the Cold War era as a whole, a good deal of this attention was paid to the 1960s in particular. A number of factors contributed to this focus, not least of which was the centrality of the 1960s to the Cold War era, in terms not just of chronology but also of meaning. The protests against the war in Vietnam, the counterculture, the latter years of the civil rights movement and the rise of black nationalism, the women's movement, the violence of assassination and riot—the 1960s challenged what America thought about itself in the Cold War era. Since the end of the 1960s, the meaning of the Cold War, of America, has had to be filtered through the 1960s. The 1970s, of course, witnessed the disillusionment of 1960s hopes, the rollback of many of its political gains, and the beginning of the fall of its stock. Reagan conservatism drove it down further by demonizing the 1960s, preaching a return to a mythical version of the values of the 1950s, to the time before what was seen as the corruption of American social life. The 1990s, then, coming at the end of the Cold War era, at the center of which was the 1960s, was a time for interpreting not just the Cold War but also the 1960s, the Cold War as seen through the 1960s, and the 1960s as seen in the decades following. As Stephen Paul Miller writes, Americans in the 1970s dealt with the 1960s by "ambivalently reconsidering older (ostensibly pre-sixties) organizing mechanisms. . . . [T]he sixties and a naive sense of the fifties, or pre-sixties, [were] reimagined through one another" (30). In subsequent years, the 1960s have continued to be reimagined, against earlier times and in light of the later times through which the decade is seen, in the larger context of the now-ended Cold War and the ongoing course of American history. Highlighted in the 1960s are themes present in the Cold War—the exclusion of the other, internal surveillance, the dream of a unified, homogeneous community safe from attack or infiltration—and present in American history from the start.

The importance of the 1960s to the public life of the 1990s could be seen in the major American events of the latter decade. Beginning in 1991 with Rodney King's beating and the trial of the policemen who delivered it, the hearings on Clarence Thomas's nomination for the Supreme Court and Anita Hill's testimony against him, and the tumult of the Clinton campaign and the past dredged up to be used against him, American public life in the 1990s was centered on events whose interpretation pivoted on themes identified with the 1960s. The issues raised by these very public spectacles included race and gender equality, sexuality, and draft dodging—all of which had been contested in the 1960s. The battles of the 1960s, in other words, were refought at the start of the 1990s. The Clinton reforms of the early years of his first term and the Newt Gingrich–led "Republican Revolution" of 1994 followed this pattern, repeating the struggle between what could be identified as 1960s and 1950s views of society. What America was, what it was supposed to be, and who was and who was not an American were again questions of the day. These questions were asked throughout the decade, as could be seen in the trial of O. J. Simpson, the Oklahoma City bombing, the Million Man March, the attempted impeachment of Clinton, and the protests over the World Trade Organization. One thread running through these disparate events, as well as those of 1991, was the relevance of the 1960s, the recourse made in interpreting contemporary events to events and movements and debates twenty or thirty years old. The place of African Americans in American society, the place of the government in the life of individuals, the place of sexuality in social life, and the place of America in the world are issues with roots in the oldest American themes of paradise and exclusion, and they are at the center of the work of Morrison, Pynchon, Roth, and the other writers who are the subject of this book. Their novels of the mid-1990s do not simply show the importance of the past to the period. Pynchon's insistence on the connections between historical periods across American history in a novel as much about the 1860s and 1960s as the 1760s in which it is set, Roth's framing in the 1990s of a novel set in the 1960s, Morrison's reading of the 1960s through the culture wars of the 1990s, O'Brien's drawing of parallels between Vietnam-era war atrocities and those of the Revolution and the Indian Wars, Didion's connection of mid-1980s American covert activity to its long history of adventurism, DeLillo's tracing of the career of Bomb fear since the 1950s—all demonstrate an attention to the past that is neither antiquarian nor presentist but rather sees the American past's inextricable connections to the present, connections that reactions to the end of the Cold War were so keen on denying.

The study of culture, politics, and history has of late often been reframed in global rather than national terms. Appearing under different rubrics, such as the postnational or the transnational, this global focus has taken many forms. Some working in this area identify nation with nationalism and desire rejection of the nation as exclusionary, while others equate the current and past globalization of corporation and culture with the erasure of difference. In this climate, then, one in which the very idea of the nation is in question, a critical study framed in national terms, as this one is, may appear limited, restricted to arbitrary hegemonic boundaries, even an example of American exceptionalism.[5]

Disciplinary conventions aside, regardless of how we understand or value the idea and fact of nation, we cannot escape its significance either as an idea or as a legal entity. Nationhood is a meaningful historical category, and citizenship is a significant component of daily existence and personal identity. While our lives may be shaped more than we realize by extranational forces and entities, our felt lives, our identifications and disidentifications, are significantly about what Benedict Anderson calls the "imagined community" of nation. Recognizing the cultural, political, demographic, and economic currents that cross borders can enrich our understanding of nation and national culture; it should not preclude attempts to reach that understanding.

The novels that are the focus of this study, at any rate, do not allow us to forget the nation. Each work is explicitly national and so forces us to remember the ongoing importance of the experience and idea of nation to contemporary life. If these novels are exceptionalist, it is because they focus on the particular, peculiar (which is not the same as special, unique, or blessed) historical circumstances of America and the peaks and pitfalls over which that history has passed. As I will argue, none of these novels ignores the darker aspects of American history (just as none claims there have been no bright moments). Each is also aware of the presence in American life of peoples and influences originating elsewhere; in fact, the way America reacts to this presence is central to these novels. The exceptionalism of these writers, if one wants to call it that, takes into account America's founding ideals and its failure to realize them, and it recognizes the strength and fragmentation of its identity.

These novels are not just concerned with nation but are also concerned with history. In fact, of course, the historical novel is, historically, national. The thinking of history in national terms is, for some, a trap from which we need to spring ourselves. Yet we continue to do it, just as our writers continue to think in terms of a national literature.[6] Central to each of these novels is the question of just how, within national borders, we imagine history. This too is a global issue, as the models of history upon which we rely are tied to the global histories of the making and remaking of nations. The historical novel, with its roots in Enlightenment Scotland, thinks nationally because it was born out of the tension between different models of national history. Asserting a national tradition against the imperial vision of progress, Katie Trumpener argues in *Bardic Nationalism*, nationalist models of history such as that found in the historical novels of Sir Walter Scott are motivated by a desire to restore indigenous identification against its erasure by extranational forces. She writes,

> Nationalist accounts . . . place their emphasis very differently, insisting on a notion of cultural tradition left out of the natural and national histories of the mainstream Enlightenment. For the Enlightenment model is evolutionary, emphasizing the inevitability with which each developmental stage, each historical culture, is replaced with the next, the more advanced one. What shapes, destroys, and replaces cultural formations is an apparently impersonal, endlessly recurring social process. The nationalist reworking of this Enlightenment model involves a sustained attempt to challenge its assumptions about inevitability, agency, and progress. When cultures change, nationalists argue, it is often due to the violence of outside forces, rather than any inevitable internal dynamic. (28–29)

The violence of outside forces is, here, global. The history of the nation, told in the historical novel, reminds us of the global context without asking us to forget the nation—in fact, it begs us to remember it.

The novels that are the subject of this study do not follow Scott in reasserting traditional culture against imperial erasure. They do, however, examine their nation's past not just as it happened but as it survives, as it is retold and understood, and so as it shapes the way people live in the present. They ask how American people remember, how they imagine the future unfolding from the past, and how they do these things not only as individuals but also as communities and as a nation made up of communities. An inextricable part of these questions, then, is the question of who these people are, of who is American. Crucial to this last question, to these novels, and to an understanding of American history are the ways in which the idea of America as New Eden has led and continues to lead to an exclusionary orientation not just toward those outside our geographical borders but also toward some within. When these novels examine the drawing of the Mason-Dixon line, as Pynchon's does, or the line that is the hyphen between Jewish and American or African and American, as Roth's and Morrison's do, or the lines between female and male, immigrant and native born, black and white, as Eugenides's and Lethem's do, they do so in the light of this idea. Similarly, when these novels explore the historical paths the nation has taken through wars declared and undeclared and how it has remembered and forgotten the acts committed along the way, as O'Brien's and Didion's do, they do so in the light of the same idea, as it helps shape the way individuals think of the exceptional path the U.S. has been said to be on—and, as constituents of that nation, the way they think of themselves. While it is crucial to think about how attention to the lines nations have drawn around themselves obscures recognition of larger realities, the fact that identities still form within them is inescapable. It is impossible, these novels demonstrate, to think about American identity without looking at the past out of which that identity is formed—and at the way Americans have written the history of that past.

There has long been a tendency in discussions of the novel to emphasize its referentiality, to think about the novel and its history in terms of its representation of reality. This is a temptation for the historical novel—for the obvious reason that the historical novel carries with it the implication of factual historical representation —and so for the historical novels of the 1990s. A number of voices in recent decades have said that the novel generally cannot do what it used to do. Many of the variations on this claim about contemporary literary history base their arguments on contemporary social history, saying that changes in the world have made the novel unable properly to represent it. While this argument (the most influential of which is Fredric Jameson's) has not seemed to bother novelists or readers too much, it has had great impact on the academic study of the novel and so has the potential to color the way academics and critics who pay attention to academics read the novels that are this book's subject. A brief rehearsal of the history of this conversation will help to isolate the main arguments and situate my own approach to reference. It will also bring in the thread of this conversation that pertains specifically to the special brand of reference that focuses on the past.

Literary-historical arguments claiming that the contemporary novel fails to engage reality range from the more literary, beginning from the evidence of contemporary novels, to the more historical, beginning from the evidence of the contemporary world. They end in roughly the same place, though, with the conclusion that while novels used to be able to present the truth about the world, the world has changed so much that they can no longer do so. Among those who early in the postwar period saw the difficulty of representing American reality was Philip Roth himself, who commented on this difficulty in an often-quoted line delivered in 1960 at a Stanford symposium entitled "Writing in America Today": "The American writer in the middle of the twentieth century has his hands full in trying to understand, describe, and then make credible much of American reality. It stupefies, it sickens, it infuriates, and finally it is a kind of embarrassment to one's own meager imagination" (*Reading* 120). Critics such as Ihab Hassan and Leslie Fiedler began to refer to the characteristic features of contemporary fiction, listing the ways in which it was different from the fiction of the first half of the century. Contemporary fiction, they argued, constituted a radical break in its form and content from the fiction that preceded it. They pointed to the fictions of John

Barth, Thomas Pynchon, Kurt Vonnegut, and John Hawkes as examples of the turn away from this stupefying contemporary reality and toward textuality, self-reflexivity, and metafiction. While prewar fiction strove to dive deeply into human consciousness, their argument ran, postwar fiction instead played on the surface of existence, eschewing the depths to skate playfully, ironically, or resignedly above them. This fiction did so, it was argued, either because literary possibility was exhausted, to use Barth's word,[7] or because postwar life was exhausting after Auschwitz and Hiroshima and as the world grew smaller, moved faster, and became more complicated and less comprehensible. There was too little left to do in fiction and too much to understand in the world.

In an interview thirty years after Roth's statement, Don DeLillo said much the same thing: "What's been missing over these past twenty-five years is a sense of a manageable reality" (Lentricchia 48). American reality has changed so rapidly, DeLillo argues, that writers are unable to get any kind of handle on it. After the assassinations of Kennedy and King, after Vietnam and Watergate, the novel would seem to have before it an impossible task. Writers and critics continue today to say what was being said decades earlier: the world is not just too much with us but just *too much*, and our literature reflects this experiential, epistemological surplus. For some of these observer-participants in literary culture, American reality serves as a welcome impetus for artistic inventiveness; Roth and DeLillo certainly see themselves as inspired to do new things to try to capture their changing world. For others, it serves only as a lamentable curb on realism. Both the metafictional funhouses of the 1960s and the minimalist sketches of the 1980s have been read by some as capitulations to the world's complexity, escapes into either amoral play or deadpan domestic dramas, sans drama.[8] Still others lament the failure of contemporary fiction to display realist tendencies but don't buy the connection to changes in American social life. Tom Wolfe is one, and he has made a small industry of his pronouncements against contemporary literary figures who, he feels, have dropped the realist baton. In a complaint he has made as recently as 2000, Wolfe argues that American writers have turned away from the tradition of painting on broad social canvases, as did Dickens and Twain and Dreiser; in this most recent complaint he oddly names John Updike, Norman Mailer, and John Irving as three primary offenders.[9] For him, their failure to be realist is a failure of nerve, or fashion, or politics; it is not the inevitable result of the way things are.

While Wolfe's assertion that contemporary American fiction is not driven by the realist impulse is mistaken, as the novels I read in this book attest, the implicit belief on which the assertion is made—the belief in the continuing availability of the American present as an object for the realist impulse—is not. Of course, it makes sense that he does not find the present so incomprehensible that it cannot be represented: the New Journalism that he championed in the 1960s grappled with the difficulty of representing new and strange phenomena in print and did not just overcome this difficulty but thrived on it. Using the techniques of fiction in nonfiction, and vice versa (witness the subtitle to Mailer's *The Armies of the Night: History as a Novel, The Novel as History* [1968]), these writers covering the cultural dislocations and ruptures of the 1960s enlivened journalistic and fictional prose and in the process implicitly questioned the theoretical validity of an absolute distinction between the two. In his 1973 collection *The New Journalism*, Wolfe displayed the wares of a variety of writers producing similar work and argued in his preface that the New Journalism was picking up the baton dropped by novelists. Nearly thirty years later, he is still arguing the point. What the actual work in the collection shows about its time, however, is not that novelists had stopped being concerned with realism (which, outside of a few experimental writers, was not really the case). What the New Journalism showed, besides the fact that the techniques of fiction were still useful at the time for writing about reality, was that reality was still representable.

Literary theorists have of course made their own arguments against realism, some of which were formulated at the time of the New Journalism and some more recently. In the late 1980s and early 1990s, Jameson made his particularly influential challenge, which grew out of an older Marxism as well as other, younger developments in theory. The general antirealist drift in theory began, of course, as structuralism spread into the study of narrative itself; the work of narratologists such as Gérard Genette (in *Narrative Discourse* [1980]) broke down the workings of reference in narrative, revealing it to be the work of a system of codes. While Genette saw his attempt to delineate the structure of narrative as scientific, Roland Barthes's *S/Z* (1970) more plainly strove to debunk realism by exposing the plurality of meaning behind the pose of single, unified meaning (which makes possible the fiction of direct representation). After Derrida's critique of structuralism (in *Writing and Difference* [1978]), poststructuralism's historically particularized understanding of linguistic structures once thought universal encouraged critiques of realism along historical lines. Poststructuralist ideas led to critiques of representation attentive to the differences between distinct times. As the Frankfurt school and others had debated the merits of modernist literature, arguing over what if any representation (and so criticism) of the modern world it was able to achieve in comparison to that which the realist fiction that preceded it achieved, so a younger cohort of postwar theorists debated the ability of the literature of their own era to mount any kind of representation (and so, again, criticism) of their times, in comparison to that achieved by realist and modernist literature.

Chief among these theorists is Jameson, who fashioned a theory of art as shaped by ideological strategies of containment, thus bearing what he names, in an influential formulation, a political unconscious, and a theory of contemporary culture that he described as postmodern. Postmodernism, which Jameson calls the cultural dominant of our age, is the product or expression of the latest stage of modern societal development, according to Ernst Mandel's three-stage theory of capitalism. Insisting on the existence of some kind of mediation between base and superstructure, against Althusser's rejection of such a relationship, Jameson sees a mediated (if not homologous, à la Lucien Goldmann) relation between early market capitalism, later monopoly capitalism, and present-day multinational capitalism, on one hand, and, respectively, realism, modernism, and postmodernism, on the other.[10] Under the current cultural dominant, Jameson argues, the realism that was already compromised under monopoly capitalism has become un-achievable. It is unachievable because under the cultural logic of late capitalism, the fragmentation of experience has led to the dis-integration of the bourgeois subject, who is then in turn unable to forge a unified understanding of her world. The apprehension of contemporary reality that is lost to realism is thus available, ac-cording to Jameson, only through dialectical interpretation, which can identify repressed content in a text's contradictions. Because global capitalism destroys the links between individual experience and reliable knowledge of the total shape and structure of society, he argues, writers cannot offer in their work any kind of realistic portrait of society, any understanding of the relations of produc-tion, of the present as historically shaped and situated, or of indi-viduals' place in the world system. As a result of our lack of contact with historical reality we produce art that, try as it might with any variety of techniques (hence the experimental, metafictional work often identified as postmodern), can tell us nothing about the world except when read for social information produced as a symptom of our divorce from reality.

Jameson's theoretical understanding of postwar art has provided a touchstone for critics, a name to invoke and a framework to plug into when reading contemporary fiction. This framework, however, has ramifications beyond the contemporary period. Accepting the Jamesonian understanding of postmodernism when reading con-temporary novels like those I read in this book means accepting his broader model of the relationship of literature to reality.

In an early statement of his postmodernism, Jameson writes of the contemporary "disappearance of a sense of history" ("Postmodern-ism" 125).[11] Identifying the modern with newness, with change — with modernization and its concomitant uneven, heterogeneous development — and the postmodern with the completion of mod-ernization and so with a loss of this sense of change because of a homogeneity of development, Jameson argues that the postmodern subject has lost any sense of history. The loss of this most basic of *grands récits*, in Lyotard's phrase, is the fundamental characteristic of the age and is the loss he and other postmodern thinkers must overcome: "It is safest to grasp the concept of the postmodern as

an attempt to think the present historically in an age that has forgotten how to think historically in the first place" (Jameson, *Postmodernism* ix).[12] Attempts by novelists to overcome the loss of a
sense of history are not successful; they are not even encouraging
evidence of a persistent impulse to understand the world. Rather,
they are simply proof of the present futility of this impulse. This
judgment is made not only generally of contemporary fiction but
also specifically of contemporary historical fiction. Jameson's take
on postmodern fiction does not accept the idea that history's being
in some ways lost to us provides fruitful creative or, more importantly, political possibilities for the historical novel. It does not
allow for the possibility that what he calls "postmodern 'fantastic
historiography'" puts us in any contact with historical reality; instead, he argues, this kind of work is "no doubt the symptom of social and historical impotence, of the blocking of possibilities that
leaves little option but the imaginary" (*Postmodernism* 368–69).

Linda Hutcheon, among others, has disagreed with this conclusion, claiming that the "blunt, overt work of historical redescrip-
tion performed by many postmodern texts ought to be viewed as
a complicated narrative strategy and not, as Jameson would hold,
a symptom of an enervated nostalgia" (176). Again, Hutcheon calls
this kind of work "historiographic metafiction" and reads it as able
to confront reality, after a fashion, though she is not a believer in
reality as a single, graspable entity in the way Jameson (as a Marx-
ist) must be. In contradistinction to Barbara Foley's claims for the
aspirations of what she calls the "documentary novel," Hutcheon
says that postmodern fiction "does not 'aspire to tell the truth' . . .
as much as to question *whose* truth gets told" (123).

Hutcheon is also among those who have written about the connections between the rise of poststructuralist theory and developments in the practice of history as a discipline on the one hand
and the evolution of the historical novel on the other. In addition
to the general poststructuralist questioning of representation and
realism discussed above, the work of Foucault, particularly his
concept of historical epistemes (the structures of thinking that
make certain ideas possible and certain ideas impossible), and the
work of Lyotard, especially in his notion of the postmodern event

(the historical event that history cannot explain), posed challenges to traditional understandings of history. Even before these developments, though, the rise of a number of new approaches to historical study brought a new challenge to notions of traditional, linear, objective accounts of the past. The *Annales* school of history, which had roots earlier in the century in France but became more prominent in the 1960s, deemphasized "great man" history and accounts focusing solely on governments and states and the corresponding use of official documents as historical sources. Instead, these historians argued for and modeled a "new history," a practice that focused on social history, on the kinds of historical sources (such as oral histories recounting the everyday lives of regular people) that could provide information about social history. For many practitioners and champions, especially later ones like Jacques LeGoff, the earlier new history's quest for a method that would provide a total, social scientific account of the past gave way to skepticism about the possibility of a single, objective account of the past. In fact, as Amy Elias and others have noted, this is not just a shared notion among later new historians and poststructural theorists. Elias points to a claim made by LeGoff that sounds an awful lot like Foucault (whom he in fact claimed as an influence): "Historical facts are made and not given, and historical objectivity cannot be reduced to pure subservience to facts" (qtd. in Elias 33).

Another whose work in history offers parallels to both poststructuralism and the contemporary historical novel, Hayden White, in his work on emplotment, develops the idea that all knowledge of the past, all historical writing is in the end not about facts but rather about the construction of narrative. Hutcheon and many others have noted the ways in which White's *Metahistory* and *Tropics of Discourse* describe what the contemporary historical novels Hutcheon calls historiographic metafiction assume—that all we have of the past, we make—that is, all we have are stories. The degree to which the recognition of this situation implies a constructivist take on the nature of reality varies, but the idea that history, the past, is something in some way always lost to us informs much of this thinking.[13] Elias herself, in her recent attempt to bridge the gap between the schools of thought she identifies with Hutcheon on the one hand and Jameson on the other—one school seeing the possibilities of postmodern history-making, the other lamenting the impossibility of historical knowledge—relies on the notion of the historical sublime, of the past as something unknowable and therefore unrepresentable. Elias's "metahistorical romances," like Hutcheon's metafictional historiographies, do not aspire to or believe in telling the truth; but rather than presenting multiple truths, written from multiple points of view, she argues, metahistorical romances "recuperate the sublime as an aestheticization of History"(53)—that is, they don't represent the past, they represent the desire for it.

Jameson's dismissal of the idea that a more accurate understanding of the past is possible in this kind of contemporary historical novel (as well as, it could be argued, Hutcheon's and Elias's own dismissals) is due, in part, to the adherence to his theorization of the development (but not progress) of capitalist society outlined above. It is also due to a commonly used but inaccurate model of Western literary history (across which he maps Mandel's model of capitalist development). This view of the modern career of the Western novel is summarized by John Brenkman:

> The reigning view of the novel tells . . . a tidy little story: in the beginning was realism (naive nineteenth-century representations of vulgar social reality); in the middle was modernism; in the end, postmodernism. Antirealism becomes the defining feature of twentieth-century fiction: modernism supersedes realistic representations with stream-of-consciousness and formalistic rigor, and then postmodernism fractures or deconstructs representation, consciousness, and form. Accordingly, innovation removes the novel even farther from realism. ("Innovation" 810)

The understanding of realism assumed in the narrative Brenkman recounts here is bound to a period- and technique-restricted definition, one that leaves out the role imagination can play in literary explorations of reality. It is also bound to a simplistic narrative of decline, since a movement away from realism can only be, in this narrative, a movement away from an understanding of the determining power of historical forces.

Approaches to contemporary fiction based on a theory that sees imagination as a poor last resort can produce poor readings. We have seen how an insistence on politics as the first basis of judgment can misshape criticism, just as we have seen how an insistence that politics has no place (itself a political stance, of course) can have similar effects. The insistence on social realism in the 1930s and the bias against it following the Left's disenchantment with Stalin are illustrations. The exclusion of Dreiser and other turn-of-the-century American realists and naturalists from the canon by Lionel Trilling and others in favor of what were seen as the more universal romances of Melville and Hawthorne betrayed a discomfort with politics that led critics to ignore a large slice of American writing.[14] As Marx's effect on late Lukács illustrates, reading only for the revolution can make critics ignore things, such as the central importance of imagination to literature.[15] Jameson's version of postmodernism, understanding contemporary culture as part of a dialectic leading teleologically to a resolution of the contradictions inherent under capitalism, leads him to ignore important things, including a crucial lesson literary history teaches us.

The aspect of literary history that Jameson and others do not sufficiently take into account is the fact that the novel, far from only recently having somehow lost the ability to represent reality, has always questioned it. As Bakhtin argued, the novel, the only literary form born in the modern world, has been more of a force than a fixed genre, crossing generic boundaries, swallowing other forms of discourse in its hunger to grow and change as the world grows and changes. In part, this hunger, there from the start, was a hunger to incorporate other forms of discourse. The novel has been a mixture, in different instances and for different theorists, of many things: of account book and spiritual confession for Ian Watt; of history, romance, and news for Michael McKeon; of "biography" (narratives of life history such as the confession or the psychoanalytic case study) and "chronicle" (narratives of collective history such as the epic or genealogy) for Lucien Goldmann (*Towards*). In part, this hunger, before John Barth and even before Laurence Sterne, has turned the novel back on itself. The novel was born a cannibal. From the hints of self-consciousness in pro-tonovels such as the second century's *The Golden Ass* and the six-teenth century's Spanish picaresque to the overt self-exposure of Diderot's *Jacques the Fatalist* (1796), the novel has from its incep-tion devoured itself, questioning its own motives and methods, at times doing so through the use of different genres and forms of discourses, through the use of its own hybridity. This playful exposure of the man behind the curtain first appeared in the same early stages as attempts to hide him through documentary ges-tures, such as pretending to reprint found diaries or letters, as in the work of Richardson and of DeFoe.[16] All this self-questioning ultimately challenged the novel's claim to realism. From birth, the form that has been alleged to hold a mirror up to the world—"a mirror being carried along a highway," Stendhal called the form,[17] while Auerbach called the modernist novel "a mirror for the de-cline of our world"—has turned that mirror back on itself.[18]

This aspect of the history of the novel does more than remind us that postwar writers did not invent metafiction and, therefore, that postwar fiction's peculiarities cannot be so easily explained as a result of the state of the postwar world. It also calls into question the idea that the contemporary novel represents a new stage of lit-erary evolution and highlights the linearity that literary histories based on formal evolution and those based on social history share. Writers such as William Gass and Milan Kundera have questioned the postmodern explanation of metafiction by arguing against the literary-historical narrative of avant-gardist radical breaks, saying that postwar novelists have not been inventing new forms but rather have returned, cyclically, to these old forms in order to continue to say things about the world. Of the early masters of the form, Kundera has said,

> Sterne and Diderot understood the novel as a great game. They discov-ered the humor of the novelistic form. When I hear learned arguments that the novel has exhausted its possibilities, I have precisely the op-posite feeling: in the course of its history the novel missed many of its possibilities. For example, impulses for the development of the novel hidden in Sterne and Diderot have not been picked up by any succes-sors. (qtd. in Roth, *Shop* 93)

This is not because successors cannot do so; in fact, the statement assumes that they can, but for one reason or another have not. Impulses found in the work of other writers, even other impulses in Sterne and Diderot, have been picked up and incorporated into new works. This recognition of the novel's history of incorporating other forms, of changing in order to relate to an always changing reality, sometimes by returning to old forms, forces us to see that Jameson's view of the contemporary novel's decline—its sudden alleged inability to represent reality—is not only mistaken but is based on a view of the novel that is itself mistaken.

How should we see the novel, then, and particularly the historical novel, in these latter days? In Don DeLillo's 1990 novel *Mao II*, Bill Gray, famous reclusive novelist, claims that terrorists have replaced novelists. In a world that no longer reads, where people are more attuned to the image and more susceptible to the mass appeal, Gray says, novelists can no longer affect the way people see the world. The kidnapping, the bombing, the single violent act repeated over and over on the television news are the novel's successors.

The morning of September 11, 2001, tested Gray's hypothesis. The images of the Towers being hit, burning, and collapsing in gray clouds have become inescapable. They have been burned into the American consciousness, beyond words. A few writers have since questioned the importance of literature, relative to the enormity of the events, and, it seems likely, in response to the power of these images. Part of Gray's argument seems correct. The impact of these attacks on American consciousness does attest to the power of the image and the terrorist. But there is another way to look at the role of the novel in contemporary American culture, and it is one that recognizes the connection between the power of imagination and the ability to understand the world historically—to tell stories about the things that have happened and that continue to happen. For the historical novel, that means to do so not simply in order to offer a play of irreconcilable competing perspectives, as Hutcheon would have it, or to attest to the desire for the knowledge of the sublimely ungraspable past, as Elias would have it, but rather to explore, through imagination and narrative, the connections between the world that is and the world that was and the ways those connections can be missed when the stories know their moral—their ending—before they even begin.

In *From the Civil War to the Apocalypse: Postmodern History and American Fiction*, Timothy Parrish calls the writers of these contemporary historical novels "novelist-historians" and argues that they "write history as a form of fiction" (2). Parrish separates himself from Hutcheon on this point, arguing that her claim that postmodern fiction "demystifies" history implies an acceptance of the generic line between the two. Parrish, on the other hand, believes the novels that are his subject "aspire . . . to the narrative status that was once accorded to history" (6). I agree that Hutcheon sells the power of these novels short, but I also separate myself from Parrish on this point, as I do not believe that the explorations these writers undertake are histories; they are novels and do what straight history, even in its recognition of its narrative nature, cannot. Nor does writing the kinds of novels they write engage them in the explicit call to arms Parrish claims they are making when he says that each of these novels "tell us that history is always a form of social action and as such obligates readers either to accepts its call to action as true or fight its claims" (2). These novels are neither straight histories nor ultimatums issued to readers; to try to be either would be to pretend to an ability to fully understand human experience that is impossible to claim at this late date. Neither, however, do they offer new stories of the past that are as good as any others or stories that express how unknowable the past is. I see them instead as implicitly arguing, through their own performance of it, a return to the familiar stories, a resistance to their conclusions, an insistence on recognizing the deforming shape of certain narratives and on using imagination to redraw the connections those narratives wish to cut.

In the Cold War's wake, the absence of an overarching narrative about history and the role of the United States in the world after the end of the Cold War led to discussions about American history that included voices as different as Fukuyama, Jameson, and Michaels. *After the End of History* argues that the historical novels of the 1990s joined this conversation. In their imaginative recreation and exploration of American history and their restoration of its connections to the contemporary state of the nation, these novels resist a number of strands of the conversation, holding instead that the course of the nation cannot be understood simply as a long victory march, that it cannot be seen as entirely lost to our understanding, that it cannot be said that we are no longer interested in it at all.

Novels such as *Mason & Dixon*, *American Pastoral*, *Paradise*, *In the Lake of the Woods*, *The Last Thing He Wanted*, and *Underworld* are of interest because they reflect a general retrospective turn evident across the culture in the 1990s; but their special significance for this book comes from their explorations of the way our constructions of the past are tied to conceptions of the U.S. as a nation and a people. Reexamining important flashpoints in the nation's past from its early years to the upheavals of the 1960s, these novels respond to the public narratives told about the end of the Cold War by constructing counternarratives tracking the careers of American exceptionalism, triumphalism, and national identity generally through the nation's history. As this book's readings will demonstrate, each of these novels tells a story about the effect of historical forces on the lives of individual characters and on the way they construct their understanding of their personal and national pasts, and each sees this act of construction as deeply shaped by dominant national narratives. This book will also show that taken together, these novels refute a number of importantly wrong statements about contemporary American culture. One of these, again, is Jameson's dismissal of postmodern historical novels as inevitably doomed failures. Another is Fukuyama's statement concerning the end of history. A third is Walter Benn Michaels's negative take, in his *The Shape of the Signifier: 1967 to the End of History*, on the historical character of the contemporary novel, which he calls, following Fukuyama, "the novel at the end of history" (80). This "posthistoricism"—which comes in a variety of flavors in literature and the larger culture, so that Michaels can use it to describe both Morrison's approach to history and Huntington's approach to geopolitics—is the result, for Michaels, of an identitarianism he believes is due in part to the end of the Cold War.

After the End of History also looks at the two post-9/11 novels

Middlesex and *The Fortress of Solitude* in order to examine the ways in which American history and the construction of stories about it continue after the decade defined by history's alleged end. Reading these books against the events of fall 2001 and their aftermath shows that in an America newly anxious about its relationship to the world around it, specific concerns about the nation's future shape the way personal and national history are constructed. A concluding return to the late 1990s and Don DeLillo's *Underworld* makes clear what lies underneath these specific concerns, namely an anxiety over the bomb that has never really disappeared. The recognition that the fear of nuclear apocalypse at the center of the Cold War (and DeLillo's novel about that time) is another thing that did not end with the dissolution of the Soviet Union aids the realization that this same fear can be found just beneath the surface of many Americans' understanding of the events of 9/11—and also beneath the surface of the historical imagination of the 1990s. In connecting stories of the past not only to the present in which they are constructed but also to the uncertain future, these post–Cold War novels show that history does not end—that historical narrative, as it is constructed, received, and revised, continues to shape in very particular ways how Americans see themselves and, so, how they act in the world.

CHAPTER 1

After Enlightenment

Mason & Dixon and the Ampersand

The project of modernity as it was formulated by the philosophers of the Enlightenment in the eighteenth century consists in the relentless development of the objectivating sciences, of the universalistic foundations of morality and law, and of autonomous art. . . . Partisans of the Enlightenment . . . could still entertain the extravagant expectation that the arts and sciences would not merely promote the control of the forces of nature, but also further the understanding of self and world, the progress of morality, justice in social institutions, and even human happiness. Little of this optimism remains to us in the twentieth century. But the problem has remained: . . . should we continue to hold fast to the intentions of the Enlightenment, however fractured they may be, or should we rather relinquish the entire project of modernity?

Jürgen Habermas, "Modernity: An Unfinished Project"

1: The world is all that is the case.
Ludwig Wittgenstein, *Tractatus Logico-Philosophicus*

"Christ, Mason. . . . Where does it end?"
Pynchon, *Mason & Dixon*

The story goes that Thomas Pynchon was heavily involved in the graphic design of his 1997 novel *Mason & Dixon*, inside and out. In particular, he is said to have been involved in the making of the novel's cover (Mxyzptlk). The dust jacket comes in two parts, a paper jacket and a transparent overlay. The paper jacket features the title, in an eighteenth-century–looking typeface, magnified and spread across the front and back. On the front of the transparent overlay are the more legibly sized author name and title running across the top and bottom. It is a distinctive design, but it may also serve a purpose other than marketing. Without making too much of something as (by definition) superficial as cover design, we are given space to think about its significance by the fact of Pynchon's attention to its details. One particular detail that I believe is significant results from the way in which the title is expanded and placed—the ampersand that fills the space between author name and title. In effect, the centrally placed ampersand is magnified to the point that it moves from the background to become the central element, more illustration than typography.

The emphasis on the ampersand is likely no accident, because it points to what I will argue is a central idea in the book, one that is essential to its vision and so, also, to its difference from its author's earlier works. *Mason & Dixon*'s ampersand is more than historically accurate; it expresses the shift in Pynchon's thinking that the novel represents, a shift that is deeply influenced by the novel's historical moment. As he spins a picaresque historical tale in *Mason & Dixon*, Pynchon also tells a new, more hopeful story about America, emphasizing relation, connection, and possibility, a story he would not have told the same way before the end of the Cold War. At the center of this new story is the ampersand.

Mason & Dixon is in many ways a novel about lines. It is the story of Charles Mason and Jeremiah Dixon, astronomer and surveyor, who from 1763 to 1767 were in charge of drawing and blazing the 233-mile latitudinal line dividing the Penns' Pennsylvania and Lord Calvert's Maryland, the line that later came to divide North from South, free states from slave. The novel follows them, in part 1, "Latitudes and Departures," from their meeting in 1760, when they travel to Cape Town to observe the Transit of Venus between the earth and the sun and help determine the Solar Parallax, to Mason's side trip to St. Helena for further measurement, to their return to London, and finally, in part 2, "America," to their acceptance and execution of a commission to chart the disputed southern border of Pennsylvania. The novel ends in part 3, "Last Transit," with their return to England, Dixon's death, and Mason's eventual relocation to America. The tale is told by the Rev. Wicks Cherrycoke, who was a member of the expedition and who has come to stay (and stay and stay) with family on the occasion of Mason's demise in 1786. Mason, as astronomer, and Dixon, as surveyor, are professionally dedicated to the measuring, charting, and drawing of lines. The task that occupies the majority of their time in the novel is to plot and cut an eight-yard-wide line.

But this is only the first and most obvious way in which *Mason & Dixon* is about lines. Pynchon's telling of their story and the story of pre-revolution America contains many kinds of lines, as do the larger contexts within which the story is set. To argue for the ampersand's place as an important figure in the novel, I will first sketch the ways in which the novel is so marked, the ways in which Pynchon understands these stories and their contexts in terms of the metaphor of the line. This metaphor has thus far understandably dominated the novel's reception by reviewers and critics. It is, after all, the word most closely associated with the names of the title characters, in the name given the swath they cut (a name given, interestingly, only long after they created it and never in the novel itself). I will first read *Mason & Dixon* in this way because it has been the dominant reading in the few years since its publication, with good reason, and because it is in relation to Pynchon's use of the line that his use of the ampersand makes sense, and, ultimately, vice versa. The ways in which the ampersand responds to the line, the ways in which connection and possibility answer division and difference, make *Mason & Dixon* something truly new for Pynchon.

Even before the two title characters receive their assignment in the colonies, *Mason & Dixon* is filled with geometry. The first sentence of the novel begins, "Snow-Balls have flown their Arcs" (5). The phrase seems a humorous allusion to the opening of *Gravity's Rainbow* (1973): "A screaming comes across the sky" (3). There is of course a bathetic drop from the latter to the former, or perhaps an ostensible lightening not just of mood but also of stakes. As becomes clear once the book gets rolling though, Pynchon brings the reader past or more exactly through the playful and apparently (mostly) accurate eighteenth-century English of his narrator and other characters, and his almost compulsive punning, to arrive at the serious ideas he explores in the novel.[1] While he is clearly being playful—a mood hardly new for his work—and may be establishing a warmer tone than exists in his earlier work, Pynchon is certainly from the start creating a serious world. It is also, from the start, a geometrical world.

As has been noted by many readers, Pynchon's big novels have all had central geometric figures, which are even referred to in their titles: *V.* (1963) has the chevron, *Gravity's Rainbow* has the parabola, and *Mason & Dixon* has the line. From the arc of the snowball to the Transit of Venus and the Solar Parallax to the equator Mason and Dixon cross in their travels to chart these celestial phenomena, the world of the novel is from its beginning crossed by these straight lines, curved along hemispheres or orbits.

An important aspect of this crisscrossing in the novel is that the lines do not in one sense exist independently of the astronomers and surveyors who chart them and so, in effect, create them. Geometry exists in the abstract, as do laws of gravity and movement; all are assumed to be independent in their own right. However, in their embodiment in concrete particular instances, they depend on people believing in them, understanding them, and applying them. From particular positions and with precision instruments, Mason and Dixon are able not just to chart the movement of heavenly bodies but also to divide the earth by degrees, to establish where every part of the earth is in relation to every other part, but their ability depends in the end on their belief. Their ability, therefore, provides an apt metaphor for their times. In a nascent America, a creation of the Enlightenment, their applications of science to government, of rationality to the wilderness embody the claims of the Age of Reason. While the drawing of the line is on a (literally) mundane level, mere surveying and cutting (as the unhappy, stargazing astronomer Mason sometimes sees it), it depends on a belief in the human ability to domesticate the natural.

One important context for the story of this line, then, is the story of the Enlightenment. Pynchon's telling of it is less celebratory than the traditional version and more nuanced than the usual revision. One way to think about Pynchon's version is, conveniently, in terms of lines. The understanding of the Enlightenment that in the twentieth century came under attack saw the eighteenth century as the time, in Kant's words, of "man's emergence from his self-incurred immaturity," as a time when reason reigned supreme, and when, as a result, civilization built up a great, improving head of steam called progress (54). Fundamental to this story are at least two kinds of lines. First is the line of progress, the inexorably upward-moving line charting intellectual, social, and material improvement. The second kind consists of the lines drawn between concrete things and people. There are the lines of classification and division with which Western science understands the world. These are the lines between the enlightened and the unenlightened, the civilized and the uncivilized, the included and the excluded, and those drawn between abstract ideas—the provable and the unprovable, the rational and the mystical, fact and fiction. The Enlightenment, not just in its intellectual projects— Diderot's *Encyclopédie*, Johnson's dictionary, Linnaeus's taxonomy

—but also in its revolutions, French and American, and its imperial and colonial manifestations, depended on and in fact championed the drawing and maintaining of lines. The upward-tending line of progress, then, depended on the drawing of lines of division. As this kind of "progress" continues to be made, this story of the Enlightenment continues to be told.

Theodor Adorno and Max Horkheimer told a different story in the middle of the last century. In their *Dialectic of Enlightenment*, they argue that what has been called Enlightenment and hailed as progress in fact led to the gas chambers. With roots in Marx and Nietzsche, Adorno and Horkheimer and others in and outside of the Frankfurt School saw the belief in human mastery through reason and attempts to impose it on the universe, or "instrumental reason," as the root of the miseries of their contemporary world, miseries that they could not cite as evidence of progress. As Walter Benjamin (also associated with the Frankfurt School) wrote in his "Theses on the Philosophy of History," "There is no document of civilization which is not at the same time a document of barbarism" (*Illuminations* 256). Earlier, Max Weber had told his own version of this story, noting that the classification of the natural world and organization of the human world, what he called the "rationalization" of the world, in effect "disenchanted" it. By drawing lines across experience, Weber argued, the Enlightenment project of understanding and domesticating the world had the unfortunate effect of robbing it of its magic.

Both versions of this story, the traditional and the revised, are recognizable in *Mason & Dixon*. The question of what to think of these ideas follows closely behind, carried most prominently in the question of what to think of the line, or "visto," but present also in many of the novel's factual and fantastic, tangential and strangely germane subplots, incidents, and mysteries. However this question is raised, at stake ultimately is the value of the drawing of lines and all that this action comes to symbolize in the novel, including not only division and classification of the natural and social worlds but also the rationalization of space and time. A focus on the line as the dominant figure in the novel can lead to a reading of Pynchon as squarely on the side of Adorno,

Horkheimer, and others in condemning the Enlightenment as the cause of many modern ills. This condemnation would square with the readings many have made of *V.* and *Gravity's Rainbow* as depicting worlds disfigured by science and modernity. Reading *Mason & Dixon* only through the figure of the line yields this same reading, as I will show first. Reading it through both the line and the ampersand, however, complicates things. A thorough condemnation of the period in which he sets this novel is not, I will argue, what Pynchon is making.

As Mason and Dixon progress westward in their cutting of the visto, into the unsettled yet not unpopulated frontier and away from the fast-dividing East, the significance of the visto as embodiment of the Enlightenment is raised in stark relief. Among the more direct ways is the opposition of the Chinese *feng shui* expert Captain Zhang, who, upon learning of their project, asks Mason and Dixon, "You two crazy?" He continues,

> Ev'rywhere else on earth, Boundaries follow Nature,—coastlines, ridge-tops, river-banks,—so honoring the Dragon or *Shan* within, from which Land-Scape ever takes its form. To mark a right Line upon the Earth is to inflict upon the Dragon's very Flesh, a sword-slash, a long, perfect scar, impossible for any who live out here the year 'round to see as other than hateful Assault. (542)

Zhang recognizes the brutal, incongruous regularity of the line as an attack on the very nature of things. The Dragon within the earth is dishonored and wounded by the incising of a right line into its flesh, into the living flesh of nature. The Enlightenment roots of the line are here expressly criticized from a non-Western perspective.

Zhang's criticisms go beyond the nature of the line itself to a more pointed indictment of its effects. He asks, "Shall wise Doctors one day write History's assessment of the Good resulting from this Line, *vis-à-vis* the not-so-good? I wonder which list will be longer" (666) and later characterizes the line as a "conduit for Evil" (701). The list enumerating the not-so-good effects of the visto—and of the other lines it comes to represent—can be drawn from many parts of the novel. Lines to which our attention is drawn include those between black and white, which we encounter early in Cape Town, later in the colonies, and in the backs of our minds whenever we remember what the Mason-Dixon line came to divide; the related line between Native Americans and the settlers and colonists who pushed them westward; that between Old World and New, between hoary, tradition-bound Europe and the New Eden of America, which the founding-fathers-to-be and would-be Adams into whom Mason and Dixon run are intent on fixing; the line between those included in this new paradise and those excluded; the line between Elect and Preterite; the line between the empirically known and the possible unknown, what the novel calls the indicative and the subjunctive the former of which they set out from in the form of the governed, measured world of bureaucratic administration and the latter of which they quickly emerge into in the form of talking dogs, amorous mechanical ducks, the eleven lost days created by the switch from the Julian to the Gregorian calendars, the race that lives on the inside of the earth, the ghost of Mason's wife, and many other fantastic yet plausibly presented phenomena; and the line between fact and fiction, history and romance in eighteenth-century terms, a line highlighted by the form of the novel itself, which takes the strands of actual historical events and weaves fiction from them.

Each of these lines can be read as Zhang reads the visto, as conduits for evil. The line between black and white is first examined during Mason and Dixon's stay in the Cape Town home of the Vrooms, where Mason is recruited to impregnate one of the family's slaves to help produce light-skinned stock. It reappears most plainly for them in America, prompting Dixon at one point to say,

> and now here we are again, in another Colony, this time having drawn them a Line between their Slave-Keepers, and their Wage-Payers, as if doom'd to re-encounter thro' the World this public Secret, this shameful Core. . . . Christ Mason . . . Where does it end? No matter where in it we go, shall we find all the World Tyrants and Slaves? America was the one place we should not have found them. (692–93)

Finding all the world tyrants and slaves means uncovering a shameful secret, a concealed truth of the Enlightenment world, namely that freedom is reserved only for some. Even an incipient America, a land soon to proclaim all men equal, hides this truth, and not very well. Near the end of their time in America, Dixon tears the whip from the hand of a slave driver busy beating his property, whom Dixon frees. The act is clearly heroic and is a judgment of the place in which it occurs. This line between black and white is most clearly represented by one significance of the visto (that, because of chronology, can never be made quite explicit within the novel) as the popularly designated divider of Union from Rebel states in the Civil War. The absence from the novel of the name by which the line came to be known underscores this implicit knowledge.

The ill effects of the line drawn between Native Americans and colonists become clear as Mason and Dixon and their party progress westward. But it is not just a phenomenon of the frontier. Long before they stop the line rather than cross the Great Warrior Path—the crossing of which, their new Mohawk companions inform them (through a translator), "would be like putting an earthen Dam across a River"—the presence of natives and the effects of contact are clear. The division of Indian from settler was enforced from the moment of settlement, a fact to which Mason and Dixon's visit to Lancaster alludes (647). They are there to inspect the site on which an Indian massacre occurred the year before; however, as Cherrycoke mentions when explaining why Mason did not go alone as originally intended, Lancaster, the location of more than one Indian fight, is "a Town notorious for Atrocity" (341). Among the more notorious atrocities is the 1676 Indian attack on Lancaster, which took place during Metacom's or King Philip's War. While the hanging of three Indians for the murder of another, converted Indian was the proximate cause of the war (still the most devastating in terms of fatalities as percentage of population in American history), the real cause was the encroachment of the settlers. The attack gained fame in America and especially in Britain from a book published as *The Sovereignty and Goodness of God* (in England, *A True History of the Captivity and Restoration of Mrs. Mary Rowlandson*). A first-person narrative of Rowlandson's captivity, it provides a historical record of Puritan attitudes toward the Indians, including both the missionaries' desire to convert them and the belief of Rowlandson and others that the natives were a race of unredeemable savages. Rowlandson's book helped win the day, and many subsequent years of American history, for her racial attitudes.

Pynchon's allusion, then, is to a long history of American attitudes toward its original inhabitants, attitudes that led to results such as those of Metacom's War, which killed 40 percent of the local Indian population. This line is related, like all the others in this book, to one that many Americans were intent on fixing: the line between themselves and Europe, the Old World and the New. This line appears behind much of the intrigue and paranoia Mason and Dixon encounter on their arrival on America's shores, in the street and in coffee houses—conspiracies and plots they first hear of from Benjamin Franklin, whom they meet in a drugstore running a brisk trade in opium, and then from a Colonel George Washington, between puffs from his hemp pipe. Like the plotting they have encountered and imagined in their earlier travels, these plots depend on division, on nations and factions; this line in particular, though, is one many Americans are soon to draw in indelible ink. The line between America and not-America, that which it will leave behind and that which it will exclude, has, like the line drawn between slave states and free, old roots. Of these shared roots, Tony Tanner writes,

> "North and South" is just one more example of the pernicious binary habit of thought, which Pynchon sees as having been so disastrous for America. He traces it back to the Puritan division—or line of demarcation—between the Elect and the Preterite, the Saved and the Damned, Us and Them. (*American Mystery* 288–89)

The significance of the Revolutionary line, like that of the line between Pennsylvania and Maryland, is one more example of what Tanner rightly identifies as binary thought, a phenomenon Pynchon has spent much time anatomizing elsewhere. Here it is the delineation of a New Eden; everything else is without, unsaved. The line between the elect and the damned preoccupied the Calvinist-descended early settlers, whose anxiety led them in their lay doctrine to work around predestination by sneaking the doctrines of work and faith back in under cover of signs of election. Their profound anxiety found some release, then, in works, faith, close attention to who would receive grace, and attempts to define their earthly version of paradise as open only to those who could call themselves the English, as they referred to themselves. The scrutiny on identity defined by group membership and the defensive stance against the external continue, one hundred years later, to shape attitudes about nation, religion, race, and countless other arenas in which lines of exclusion could be drawn.

The line Mason and Dixon draw, then, shares two things with the line America draws both around itself and against those within its borders it would prefer were without: an inheritance and an essential structure. Also related to the line that defines America is a line that appears and reappears throughout *Mason & Dixon*, a line that also can claim a long descent: that between what Pynchon calls the indicative and the subjunctive. This line is not so much grammatical as metaphysical, though the deep connection of the former to the latter is noted in the borrowing of terms: it distinguishes between what we can say "is" and what "might be." The connection of the American line to this line between what is and what might be — of America's self-definition and differentiation to the line between the known and the possible — is best seen in a passage set, fittingly, during the visit to Lancaster:

> Does Britannia, when she sleeps, dream? Is America her dream? — in which all that cannot pass in the metropolitan Wakefulness is allow'd Expression away in the restless Slumber of these Provinces, and on West-ward, wherever 'tis not yet mapp'd, nor written down, nor ever, by the majority of Mankind, seen, — serving as a very Rubbish-Tip for subjunctive Hopes, for all that *may yet be true*, — Earthly Paradise, Fountain of Youth, Realms of Prester John, Christ's Kingdom, ever behind the sunset, safe till the next Territory to the West be seen and recorded, measur'd and tied in, back into the Net-Work of Points already known, that slowly triangulates its Way into the Continent, changing all from subjunctive to declarative, reducing Possibilities to Simplicities that serve the ends of Governments, — winning away from the realm of the Sacred, its Borderlands one by one, and assuming them unto the bare mortal World that is our home, and our Despair. (345)

America as possibility—as the New World, as the place that allows what Europe cannot—is the dream of the Old World, and like a dream it is not true, but might be. But although it is Britain's dream, America keeps awakening itself, as it turns frontier into settlement into colony, curtailing its possibility, consigning hopes to its rubbish heap. The western frontier was only seemingly boundless. As long as it seemed so, America could be the place where the West in the larger sense could escape the Enlightenment reduction of possibility. When the western frontier's apparent boundlessness was revealed as only ostensible—when lines were measured and laid down across it, disproving its infiniteness—this escape route was cut off. Mason and Dixon run into a number of examples of the subjunctive, both before they begin their line and as they blaze it across the frontier, discovering what would seem impossible and its near simultaneous disappearance or destruction—its absorption into the bare, mortal world. When anything seems possible, the Enlightenment certainties, it seems, reassert themselves.

In their travels, Mason and Dixon come across, among many other unlikely phenomena, a talking dog, a flying mechanical duck with a crush on an unwilling French chef, a giant cheese, the ghost of Mason's late wife, and a race of people living inside the earth. Each of these exceeds the conditions of Enlightenment understanding, as does Mason's experience of the eleven days "lost" when the calendar was switched from the Julian to the Gregorian in the "Schizochronick" (192) year of 1752:

> 'Twas as if this Metropolis of British Reason had been abandon'd to the Occupancy of all that Reason would deny. Malevolent shapes flowing in the Streets. Lanthorns spontaneously going out. Men roaring, as if chang'd to Beasts in the Dark. A Carnival of Fear. Shall I admit it? I thrill'd. I felt that if I ran fast enough, I could gain altitude, and fly. (559–60)

The occupancy of America by all that reason would deny dramatizes its status as the land of possibility. The loss of these phenomena, their eviction, dramatizes the loss of this possibility. Dixon's visit to Hollow Earth makes plain that it is eviction:

"Once the solar parallax is known," they told me, "once the necessary Degrees are measur'd, and the size and weight and shape of the Earth are calculated inescapably at last, all this will vanish. We will have to seek another Space." (741)

Even though we know such a world could not exist, we still feel its impending loss; it is as if the loss of possibility is doubled.

The line between subjunctive and indicative, then, is crucial both to the book's understanding of the Enlightenment—as the demarcation between what the Enlightenment can know and what it cannot and so between what is and is not—and also to its understanding of America, as the demarcation between what America might be and what it can no longer be. The visto Mason and Dixon draw, as it cuts through America, is the vehicle through which the novel encounters the ways America is built on lines, and, more importantly, through which it—and we—are able to think about how America became marked by these old lines when at first it seemed open and unlimited. It was one place we should not have found them. The disenchantment of America, the turning of the New World into just another part of the Old, is the turning of subjunctive into indicative.

The fate of the Indians illustrates this aspect of the line. In the end, the mysteries of their world, while given a reprieve by Mason and Dixon's party, seem surely doomed. Mason and Dixon turn back east, giving up the visto, when they reach the Great Warrior Path, an ancient north-south road reported to have a power that science does not recognize. They learn of the Path from Hugh Crawfford, the white man who accompanies the band of Indians that joins them toward the end of their journey. He tells them that it is sacred and that they will not be allowed to pass. At this point drawing the line becomes fraught with tension. They do not want to stumble upon the Path, but they have only an inexact idea how far they are from it because they do not know its precise location and because, as Crawfford says, "Distance is not the same here, nor is Time" (647). Out in this still unmeasured wilderness, occupied by the Indians with their unenlightened worldview, the impossible is still possible, and the laws of Western science may not apply.

We all feel it Looming, even when we're awake, out there ahead some-place, the way you come to feel a River or Creek ahead, before any-thing else,—sound, sky, vegetation,—may have announced it. Per-haps 'tis the very deep sub-audible Hum of its Traffic that we feel with an equally undiscover'd part of the Sensorium,—does it lie but over the next Ridge? the one after that? We have Mileage Estimates from Rangers and Runners, yet for as long as its Distance from the Post Mark'd West remains unmeasur'd, nor is yet recorded as Fact, may it remain, a-shimmer, among the few final Pages of its Life as Fiction. (650)

As Cherrycoke notes when they reach the Path, the frontier is "the Membrane that divides their [Indians'] Subjunctive World from our number'd and dreamless Indicative" (677). As soon as they come to the Path, as soon as they are able to fix it in latitude and longitude, the dream will be over, it will be Fact. Like the Hollow Earth, it will cease to exist. Again, applying geometry is, in Michael Wood's words, an "imperialist gesture, an administrative onslaught by the numbered on the unimagined" (128). The unimagined, when seen and counted, must by definition cease to exist as such.

As do the Indians, at least the way they were, untouched by the Old World. When the party finally reaches the line, Mason wants to continue, thinking that the Indians who travel the path and live beyond it will not threaten them once they see that they are harmless. Dixon, on the other hand, wants to stop.

They don't want any of thah'? They want to know how to stop this great invisible Thing that comes crawling Straight on over their Lands, devouring all in its Path. . . .

A tree-slaughtering Animal, with no purpose but to continue creat-ing forever a perfect Corridor over the Land. Its teeth of Steel,—its Jaws, Axmen,—its Life's Blood, Disbursement. And what of its inten-tions, beyond killing ev'rything due west of it? do you know? I don't either. (678)

After some disagreement, the line is ended, and the party turns back, but the Indians by whose war parties they are surrounded at the end will not be able to turn back those who sent Mason and Dixon.

The unlimited possibility of America, of the New Eden, the land not just of the free but the equal, will not survive either. As is seen in the novel's frame, Wicks Cherrycoke's 1786 telling of the story of Mason and Dixon, its great promise will not be met. He says, "This Christmastide of 1786, with the War settl'd and the Nation bickering itself into Fragments, wounds bodily and ghostly, great and small, go aching on, not ev'ry one commemorated,—nor, too often, even recounted" (6). After the American Revolution, we see the failure of this promise, and this failure is seen specifically to take the shape of lines. The fragments into which the nation is dividing, the wounds that go aching on existed long before the revolution, as Cherrycoke's story illustrates. Though he is not re-counting the story of the contemporary wounds, the story Cherry-coke does tell clearly applies. The American mania for drawing lines and for thinking them progress is not specific to the 1760s.

Nor is it specific to the eighteenth century. From the retrospec-tive moment of the 1990s, Pynchon is reading not just a historical moment but also all of American history. The drawing of lines that characterizes the birth of the nation is explicitly linked to a more recent time, one hundred years after the time of *Mason & Dixon*. The Civil War was another moment when the various lines divid-ing the country were contested. The racial lines drawn at Amer-ica's birth remained, despite military, legal, and social efforts to erase them, and just as they persisted through Reconstruction and resurfaced in Jim Crow, Pynchon seems to believe, these lines are still evident today. His concern for racial prejudice and systemic discrimination can be seen in his novels, his early short fiction, such as "The Secret Integration" (1964), and even his nonfiction, such as his 1965 essay in the *New York Times Magazine*, "A Journey into the Mind of Watts." We are thus led to ask how the century of *Mason & Dixon*'s writing fits into this pattern of Pynchon's, how in the second half of the twentieth century we see possibility raised and unrealized. How does the tendency to draw lines, the binary habit of thought seen as dominating American history, exist in our time? To address this question, we need to go beyond a reading of *Mason & Dixon* solely as a novel of lines, as a reckoning of the costs of America's addiction to binarism. To get at other ways of thinking and being that *Mason & Dixon* might entertain, we have to focus on the other figure that dominates the novel.

The ampersand is an ancient Roman symbol derived from the ligature or combination into one character of the *e* and *t* in the Latin *et*, meaning *and*. In modern English usage, it continues to serve as shorthand for *and*. Its English name is a corruption of the words English schoolchildren used to recite at the end of the alphabet: "X, Y, Zed, and per se and." The last phrase refers to the ampersand character, which is per se (by itself) the word *and* and which came to be pronounced "ampersand." Modern typefaces have variations on the ampersand in which the original *e* and *t* have become lost. Eighteenth-century typefaces, such as William Caslon's, preserved the distinction between the two letters, linking them only at the end of the second, bottom stroke of the cursive capital *E* and the *t*. The ampersand on the cover of *Mason & Dixon* is Caslon's.

Pynchon's choice of this variation of the character is worth noting because of its symbolic importance to the novel. A character whose meaning is equal to *and*, it is not, however, *and* itself. It is a character that means "and" but that has a physical form and a name that can both be read to express certain ideas of and-ness. The ligature of the two letters expresses combination, connection, while the separate recognizability of the letters in the eighteenth-century version expresses the preservation of distinct identities, of difference. The name, which again literally means that the character itself means "and," conveys both by itselfness and its opposite— because the ampersand is not *and* itself but rather is joined to *and* as signifier to signified, so that when we see it, we think "and." In other words, the name of the ampersand holds the same potentially paradoxical meaning as its form, namely, the simultaneous coexistence of the ideas of distinctness and unity, of difference and individual identity. This meaning is paradoxical, though, only if it is assumed that such a thing is impossible.

As I have tried to show, *Mason & Dixon* can be read as a book about the destructive prevalence of the setting up and maintaining of binary difference in American history. But from the choices made on its cover to the story told on its pages, it is also a book about the possibility of connection, relation, simultaneity; about possibility itself; about the ideas expressed in the character that dominates its cover. A good place to start examining these ideas would be this first expression of them, paying attention not just to the particulars of the character itself but also to the immediate context in which it appears, the title, between the names of the novel's heroes.

The binary created in the title could be said to capture the geometric form of the line, since what is emphasized is the line between the two names, the distinction between the characters. But by using the ampersand rather than the word *and*, Pynchon expresses something else: the connection between these two distinct characters, just like that between the *e* and *t* from which the ampersand derives. The differences between the two men are clear from the start. Mason is a top-flight astronomer from the south of England, a deistic Anglican. Dixon is a surveyor, a Geordie, a Quaker. Temperamentally, they are also quite different: one attuned to mystical possibility, the other a good Enlightenment rationalist; one reserved, one loud and convivial; one a wine man, the other fonder of beer. However, as many reviewers noted, these differences do not drive them apart. Joined by circumstance, they become an instance of "the classic comedy team of straight man and flake" (Boyle); as John Leonard put it, "like *Huckleberry Finn*, like *Ulysses* . . . one of the great novels about male friendship in anybody's literature" ("Crazy Age of Reason" 68).

The relationship between these two is one element of *Mason & Dixon* that makes it new in Pynchon's corpus. It is generally accepted that *V.*, *The Crying of Lot 49* (1966), *Gravity's Rainbow*, and *Vineland* (1984) are not marked by the creation of and attention to fully rounded characters. As one review of *Gravity's Rainbow* put it, "Pynchon doesn't create characters so much as mechanical men to whom a manic comic impulse or vague free-floating anguish can attach itself, often in brilliant streams of consciousness." This reviewer finds the absence of more typically novelistic characters appropriate to the worlds their author creates in his fiction, worlds in which only mechanical men have a place: "In Pynchon's world there is almost no trust, no human nurture, no mutual support, no family life" (Locke 12). This characterization of Pynchon's fictional worlds is also generally accepted: though there is much humor in the novels and much attention to the prevalence of human indecency and unkindness, there is not much warmth. Though some demur, Pynchon's work up until *Mason & Dixon* has been largely seen as relatively cold; in its attention to large ideas, national and international histories of ideas and systems, and in its painting pictures of the world as a place riven by conspiracy or suspicions thereof, his work has had neither the time nor the inclination to present round, sympathetic, engaging characters.[2]

Mason & Dixon has been widely seen to have a warmth lacking in these earlier works, and this perception is due in large part to the way Pynchon draws these two men, separately and together. The stories of their lives before and after their partnership create sympathy for them as individuals; and their story together — stumbling across America, completing a task whose meaning dawns slowly upon them, and supporting each other as it does — creates sympathy for them as a pair. As Michael Wood writes, we see them

> arguing, Anglican against Quaker, mystic against rationalist, and finally discovering that their need and respect for each other, in spite of the frequent acidity of their exchanges and their constant mutual fending off of real intimacies, the drawing of a sort of line between Mason and Dixon, add up to a form of passion, indeed the central passion and care of their lives. (124)

The line between them, the binary expectation set up by the juxtaposition of their names and the difference in their characters, becomes instead a connection, a relationship between two men who still remain distinct.

The possibility of connection across difference, illustrated in the relationship between these two men, is an important subject of *Mason & Dixon*. It is a possibility that applies not just to the main characters but also to America, not just to the line drawn between these two people or any two people but also to the lines drawn between kinds of people, between aspects of experience, between times and places and ideas, between what is and what might be. What Pynchon sees in the relationship between Mason and Dixon, he sees in American history; and what he sees in American history, he sees in the American present: not just the age-old fact of division but also the possibility of something else.

The relationship between Mason and Dixon is important because they connect across their difference. Just as their differences make for the texture of their bickering and, in the end, their friendship, so the division, rather than deserving only condemnation, is valued positively for making the connection possible. For the novel as a whole then, lines are not simply to be condemned. They make possible many things, including the existence of connections across them.

Without lines, we would have a world without difference. And in some ways we are moving closer to such a world all the time. Louis Menand sees *Mason & Dixon* as a novel about colonialism and an adaptation of Pynchon's favorite multidisciplinary metaphor, entropy. He calls the novel an American *Tristes Tropiques* because Pynchon seems to be practicing an anthropology like that of Lévi-Strauss, which Menand says might as well be called "entropology" because it sees history as the process of increasing homogenization through contact (24). Homogenization—a world without lines—is not for Pynchon a victory over division but a defeat of energy, of motion, of change. It is also, in the process by which it occurs, a victory for cruelty.

Seeing the American frontier as Britannia's dream, as the place where it seemed that the impossible might be possible, Pynchon explores the simultaneous opening up and shutting down of possibility that America as frontier came to represent and that the Mason-Dixon line symbolizes. As they travel westward, Mason and Dixon encounter the fantastic possibility of America beyond the New Eden of the New American Adam, the mysterious, mystical world both excluded and in a way created by the Enlightenment. As they encounter it though, the line they blaze into the heart of this frightening and wonderful darkness brings a harmful light. Thus the moment of expansion is at the same time the moment of contraction, when that not normally seen is glimpsed and quickly domesticated. When Pynchon entertains us with tales of the impossible and in so doing laments its loss, he might seem to be resigned to this inevitable process, as we all must be resigned to the final loss of possibility that ends the book, the deaths of its heroes. What happens in the fantastic lives of Mason and Dixon and in the fantastic life of America might seem inevitable, as might the cruelty that sometimes results from America's old binarism.

This sense of the inevitable—that people die, that cultural entropy occurs, that bad things happen to good people for no good reason—is undeniably part of *Mason & Dixon*. And the movement in *Mason & Dixon* beyond what readers of Pynchon over the years have called paranoia or conspiracy certainly contributes to this sense of the inevitable. Rather than a grand conspiracy, there is simply history. Mason and Dixon are not pawns in some great game. Dixon does ask, "Are we being us'd, by Forces invisible?" and "Whom are we working for, Mason?" (73). But this is not a paranoid book. The Jesuits, the trading companies, Captain Zhang, Royalists, many different forces and causes and organizations try to influence history, and while there may be trends, no mysterious master plan is in evidence. As Menand writes of this sentiment in the novel, "This is just the direction human history happens to run" (25).

But Pynchon's paranoia has not been replaced by an equally unknowable, unalterable historical inevitability. In *Mason & Dixon*, Pynchon presents a different sense of history. The old search for the conspirators in Pynchon's work is here, at bottom, explicitly what it was sometimes only implicitly in its earlier incarnations: a search for the answer to the question of the impossible. As is made clear in *V.*, when Weissman deciphers an atmospheric message spelling out Wittgenstein's proposition, "the world is all that is the case," Pynchon is concerned with how we know, with the implications of whether we accept only what we see or are open to more. All the searches for transcendent patterns or forces or impossible things in Pynchon's work ask if indeed the world is all that is the case. This question is asked in *Gravity's Rainbow*—where Roger

Mexico sees no transcendent meaning, while Slothrop is open to anything, becomes Rocketman, and eventually fragments into many possibilities—and in *The Crying of Lot 49*, where Oedipa Maas must decide whether or not, beneath the surface of everyday life, there lives a great conspiracy. In the end the questions go unanswered: *The Crying of Lot 49* ends as the title event, which should reveal all to Oedipa, is about to happen. We cannot know if the world is all that is the case. The implication of this argument, which Pynchon seizes on in *Mason & Dixon*, is that we also cannot rule out other possibilities. And if we cannot rule out other possibilities, we cannot rule out different historical outcomes. Pynchon insists in *Mason & Dixon* on the possibility that other worlds might exist in order to ask if things might have turned out differently, or might still. If this is the way history has happened to run, it does not follow that it has had to. The cruelty that fills history does not always, in every instance, have to happen. Those who try to stop it—as Dixon does when he challenges the slave driver—are not fools. They are simply open to the possibility of what might seem historically impossible.[3]

This is openness not just to difference—to recognizing both the existence of difference and also the possibility of connecting across it—but also to a history that could have turned out differently and can still. Seeing this kind of history in *Mason & Dixon* requires seeing not just the line but what the line makes possible, seeing not just an anatomy of loss but also a celebration of continued possibility.

The course of history runs, in *Mason & Dixon*, up to a present that is multiple. There is the present of the novel's frame, that is, the 1786 from which Cherrycoke looks back and thinks about the lost promise of pre-revolution America. There is also Pynchon's present, about two hundred years later, the implicit frame around Cherrycoke's frame, which is all that has happened since. Thus the retrospective takes on a wider focus, including the Civil War and the postbellum years as well as the turmoil of the 1960s and the years between that turmoil and the time of the novel's publication. All of America's past between then and now, from Lancaster to Gettysburg to Kent State, is part of the story.

The structure of the novel, then, makes possible a way of thinking about America that crosses the lines between eras, making American history a single connected story. It also makes possible a way of thinking about history itself, about its connections and cycles. The picture of history we see in *Mason & Dixon*, like the relation of all the pasts and presents in the line of the novel, is not linear, nor is it progressive. The literary-historical argument implicit in Pynchon's use of forms from the eighteenth-century novel is that the road the novel takes through literary history is not one of progressive innovation but of recyclings, repetitions, adaptations. It is itself ampersandic. The larger historical argument implicit in Pynchon's use of forms is the same. While it seems not to accept the traditional Enlightenment, progressivist model of history, *Mason & Dixon* does not draw a downward line either. It does not tell a story of descent or degradation. The story this novel tells is one of repetition, of repeated moments of potential change, of utopian promise followed by failures to fully realize that promise. Each of these moments is at bottom about changing the ways in which America wants to deal with the lines it has drawn down the middle of itself and around itself, about the promise of constructing difference less divisively. And each of these subsequent failures of possibility—of these moments when the subjunctive is reduced to the indicative—is about the failure to remain open to alternatives, particularly to the alternative of connection.

As Tony Tanner notes, *Mason and Dixon*'s 1760s, the important moments in the Trystero's history in *The Crying of Lot 49*, and the moment in the German Zone in *Gravity's Rainbow* can all be seen as "explosions of change" (*American Mystery* 235).[4] All are times when much seemed possible, when barriers were down, boundaries fluid. The American 1860s and 1960s were also explosions of change. *Mason & Dixon*'s interest in slavery and the Civil War is clear. And while Pynchon's concern with the issues debated in and now identified with the 1960s may not be as evident in *Mason & Dixon* as it is in his earlier works, it is nonetheless at the center of this novel.[5]

Mason & Dixon is the product of Pynchon's continued exploration of the drawing of lines, an exploration apparently motivated in large part by the hopes raised and disappointed by the 1960s. It asks us to see the persistence of this American way of thinking by linking the 1760s, 1860s, and 1960s. What *Mason & Dixon* does not ask us to see, I am arguing, is its inevitability. Unlike Pynchon's earlier works, it accepts neither paranoia nor hopelessness nor unknowability. It does not accept the failure of the 1960s to fully realize its utopian visions. Lines will always be erased and drawn again, but the way America deals with them has changed many times and can continue to do so. It changes when America remembers that history, its history in particular, is not finished. *Mason & Dixon* is the first novel in which Pynchon can look back historically on the decade that raised so many of the issues at the center of his work: the Cold War has ended, the century's end approaches, and the 1960s appears as the decade at the chronological and ideological center of the Cold War era in a way it could not have appeared at the time he wrote *Vineland*. In retrospect, the 1960s have stood as a kind of running historical Rorschach test, with successive decades and different political orientations rereading the 1960s according to their needs.[6] The retrospective stance on the 1960s and on American history as a whole in *Mason & Dixon* is not nostalgic, as in *Vineland*, or merely allusive. This novel is a reminder, in a post–Cold War America grown complacent in its ostensible victory, that history is not over. In the face of the triumphalist 1990s, *Mason & Dixon* insists that history continues, that no telos has been reached, no real war won. As America in the 1990s experienced a national retrospective mood, Pynchon's novel insisted that the past is still tied to the future, and utopias imagined and grasped for in the past can still be imagined and grasped for.

Michael Wood interprets the tension in the novel between indicative and subjunctive in this way: Pynchon is suggesting that what we "miss is not a mystical revelation or an ancient wisdom, and not the grand conspiracy underlying all things, but a sense of 'Human Incompletion'" (129). This incompletion, he argues, is what we need to remember if we wish to avoid the errors and cruelties of American history, the ways of dealing with division that have led to so much that is regrettable in our past. Perhaps we need to remember that there are things we don't know, that what lies on the other side of the line is not inherently worse than what is on our side, that we ought to see America always as frontier, in its most hopeful sense. America as frontier does not have to be the America that acts as if everything is new and what is previously established—ideas, communities—does not matter. America as frontier can simply be America as possibility. What America remembers, when it remembers that it is unfinished, is possibility; what it forgets, when it forgets to see its past and present as continuous and ongoing, is that whatever is, is not inevitable, that the world may not be all that is the case.

This sense of incompletion, of unfinishedness, can keep us open to possibility, a way of thinking represented in *Mason & Dixon* by the imagined world inside the earth. As one resident says,

> And wherever you may stand, given the Convexity, each of you is slightly *pointed away* from everybody else. . . . Here in the Earth Concave, everyone is pointed *at* everyone else,—ev'rybody's axes converge,—forc'd at least thus to acknowledge one another,—an entirely different set of rules for how to behave. (741)

This is also a set of rules for how to think, a way of seeing the world not just in terms of possibility but also in terms of relatedness. If each of us on the Earth Convex, in this Terra Concavan's terms, stands on the outside of an outwardly curving earth and so points slightly away from each other, then we can ignore each other and act accordingly; those on the inside of the inwardly curving Earth Concave are forced to act with others in mind. The former way of thinking and acting is presented in the novel as Mason and Dixon's: the line they draw ignores its effects on the lives they draw it through. By extension, it is an American way of being, an Enlightenment way of being, a Western way of being. The Earth Concave's alternative is thus presented not only as an alternative to American exceptionalism. Acknowledgment of the crossing of lines that is the world's reality, of the world's ampersandic actuality, is wanting everywhere. This acknowledgment is not an unfinished task only for America.

Just as the unending road of *Mason & Dixon*'s picaresque form lends a sense of unfinishedness, so too do its other borrowings from the past. The novel's intentionally anachronistic references and language are crucial to its sense of history not as simply unfinished but also as recrossing itself, as cycling back and crossing over its own past like the line of our contemporary ampersand. This sense of history can be seen in two of Pynchon's anachronistic uses of caffeinated beverages and other addictive luxuries: the last name of the narrating Rev. Cherrycoke and the Starbucks-like All Nations coffeehouse with its half-caf ordering. The first anachronism alludes to Coca-Cola, of course, the caffeinated stuff that empire now spreads around the globe. The second anachronism links the eighteenth century to the contemporary corporate homogenization exemplified by Starbucks. These two moments are connected across time and space to a present concern when Mason and Dixon stand before a tableful of coffee and sweets that a Quaker gentleman reminds them is "bought . . . with the lives of African slaves, untallied black lives broken upon the greedy engines of the Barbadoes" (329). The Quaker's remark echoes the moment in *Candide* when Candide comes across a maimed slave lying at a crossroads, who says of the hand and leg he lost in the cane fields of Surinam, "this is the price of the sugar you eat in Europe" (Voltaire 40). When Candide breaks into tears and wonders for a moment if maybe this is not, as Pangloss has taught him, the best of all possible worlds, he cries not just for the slave (or for himself, finding another instance of Pangloss's error) but because he is confronted by this disturbing evidence of empire's effects. The eighteenth-century concern over the deleterious effects of globalism raised by Pynchon's allusion echoes our own contemporary concern over globalization and connects the substances that fueled empire and revolutionary thinkers like those in Pynchon's inn—the coffee, sugar, and tobacco firing their dreams of freedom, democracy, and untaxed profits—to the substances that fuel today's workers and their empire.

Pynchon's ampersandic history, connecting these different moments, enables further thought about how America has ended up where it has, and why, and whether it can go somewhere else. It asks whether the line of American history will endlessly recross itself, as does the line that symbolizes the infinite, or whether the opening in one loop of our contemporary ampersand can be taken to signify the possibility of things taking off in another direction. The line of empire America has blazed across the North American continent and the world stage, according to *Mason & Dixon*, has not ended so much as paused, ready perhaps to loop back on itself once again and then continue on as before or, perhaps, head off on another path. Perhaps, this novel asks, the recognition in our post-Vietnam, post-Reagan, post–Cold War time that we have in many senses been here before will force the realization that we are more concave than convex, more pointed toward each other than away. Once that realization sets in, perhaps we will be forced not just to acknowledge each other, as the resident of Hollow Earth puts it, but to see that in our still divided yet ever more connected world, our axes converge.

Ultimately, if attention is paid only to the meanings of the line in *Mason & Dixon*, what is missed is the historical sense emblematized by the ampersand—awareness of the connections between disparate moments from across American history, the feeling that these explosions of change are repeated resurfacings of possibility, of alternative outcomes for an only seemingly inevitable future. These moments resurface in the midst of forgetting, a historical amnesia that results not only when America ignores its past entirely or when it sees in that past only the glorious story of its founding followed by the upward path leading to its triumphant present, but also when it sees in its past only the inevitable cruelty attendant upon its persistent binarism. Rather than seeing our past as the story of failure to get this binary monkey off its back, *Mason & Dixon* wonders if we can learn to think in terms of possibility. Certainly, as Bernard Duyfhuizen writes, the book aims "to unravel the historical roots of the racial and social dislocations" (G4) of contemporary America. But its exploration of the past is more than a disinterment, an autopsy explaining the death of American promise. If a medical analogy is wanted, the psychotherapeutic might be more apt: Pynchon's talking cure aims to get America to realize the patterns of thought it learned in its youth, in order to get it to think differently in the future. Cherrycoke ends the paragraph, in which he describes the America of 1786 as bickering itself into fragments: "For the Times are as impossible to calculate, this Advent, as the Distance to a Star" (6). Pynchon's contemporary America might also seem to be following an old pattern by bickering itself into fragments and might seem as difficult to understand as Cherrycoke's times did to him. This phrase comes from the very beginning of the book; by the end, through telling his story, Cherrycoke may have figured a few things out. And they may be things Pynchon thinks applicable to our own era.

Mason & Dixon ends sadly, with Mason descending not just into senescence but also into paranoia. But he has, from his relationship with Dixon and his relation to the land through which they drew their line, learned some of the lessons I argue Pynchon is trying to teach. At the end of the American section of the book, both Mason and Dixon are in flux, and have learned to like it.

> Betwixt themselves, neither feels British enough anymore, nor quite American, for either Side of the Ocean. They are content to reside like Ferrymen or Bridge-Keepers, ever in a Ubiquity of Flow, before a ceaseless Spectacle of Transition. (713)

While Mason has learned a new way to think about division, to reside in transition, he cannot hold on to it forever. When he regresses to his previous way of seeing things, it is the last moment of the subjunctive: "the Event not yet 'reduc'd to certainty,' . . . [a] last morning of Immortality" (177). The inevitability of death, though, is accompanied by a reminder of the magical possibility inherent in and symbolized by America. In the words of Mason's once estranged children, words that close the novel,

> "The Stars are so close you won't need a Telescope."
> "The Fish jump into your Arms. The Indians know Magick." (773)

Any times, especially those times of retrenchment following explosions of change, can be as difficult to calculate as the distance to a star. *Mason & Dixon* reminds us that there have been times when we were closer to the stars, that they may come again, that in some ways our distance to them is always in flux. Impossibly far or unimaginably close, the stars will always be separate from us, but, like the residents of the Earth Concave, we can lean toward them, and each other.

CHAPTER 2

After the Fall
Roth and the 1960s

"The pastoral is not your genre. Your chosen fate, as you
see it, is to be innocent of innocence at all costs."
Roth, *The Counterlife*

I had dressed him for eternity in the wrong clothes.
Roth, *Patrimony*

What Ozzie wanted to know was always different.
Roth, "The Conversion of the Jews"

n an October 2002 interview, Philip Roth was asked about the events of September of the previous year. The interviewer offered, "It has been said many times that with September 11, the United States lost its innocence." Roth responded, "What innocence? That's so naive. From 1668 to 1865, we had slavery in this country. Then, from 1865 to 1955, a society marked by brutal segregation. What innocence? I don't really know what people are talking about" (Roth, Interview).

Five years earlier, Roth had published *American Pastoral* (1997), a historical novel about the Vietnam era, another time when America is said to have lost its innocence. *American Pastoral* is the first of a trilogy of novels about postwar American history and as such marks the beginning of a new phase in its author's career—a period of greater attention to national historical themes often present in earlier works but never as foregrounded.[1] *American Pastoral* is the first Roth novel to look back on the past in the way historical novels do, weaving the story of a life into a historical narrative, and the first to employ Nathan Zuckerman, a familiar narrating main character in his oeuvre, in the unfamiliar role of the teller of another's story. Written and published in the 1990s, when the end of the Cold War engaged much of America in a reaffirmation of the nation's innocence and purity, the novel was initially read by many as a conservative novel, an anti-1960s screed nostalgic for the more innocent America that preceded that allegedly ruinous decade. The novel was alternately praised and damned for this perceived conservatism, depending on readers' own attitudes toward the 1960s, which had come to stand for so much as a period in the nation's development, or decline.

These opposed reactions, however, themselves depended on the same fundamental misreading of the novel. This deceptively complex novel is not a simple historical reflection on the way things went wrong in the latter half of the twentieth century. Instead, through the use of a not especially subtle yet widely ignored framing device, *American Pastoral* self-reflexively explores the ways in which Americans during midcentury, during the late 1960s, and during the 1990s saw themselves and their nation in ways shaped — deformed — by the persistent myths of innocent, pastoral, Edenic America. The roots of these misreadings of *American Pastoral* can be found in Roth's long career as well as in public narratives of recent American history. Unearthing these roots and looking again at just how *American Pastoral* really works as a piece of fiction can help us to see that *American Pastoral* is not about the damage wrought by the 1960s but rather is about the persistence of the myth of innocence in national and personal narratives and the costs of that persistence. Like *Mason & Dixon* and other historical novels of the 1990s, *American Pastoral* isn't just about the past: it's about how stories of the past get told.

———

American Pastoral ends with a question. The narrative voice — which in the last moments has been offering readers the main character's thoughts through free indirect discourse, allowing them almost direct access to his reactions to the events of what has surely been the worst day of his life — now seems to leave him behind. This voice asks, "And what is wrong with their life? What on earth is less reprehensible than the life of the Levovs?" (423). The narrator is Nathan Zuckerman, telling the story, as he imagines it, of Swede Levov, hero of his youth. The Swede, who earned his nickname for his all-American, not particularly Jewish good looks, is a former star athlete and successful businessman who has achieved one version of the Jewish-American dream by marrying a Gentile beauty queen, Miss New Jersey no less, and moving away from the ethnic enclave of Newark and out to the country. Zuckerman tells this story in the wake of his forty-fifth high school reunion in 1995, where he learns of the Swede's death only days before. Zuckerman is thrown into a nostalgic reverie by the reunion, a reverie that is darkened not just by the news of the Swede's death but also by his learning of the 1968 war-protest bombing of the local general store by the Swede's daughter. For Zuckerman and his entire boyhood community, the Swede had embodied the possibility of oneness with America outside the parochial prison of ethnic Jewishness. Learning how the Swede's exemplary life strayed off course, Zuckerman devotes the rest of the novel to asking what went wrong. The novel-within-the-novel that he proceeds to write is his attempt to answer this question. The fact that *American Pastoral* ends with a question complicates the way it must be read. Does Roth really have Zuckerman answer his question with a question, or is the final question rhetorical?

For Zuckerman, the Swede represents the second-generation Jewish American dream of an American paradise, in both its success and its failure. What went wrong for the Swede is, for Zuckerman, what went wrong for this dream. "What is wrong with their life?" then, is a significant question. It asks not just where responsibility lies for the personal tragedy that happened to this family, and not even just where their dreams went wrong, but ultimately where America went wrong. How the landscape changed, then, how the American paradise was lost, is the ultimate question asked by Zuckerman.

Reading *American Pastoral* again, after its end, requires some thinking about how the novel answers Zuckerman's question. It also requires, a little more trickily, some thinking about whether Zuckerman's question is Roth's, or if Roth's novel is standing in a particular relationship to its narrator and his question, and if *American Pastoral* isn't in fact asking something different. Like Ozzie Freedman in his early story "The Conversion of the Jews," Roth is not asking the obvious question; what he wants to know, as Ozzie does, is "something different" (*Goodbye* 101). One way to start thinking about what he does want to know is to look back at a novel of Roth's from this historical moment, *Portnoy's Complaint*.

To read a Roth novel is to read it not simply for itself but to read it against other Roth novels. This is the case not so much because, in a fifty-year career, he has written twenty-five or so novels and novellas (one about every two years), but more because Roth returns, again and again, as some writers do, to certain themes, stories, and places. "To read a single piece of work by Philip Roth," one critic writes, "is, in more than just a metaphysical sense, to be connected by a network of interests and associations to every one" (Anastas). Roth does more than return to issues and narratives that concern him, though; he returns to the books themselves and even to responses to them, often through stand-ins authored by Zuckerman, such as *Carnovsky*, Zuckerman's *Portnoy's Complaint*. In *American Pastoral*, however, Roth does something new, returning to earlier work not simply to revisit its handling of Rothian themes but to reconsider the historical time that produced the writer and the work.

Philip Roth's 1969 novel *Portnoy's Complaint* famously ends with Dr. Spielvogel's response to his analysand, Alexander Portnoy: "Now vee may perhaps to begin." Dr. Spielvogel's response brings to an end Alex's relentless, book-long confession of sexual misadventure and family conflict. What he intends to begin, perhaps, is the process of Alex's truly dealing with his complaint; while the doctor's response is funny (it is, after all, introduced with the subtitle "PUNCH LINE"), it points to the continuing seriousness of Alex's problems. The end of the novel also begins the history of response to it. At the time of its publication, *Portnoy's Complaint* was read as an act of rebellion. It tells the story of Alex's struggle to be free from the constraints of his family, his Newark Jewish community, his larger Jewish American tradition, and from the sensibility and morality for which they stand, a struggle that takes the form of frenzied attempts at sexual liberation. In letting readers hear Alex's angst-ridden cry from the couch, Roth let them hear Alex's criticism of the world of his upbringing for themselves. In doing so, Roth rebelled, in the eyes of many American Jews, against his own community; he was accused, among other things, of "fanaticism in the hatred of things Jewish" (qtd. in Roth, *Reading Myself* 243).

With *Portnoy's Complaint*, Roth also jettisoned the solemn weight of his immediate literary tradition and his more distant literary models. The lampooning of Alex's family, sitting around the dinner table screaming about their son's bowel movements, can of course be seen as the novel's way of exposing a community and a way of life to criticism. What is less apparent but no less important to *Portnoy's Complaint* is the literary revolt, one goal of which Roth himself described as "liberating me from an apprentice's literary models," namely Henry James and Gustave Flaubert (*Facts* 157). Another aspect is that of the more local revolt against the constraints of writing as a member of the Jewish American "school" of Bernard Malamud and Isaac Bashevis Singer, a revolt assisted by Saul Bellow, whose 1953 *The Adventures of Augie March* has been cited by Roth as the book that made his writing possible. "Bellow was indeed Columbus for people like me, the grandchildren of immigrants, who set out as American writers after him" (*Shop* 143). *Portnoy's Complaint* is at least as much about defying the influence of James and Flaubert and Roth's more immediate predecessors and contemporaries as it is about defying the authority of the world of his upbringing.

The end of *Portnoy's Complaint*, then, began Roth's career in earnest. It was not his first success: *Goodbye, Columbus* (1959) and his first novel, *Letting Go* (1962), were well received. And Roth had been criticized before for his representation of American Jews: the early "Defender of the Faith" (1959) provoked accusations of providing fuel for anti-Semitic fires when it first appeared in the *New Yorker*, as did other early stories and *Goodbye, Columbus*. *Portnoy's Complaint* was also not the first time Roth had ventured into relatively more explicit territory—in his coverage of sexuality among Jews—than was common. But the prolific Roth of the 1970s and 1980s wrote novels possible only after *Portnoy's Complaint*, novels that focus unromantically on the customs and mores of the community of his youth and its offspring and do so in language his earlier, "apprentice" books would not have dared, some dealing explicitly with the personal and professional impact of having written *Portnoy's Complaint*.[2]

American Pastoral comes back, in 1997, to what *Portnoy's Complaint* truly began in 1969. If *Portnoy's Complaint* began Roth's revolt against everything that worked to define his protagonists—the middle class morality, ethnic superiority, and narrow and stifling worldview he saw in American Jewry at midcentury—*American Pastoral* represents a reevaluation of this revolt at century's end. If *Portnoy's Complaint* also began Roth's literary revolt against the constraining influence of his literary antecedents, *American Pastoral* represents a reconsideration of the value of those influences and the costs of rejecting them. In the 1990s, America's retrospective turn provided the opportunity for Roth to look back at the history his career had thus far spanned. At the center of this history was the 1960s, the decade that produced *Portnoy's Complaint*, the work that made him. In the later years of his career and in the twilight glow of the end of the American Century, Roth looks back at all that he and America chose to leave behind and wonders again about the causes and the cost. This is not the same as asking what went wrong, Zuckerman's question; it is more like asking, how did the stories we told ourselves about what was happening help or not help us to understand it and even help it to happen?

American Pastoral begins with a two-word sentence: "The Swede." In this beginning, readers see the glow of youthful hero worship the narrating Zuckerman still sees when he looks at Swede Levov, decades after their youth has ended. They see the glow then, at the baseball game where he and a grown-up "Skip" Zuckerman run into each other, and ten years later, when the Swede invites him to dinner to help him write a book about his father Lou's life. Zuckerman is maddened by the Swede's failure at the dinner to discuss the mysterious "shocks that befell [his father's] loved ones" to which he alluded in the letter containing his invitation (18). Zuckerman thinks that maybe he had been right after all about the Swede—that, while he was indeed a magnificent athlete, a symbol for the Jews of Weequahic of the possibility of succeeding as Americans, a man who had not just been a Marine drill sergeant but had married Miss New Jersey, he was not a man with much self-awareness or depth, not a man with subjectivity. The letter had raised hopes that the Swede had, in suffering, been brought to the awareness that suffering can bring; at the restaurant, Zuckerman realizes, with the resignation of a writer losing interest, that he had not.

And it is an angry resignation, as Zuckerman realizes that he wants the Swede to hold up his end of the hero-worship deal, to be more than an all-American surface, more than "the embodiment of nothing." When he asks himself, "Why clutch at him? What's the matter with you" (39), he does so because he realizes that his curiosity about the Swede is motivated by more than writerly desire to dig deeper and is about more than just the Swede: it is about Zuckerman's fascination with him as he was and with what he has become. That the "Jewishness that he wore so lightly" was responsible for Weequahic's past elevation of the Swede is obvious; his heroism lay less in his on-the-field exploits than in his "unconsciousness oneness with America" (20). The mystery of the Swede, for Zuckerman, lies in what happens to this assimilated hero, in what kind of person he becomes, in whether he really "succeeds." Does the Swede slide into complacent, superficial blandness, becoming "a human platitude" (23), or does he achieve an awareness of the harsher realities of life as it is for most humans?

What Zuckerman wants to know is whether the Swede's life "had been most simple and most ordinary and therefore just great, right in the American grain" (31), or whether, as for Ivan Ilych, the uneventfulness of his life is its own terror. The frustrated sense of anticlimax with which the dinner leaves him is a sign of the mystery's importance. For a moment, when he learns of the Swede's recent prostate surgery, he thinks perhaps the Swede will have been brought to "subjectivity" (20), to a deeper understanding, even a skepticism, by a new sense of mortality, but this hope too is quickly dashed when he sees that he is a "big jeroboam of self-contentment." Unlike Zuckerman, of course, the Swede is asked by life only "to respect everything one is supposed to respect; to protest nothing; never to be inconvenienced by self-distrust; never to be enmeshed in obsession, tortured by incapacity, poisoned by resentment, driven by anger" (29). He is the opposite of the Zuckerman Roth's longtime readers have come to know.

The chapter ends readers' introduction to the Swede and to Zuckerman's obsession with him by letting them know, again, what Zuckerman has told them before: "I was wrong" (39). In fact, he was and he wasn't. The twists in the Swede's story are not what he imagines them to be, but he was right that there was something more there. Readers learn over the rest of the novel what that something was, and they learn why it is important for Zuckerman from the particular way in which he imagines the rest of the story. But the groundwork for understanding both is laid in this opening chapter, especially in what lies just in the background, in elements seemingly brought up only to be quietly dropped. The Swede's prostate surgery leads Zuckerman to reflect on his own experience with prostate cancer: he tells the Swede of friends who had come out of surgery somewhat unhappily, either impotent or incontinent or both, doesn't reveal that the diapers were worn by him, and drops the subject. There are reflections on the manufacture of gloves, from the history of the founding of the family business to the details of making an actual glove down to the fourchette, the piece of leather between the fingers. Intertwined with this history is the history of Newark, a collection of immigrant neighborhoods such as their own idyllic Weequahic, the recreated Polish shtetl that grew more like America in the first postimmigrant generation (their fathers') and had become, by the time of the dinner and as a result of the '67 riots, what the Swede calls "the worst city in the world . . . the car-theft capital of the world" (24).

The importance for Zuckerman of the Swede's fate can be seen early on in the novel in the way the story is framed and in these more-than-atmospheric details that surround it. It is seen as the tragedy of an innocent undeservedly struck down, told by a writer becoming increasingly, immediately aware of his own mortality. Zuckerman is from the start of the novel overcome by memory, wistfully, elegiacally, but also angrily. Zuckerman's unvoiced rage against how things have turned out for him—emasculated, infantilized, and alone in his house in the Berkshires—frames his investigation into the fate of a man who has been for him a symbol of happy endings.

Zuckerman's curiosity about what happened to the Swede is also about what happened to the Newark of factories and immigrants, especially the descendants of Jewish immigrants. From the beginning of their introduction to the Swede, readers are led to see him as a hero of a particular sort, blessed with an easy Americanness, devoid of the conflict felt by the hyphenated American, possessing "no striving, no ambivalence, no doubleness" (20). The fate of such a symbol, "the household Apollo of the Weequahic Jews" (4), born out of wartime Jewish America, is from the novel's start clearly about assimilation. The Swede's fate is also about the loss of the Newark of the 1940s and 1950s, the burning in the riots, the loss of the factories to the third world and of the original families to the suburbs. And this fate itself is, for Zuckerman, the loss in the late 1960s of an America that he and his parents' generation dreamed of joining and that the Swede had apparently conquered.

Zuckerman begins the second chapter's undelivered reunion speech, written afterward, which he describes as "a speech to myself masked as a speech to them" (44):

> Let's remember the energy. Americans were governing not only themselves but some two hundred million people in Italy, Austria, Germany, and Japan. . . . Our class started high school six months after the unconditional surrender of the Japanese, during the greatest moment of collective inebriation in American history. And the upsurge of energy was contagious. Around us nothing was lifeless. Sacrifice and constraint were over. The Depression had disappeared. Everything was in motion. The lid was off. Americans were to start over again, en masse, everyone in it together. (40)

After the defeat of the Axis powers, and especially of Hitler, this was a powerful set of notions, especially for American Jews. Zuckerman goes on to describe the end of the war as "the clock of history reset . . . a whole people's aims limited no longer by the past" (41). "People" here indicates the American people, no distinctions made. This resetting of the clock is felt to occasion the erasure of old boundaries, the freeing of a people—a whole people—to pursue their dreams. These ideas of wholeness, of freedom, of time beginning again are Edenic ideas. To start over again, everyone together, is to return to the Garden.

This beginning is recreated by Zuckerman, in all its rich detail, as a response to his reunion and the speech he makes to himself.

With a nod to Proust's madeleine-inspired reverie, Zuckerman's remembering, which does not pull him out of time but sends him "rocketing to its secret core" (45), is helped along by the rugelach handed out at the end of the evening. Wolfing them down, Zuckerman recalls the "apprehensiveness of death" (47) vanishing from Proust in his own search for lost time and laments the same not happening for him. In the imagined narrative of the Swede's life Zuckerman soon undertakes, the goal is at least partly the same, to overcome death through memory. His method is similar, to supply a rich, almost overwhelming wealth of detail. The result, however, apparently will not be the same.

Zuckerman does supply the detail, though, and in so doing re-creates the new postwar Garden in his narrative. The descriptions of the neighborhood, of the glove-making business, from tanning to stretching to cutting to forming to shipping to selling, are presented not just with the glow of nostalgia but with the realist's obsessive drive to depict reality through the weight and thickness of detail. The detail is laid on so thick that it led Morris Dickstein to describe *American Pastoral* as a realist novel (*Leopards* 20). Like William Dean Howells on Silas Lapham's Boston paint factory or Frank Norris on McTeague's San Francisco office, Zuckerman's description of the Levovs' Newark glove-making concern works to convey the truth to be found in the material of life. However, as with the genteel realism of Howells and the determinist naturalism of Norris, Zuckerman's use of detail to present reality "as it is" is shaped by a particular project. If Howells's realism was driven by a democratic impulse and if Norris's naturalism revealed what he saw as the animal just beneath the thin veneer of civilization, Zuckerman is driven by his own project to shape the "objective" facts of the life of his subjects in particular ways.

That project is to recover a lost, idyllic past and at the same time to ask how it was lost—and at what cost. The thing that complicates a reading of *American Pastoral* as a straightforward realist novel is the easily missed fact that it is actually a complicated frame narrative and that the "realist" part is in fact the product of a fictional character's imagination. And it is easy to think of Zuckerman, in all of the books in which he has appeared, as an authorial stand-in (though it is possible to do so only at the risk of missing Roth's complicatedly ironic stance toward him); so it is easy to mistake his words for Roth's. For example, Debra Shostak, a critic usually perceptive to Roth's play with voices and perspectives (as the title of her 2004 book, *Philip Roth—Countertexts, Counterlives*, attests), writes of *American Pastoral*, "Like *Sabbath's Theater*, it cannot be mistaken for an autobiography, except insofar as Nathan Zuckerman reappears as narrator and, through his familiarity to Roth's readers as a writerly alter ego, may be taken as a mouthpiece for the author" (181). Taking Zuckerman as mouthpiece would in this case mean missing the ways in which the aims of Zuckerman's project shape the narrative he constructs. Roth does not simply use Zuckerman's reunion experience as an excuse with which to frame a novel about the past. Rather, in his use of this frame, Roth makes clear to readers that Zuckerman recreates his own past and the past of the Swede through an act of imagination and that it is Zuckerman's act, not Roth's own—that is, the story of the Swede is imagined through a character at some distance from Roth, a distance that allows us to think about motivation. Zuckerman is not a camera lens here for Roth, but a character, inspired in the first instance less by the documentary imperative than by a reunion and some buttery baked goods, by the death of a childhood idol, and by his own prostate cancer, and, as a result of all of these, by a need both to revisit the past and also to somehow rescue it.

These needs are intensified by the appearance of Jerry, the Swede's brother and Zuckerman's classmate, who interrupts the reunion's quiet nostalgia, what he calls "the past undetonated" (61). Jerry's news of the Swede's recent death at first only adds to the litany of losses recited at the reunion, but then he tells Zuckerman about "little Merry's darling bomb." All of Zuckerman's questions about the Swede's apparently absent subjectivity, about what could happen to a man who so perfectly and so literally embodied the dreams of assimilation and success, are raised again and reframed by what he learns from Jerry: that the Swede's daughter was, in Jerry's words, a "kid who stopped the war in Vietnam by blowing up somebody out mailing a letter at five A.M." (68). He learns from Jerry that the Swede had in fact acquired subjectivity, in the hardest way.

Jerry goes on to explain how this kind of violence could erupt in pastoral America, in the perfect life of the Swede, in three words: "That was '68." He continues,

> That was '68, back when the wild behavior was still new. People suddenly forced to make sense of madness. All that public display. The dropping of inhibitions. Authority powerless. The kids going crazy. Intimidating everybody. The adults don't know what to make of it, they don't know what to do. Is this an act? Is the "revolution" real? . . . He knew something was going wrong. (69)

But the Swede was, in Jerry's words, "just a liberal sweetheart of a father," who raised his daughter "with all the modern ideas" and who "took it and took it" (69, 70). In this world the "duty" (72) that was the Swede's central belief could not stand him in good stead because the things to which he felt responsible were crumbling all around him.

For Jerry, the shock of the bomb is due both to the Swede's misplaced sense of duty and also to the ways the world changed. For Zuckerman, it is not so easy. Jerry seems too hard, still too much the resentful little brother to trust as an interpreter of his older brother's life. While as a writer Zuckerman is continuously aware of the ways in which people get other people wrong (talking to Jerry, he calls these layers of misunderstanding caused by the inaccurate pictures people have of each other "the shit" [64]), he still feels it will take a novelist's imagination to get closer to the truth.

Dancing later with an old boyhood crush, Zuckerman reflects on what happened to the Swede's life and so to America's, on "the disruption of the anticipated American future that was simply to have unrolled out of the solid American past" (85):

> the daughter and the decade blasting to smithereens his particular form of utopian thinking, the plague America infiltrating the Swede's castle and there infecting everyone. The daughter who transports him out of the longed-for American pastoral and into everything that is its antith-

esis and its enemy, into the fury, the violence, and the desperation of the counterpastoral—into the indigenous American berserk. (86)

The Swede's attempt to preserve the American dream he'd been forced to embody was utopian, an attempt to live outside of history. Formed by history, however, by American success in World War II and Jewish success in America, he couldn't run from it, and in the end it ran him over.

While history was what ran him over, his daughter was driving, and it is with his attempt to understand her that Zuckerman begins his imagined story of the Swede. He gets there almost imperceptibly, seeming to slide into it effortlessly and almost by surprise:

> To the honeysweet strains of "Dream," I pulled away from myself, pulled away from the reunion, and I dreamed. . . . I dreamed a realistic chronicle. I began gazing into his life—not his life as a god or demigod in whose triumphs one could exult as a boy but his life as another assailable man—and inexplicably, which is to say lo and behold, I found him in Deal, New Jersey, at the seaside cottage, the summer his daughter was eleven, back when she couldn't stay out of his lap or stop calling him by cute pet names, couldn't "resist," as she put it, examining with the tip of her finger the close way his ears were fitted to his skull. (89)

So begins the story of the day in which the Swede kisses his daughter the way he kisses, in her stuttering word, "umumumother" (89). He does it because he has unintentionally mocked her stuttering request, and out of his guilt, Zuckerman imagines, he turns what had been an innocent summer-long intimacy into a moment of passion and, ultimately, paradise into inferno.

The sentence with which this narrative begins is the last in the novel in which Zuckerman's "I" appears. After, as at the end of the sentence, the rest of the novel is narrated unobtrusively by a narrator who has chosen to fade into the background, taking the first person singular pronoun with him. He absents himself at the start of his narrative, which begins not at the beginning but in medias res, with a moment for which readers are totally unprepared. It is apparently meant to stand for the liberal permissiveness of his family and of so many families of the time whose children seemed to turn upon them and their nation. But this moment, and what it is supposed to mean, should be met with skepticism because readers know that Zuckerman created it, that it is made not from the research he says provided material for other parts of his narrative but out of whole cloth.

A closer look at what critics have done with the fact of the "madeness" of the Swede's story—when they have noticed it or at least mentioned it—may help here. Some note the metafictional aspect of the novel but restrict its importance to questions of facticity, as Elaine Safer does:

> Roth's readers try to follow clues about what Jerry could have told Zuckerman, what Zuckerman could have learned himself as a youth, what must be only based on Zuckerman's imagination, and what biographical information about Newark experiences could possibly relate to Zuckerman's author Philip Roth. . . . We are looking for facts, and there are no "facts" in a literary work. (96–97)

Other critics do more with the fact of the frame than treat it as a commentary on fact and fiction, instead connecting it to the way reading one Roth work means reading it in the context of his previous work and so, in the case of *American Pastoral*, means reconsidering the treatment of the same subjects in earlier works. As Timothy Parrish puts it,

> By framing the narrative through the perspective of Zuckerman, Roth also invokes the earlier Zuckerman canon to make sense of this story. . . . Roth rewrites Zuckerman's story as a way of rewriting all of his previous Zuckerman stories. In portraying Zuckerman's perspective on the meaning of the second half of the American twentieth century through his idolatry of Swede Levov, *American Pastoral* reframes Roth's entire oeuvre. ("End" 132)

However, Parrish reads this reconsideration as amounting to blaming it all on assimilation, saying Roth "explores the deleterious consequences of forsaking one's Jewish origins" by having Zuckerman make up a story "that locates Swede's fall in the loss of his Jewish identity" ("End" 133). Parrish misses the ironic distance Roth inserts between his novel and Zuckerman's.

Still other readers argue that the frame is used to tell a story about the Swede that isn't really about the Swede. Derek Royal writes, "Zuckerman creates his hero's story not necessarily for the purpose of understanding the high school legend, but to understand himself" ("Fictional" 14). The most useful description of what Roth is up to here may appear in Ross Posnock's characterization of the first ninety pages of the novel, before Zuckerman's "I" disappears: "The circumstances that prompt Nathan's evocation [of the Swede's story] are meticulously described, especially since they will condition his act of mimesis" (*Philip* 105). In describing the structure of the novel in this way, Posnock allows room for distance between Roth and Zuckerman. However, Posnock thinks about this structure in terms of the historical circumstances conditioning Zuckerman's imagining of the Swede's story rather than in terms of Zuckerman's own active grappling with history, the motivations of which Roth explores in the larger novel of which Zuckerman's novel is part. In doing so, I believe, Posnock is unable to fully appreciate the ways in which Roth's reading of Zuckerman's writing is about art rather than determining historical conditions. I will return later to Posnock's reading, which gets the closest of these readings, in my view, to the truth of how the novel works. For now, though, because Posnock's argument and my own depend on the meaning of the 1960s as presented by Zuckerman and Roth, let's return to *Portnoy's Complaint*, Roth's book of the 1960s.

In *Portnoy* the Jewish son had his revenge. . . . A whole middle class of sons and daughters, turning and turning within the widening gyre of the nuclear Jewish family—nucleus indeed of the Jewish experience and the first scenario of the psychoanalytic drama—found in Portnoy its own fascination with the details of childhood. It was this emphasis on the unmentionable, Roth's gift for zanily working out inaccessible details to the most improbable climax, like Portnoy masturbating into a piece of liver, that was the farce element so necessary to Roth's anger. There was the calculated profanation of mother, father, the most intimate offices of the body—a profanation by now altogether healthy to those therapeutized members of the professional middle class to whom everything about the body had become, like the possibility of universal destruction through the Bomb, small talk at the dinner table. (Kazin 148)

Like most readings of *Portnoy's Complaint*, the account Alfred Kazin offers here interprets Roth's public unveiling of the heretofore private workings of bodies and families as a calculated act of revenge on his own family and on the claustrophobia-inducing Jewish family in general. In 1969, Kazin writes, the shock was palpable, carrying the weight of Roth's anger, but it was not unprepared for; the novel "captured perfectly a generation psyche which was more anchored on family, and more resentful of it, than any other" (147). This generation recognized the anger and was not uncomfortable with its vehicle of expression. The preceding generation, as reactions indicated, was not so comfortable.

To ascribe the difference between these two reactions to intergenerational conflict is sensible; Roth clearly seems in *Portnoy's Complaint* to be striking out against perceived inherited constraints.[3] Kazin, following Roth's lead in the figure of Spielvogel, sees this conflict played out on a field chalked with the new lines of psychoanalyzed culture's game, in which an outpouring of the darkest secrets and desires is only the beginning of a journey toward self-understanding. Kazin does not see Roth as a social commentator in a broader sense, however. Citing Roth's comments in his 1960 lecture (reprinted as "Writing American Fiction" in *Reading Myself and Others* [1975]) on contemporary reality outdoing the imagination of the American writer, Kazin acknowledges that Roth is aware of the great historical changes of his day. However, he denies that they are Roth's subject: "Though the 1960s closed on more public disorder than Roth could have dreamed of, he did not become the novelist of this disorder, or even the journalist of it" (147).

Roth would not have disagreed with this characterization at the time or for many years. To quote from his later discussion of the novel in *The Facts* at greater length,

[*Portnoy's Complaint*] was a book that had rather less to do with "freeing" me from my Jewishness or my family (the purpose divined by many, who were convinced by the evidence of *Portnoy's Complaint* that the author had to be on bad terms with both) than with liberating me from an apprentice's literary models, particularly from the awesome graduate school authority of Henry James, whose *Portrait of a Lady* had been a virtual handbook during the early drafts of *Letting Go*, and from the example of Flaubert, whose detached irony in the face of a small town woman's disastrous delusions had me obsessively thumbing through *Madame Bovary* during the years I was searching for the perch from which to observe the people in *When She Was Good*. (157)

In 1988 as in 1969, Roth does not disagree with Kazin: he describes his novel as less a comment on a cultural moment than an attempt to break old literary constraints. Roth's objection to what he sees as a misreading of *Portnoy's Complaint* is on one level an objection to the biographical fallacy—that Alexander Portnoy's feelings and struggles are in some way his own. As strangers on the street call out "Carnovsky!" to Zuckerman in *Zuckerman Unbound* (1981), confusing him with his Portnoyesque character, so Roth feels critics misidentify him with his character. He also objects to the critics' characterization of his book as an unreflective call for liberation.

The liberation Alexander Portnoy wants is freedom from his family, embodied especially in his mother (whose authority and presence were so overwhelming that a young Alex would rush home from school to try to catch his mother transforming from his teacher back to herself) and freedom from himself. It is a self he is still not free of at the end of the novel, when he cries, "Nothing but self! Locked up in me!" (280). He is not free of family or of the traditional sexual mores they represent for him, standing outside the locked bathroom door of his psyche, asking what he's doing in there. His affairs do not lead to a freer, guiltless existence.

Portnoy's Complaint was mistaken as a simple manifesto of the sexual revolution by critics such as Diana Trilling and Irving Howe because they failed to recognize the note of ambiguity in Roth's presentation of Alex's attempts to free himself. But the book, while not a wholehearted manifesto for liberation, is not a condemnation either. The difficulty Alex encounters in trying to liberate himself is more a comment on how hard it is to do than an argument that it is not the right thing to.

The liberation Roth wants to focus on in later comments about the novel is that from literary convention. Part of that liberation was about content, about the freedom to mention the unmentionable, and part was stylistic. Discussing in *The Facts* the "ingredients" that made up *Portnoy's Complaint*, Roth cites the "reckless narrative disclosure" he learned from his own psychoanalysis and especially notes a new kind of language inspired by

> the ferocity of the rebellious rhetoric unleashed against the president and his war, the assault that Johnson's own seething cornball bravado inspired and from which even he, with his rich and randy vein of linguistic contempt, had eventually to flee in defeat, as though before a deluge of verbal napalm. It bedazzled me, this enraged invective so potent as to wound to the quick a colossus like Lyndon Johnson, especially after my long, unnatural interlude of personal and literary self-subjugation. (137–38)

The rebellion seems here to take on a social cast, in spite of Roth's efforts to insist otherwise. In both asserting the right of full disclosure of private life (though not, he insists, his own) and also claiming a style as incendiary as napalm, Roth recognizes that in writing, he is performing a social act. While *Portnoy's Complaint* may not have been intended as social commentary at the time and Roth did not mean to be, in Kazin's words, "the novelist of this disorder," *Portnoy's Complaint* was a part of those changes. In 1969 (and 1988) though, Roth preferred not to think about his novel in those terms.

He preferred not to, but his later novels seem to have considered it in this light anyway. In *The Ghost Writer*, Zuckerman receives a letter from a family friend (a judge, fittingly) asking, "Can you honestly say that there is anything in your short story that would not warm the heart of a Julius Streicher or a Joseph Goebbels?" (103–4). While the question is hyperbolic, the idea that fiction acts within a social context is not entirely undercut. In *Zuckerman Unbound*, his work, misread, is taken by those around him as a rejection, most importantly in the (possibly misheard) last word of his father, "Bastard." Zuckerman takes it as a condemnation of his work. Any doubt he may have about what he heard is erased by his brother:

> You *are* a bastard. A heartless conscienceless bastard. What does loyalty mean to you? What does self-denial, *restraint*—anything at all? To you everything is disposable! Everything is exposable! . . . Love, marriage, family, children, what the hell do you care? To you it's all fun and games. *But that isn't the way it is for the rest of us.* And the worst is how we protect you from knowing what you really are! And what you've done! You killed him, Nathan. . . . With that book. *Of course* he said "Bastard." He'd seen it! He'd seen what you'd done to him and Mother in that book! (217)

Carnovsky, though intended by Zuckerman not as personal confession but rather as satirical comedy, is taken as an attack on his own family, on Jewish tradition, on the whole notion of family and tradition. It is this reading, as much as the world of his birth, from which Zuckerman attempts to unbind himself in the three novels and novella of *Zuckerman Bound* (1985). He does so by protesting both the employment of critical fallacies that allow readers to mistake his narrators for himself and his novels for his life and also the refusal to recognize his work as satire. It is the guilt over this perceived rejection and the reaction to it with which Zuckerman binds himself in *The Anatomy Lesson* (1983), experiencing chronic, inexplicable pain that tortures him throughout the novel, so much so that he tries to escape it by ending his career as a writer and going to medical school.

It takes another decade before Roth's novels seem to reconsider more fully the nature of his artistic and social rebellions in the context in which they took place. By the mid-1990s, this context becomes more available. As Alex Portnoy struggles fitfully to liberate himself from the physical and psychic home of his mother and father and as Zuckerman liberates himself as a writer only to be accused of literally killing his father, so Roth's more recent work seems to reconsider how his own liberation as a writer was part of a larger cultural liberation, one that came at its own costs. When Roth looks back on the 1960s in *American Pastoral*, he can see his career in the context of the times in which it bloomed and recognize that rejection and loss are inherent in liberation because the liberator can see only his own innocence and purity. In the old American pattern, the dream must be realized in toto, the old people and ideas gotten out of the way.

It is important to repeat that in exploring this theme, Roth is not withdrawing or repudiating his protests against misreading and parochial ignorance in order to say, in *American Pastoral*, that everything good was lost in 1969. The problems with reading *American Pastoral* in this way, in terms of Roth's ideas about writing or about American reality, become apparent when reading individual accounts of the book along these lines. The novel was praised by many in the press as a Reaganesque idealization of the 1950s, a Brokavian glorification of its "greatest generation," and welcomed by critics who'd smelled the odor of the self-hating Jew in Roth's earlier work. Norman Podhoretz's review belatedly welcomed Roth to the side of right thinking: "I myself, and many other people too, detected in this book a born-again Philip Roth whose entire outlook on the world had been inverted" (34). Critic Andrew Gordon lamented, "Despite his apparently thorough and unrelenting critique of pastoral myths and utopian illusions [in *The Counterlife*], in *American Pastoral* Roth suffers from a blind spot. Like so many conservative social critics in America today, he wants to blame it on the sixties" (157). Podhoretz praises Roth (in an unfortunate choice of metaphor) as born again, rightly reversing the way he saw his people and his nation and so implicitly agreeing with Podhoretz-style conservatism; Gordon also sees Roth as conservative and, similarly, sees him repudiating his past views, though in Gordon's case this is an unwelcome development. Actually, though, in the case of neither critic's reading is this repudiation seen as a development. In Podhoretz's case, it is a sudden inversion; in Gordon's, it is the result of a blind spot caused by Roth's unexplained bad politics. In both readings then, Roth suddenly changes his mind, an unhelpful supposition for a critic trying to understand any novel in the context of a writer's oeuvre.[4]

One way to think more constructively about Roth's attitude toward the times is to look directly at the part of the book most central to its sense of the 1960s—Merry's bomb or, in other words, 1960s radicalism. Some readings argue that Roth's unconvincing portrait of 1960s radicalism is evidence of what Gordon calls a blind spot. Laura Tanenbaum, focusing on the novel's inability to explain Merry's actions, reads *American Pastoral*'s politics not as antiradical but as "a throwing up of the hands" (47). Robert Boyers, as Tanenbaum notes, blames the novel's failure to explain radicalism in part on Roth's failure to sufficiently contextualize it in history (Tanenbaum 43). Ross Posnock's reading, on the other hand, more subtly understands what Roth is up to novelistically. Noting, as Tanenbaum and others have, that the portrait of Merry is unsatisfyingly incomplete, Posnock argues that, in a way, it's the Swede's fault. Referring to a section in which the Swede mentions the Weathermen, the Black Panthers, Marcuse, Fanon, and others he associates with Merry's politics, Posnock writes,

> The schematic quality of this passage instances the price Roth pays for having Swede's kitschy Americana perspective be the controlling sensibility, a decision dictated by the immanent method that requires Nathan's effacement. The Swede's political ruminations seem at once too pat and too thin as well as improbable—either as observations the Swede would make or experiences that Merry would have. In confronting the political dimensions of his daughter's violence, the Swede seems over his head, lost in sentimentality. . . . Zuckerman and his creator are as if trapped by the Swede's limits. (*Philip* 109–10)

Here, Posnock takes the useful step of separating the point of view of a fictional character, the Swede, from the narrative of which he is part. As a result, he is able to separate the Swede's analysis of the times from *American Pastoral*'s, though he does argue that the novel is trapped in that point of view. What Posnock does not do is separate another fictional character who is the Swede's nominal creator—Zuckerman—from the narrative of which *he* is part. This move would allow him to see that while Zuckerman is trapped by the Swede's limits, Roth is not: an ironic distance exists between Zuckerman's novel-within-the-novel and Roth's novel. It is in this space that Roth's self-reflexive history operates, exploring, through Zuckerman's errors, the effects of myth on the way history is understood.

The genius here is that Roth, while separating himself from Zuckerman's errors, does not pretend they are not his own — in other words, he doesn't say that they are mistakes he hasn't made himself. Susceptible to history's myths, Roth has idealized pastoral America in its founding and postwar incarnations as well as in its 1960s moment of starting over. There is a moment in *Patrimony*, Roth's memoir of his father's decline and death, in which he dreams that his dead father returns and says he is angry that his son decided to dress him for burial in the traditional shroud rather than in a suit. "I had dressed him for eternity in the wrong clothes," Roth reflects, adding that his father had been alluding to the book *Patrimony* itself; it is not a stretch to say that the allusion also extends to all the father characters in his fiction (237). In *American Pastoral*, I would argue, Roth is motivated by the idea that, in his susceptibility to the myth of pastoral in its various iterations, he has in his work also misrepresented Newark and even his nation's history. Rereading himself in *American Pastoral*, through Zuckerman, Roth explores the way we always get history — like other people — wrong.

It is five years after his daughter's disappearance before the Swede sees her again. During this period, from 1968 to 1973, he watches the newspapers. "Bombs are going off everywhere": variations of the word "bomb" appear thirteen times on one page, hammering home the violence until the word itself becomes merely a sound, a meaningless signifier, the very real, exploding referent of which is lost in repetition, as it must have been lost to the readers of the papers and the watchers of the news like the Swede (147). That it is never a completely empty signifier for the Swede becomes clear when he fears that the body found at one bombing is his daughter's. Ironically, the one thing to allay that fear is news of further bombings: "The torso's not hers! Merry is alive!" (150). Aside from raising and dashing the Swede's hopes, the bombings remind him of the violence Merry witnessed as a girl in the early 1960s, in particular the televised self-immolation of a South Vietnamese monk. Searching for an explanation for what Merry had become, an alternative to that hinted at in the beginning of Zuckerman's story about him, the Swede seizes on this moment.

Driving to find Merry in 1973 after he finds out she is living in Newark, the Swede remembers Saturday morning trips with his father to pick up piecework done in the homes of immigrant Italian families before the factory existed. These memories, of families working hard together, becoming Americans, are juxtaposed with the sight of his daughter. Merry, who has become a Jain, wears the foot of an old stocking across her mouth to avoid breathing in and so killing helpless microorganisms. She is filthy and smelly and lives in the worst part of town in a dirty room furnished only with a mattress on the floor. Her revolution, inspired by the world's violence and America's part in it, leaves her, in Zuckerman's re-creation, like this. Leaving her where he finds her, the Swede calls Jerry, who offers little in the way of comfort:

> You wanted Miss America? Well, you've got her, with a vengeance—she's your daughter! You wanted to be a real American jock, a real American marine, a real American hotshot with a beautiful Gentile babe on your arm? You longed to belong like everybody else to the United States of America? Well, you do now, big boy, thanks to your daughter. The reality of this place is right up in your kisser now. With the help of your daughter you're as deep in the shit as a man can get, the real crazy American shit. America amok! America amuck! (277)

The contrasts between old Newark and new, the Swede's life in his stone colonial-era house on Arcady Road and Merry's in the Ironbound section, are marked. For Zuckerman, the contrasts illustrate what's happened to his city and his nation. It is about historical change.

With the larger novel's network of allusions and direct references to the pastoral, however, it is also about the meaning of pastoral—not the original ancient Greek and Roman meaning, but rather its revisions. The idealized rural life championed by Virgil in his eclogues may be what the Swede envisions when he moves out from Newark, but that is not all that Roth is invoking. Since ancient contrarians pointed out the real Arcadia of the pastoral was a backward, savage place, people have been exposing as myth the invidious comparison of city to country, embodied in rustic images of bounding livestock and simple shepherds. In the seventeenth century, Guercino and Poussin contributed to this exposure in successive paintings of shepherd's tombstones inscribed with the motto "*Et in Arcadia ego.*" Even in ideal rural life I exist, says Death; even the perfect life is only life and therefore imperfect. The danger comes when a myth arises that that imperfection does not exist. The allusion to the pastoral says that there are no perfect, pure, innocent places, populated by postwar landed gentry or countercultural rebels or ideological revolutionaries. Each may think that his or her way is the only way and that the old ways must be rejected in toto, but there is death too in that rejection.

As the 1960s can be thought to have finally ended with Watergate, if one uses the shorthand of the decade to refer to the complex of protest movements and disillusionments of the time, so ends *American Pastoral*. "It was the summer of the Watergate hearings," begins the last section of the novel, a slow, closely narrated account of a dinner party. The explosion Merry's bomb was meant to effect, an explosion of American ways and beliefs, has already occurred, and the blast is beginning to be felt, the ripples spreading outward like those in films of atomic bomb tests (285). Instead of sitting on the porch watching their herd on the hill, the Swede and Dawn are watching the replay of the Watergate hearings on television with his parents. Bill and Jessie Orcutt, a couple invited for dinner, are old stock and a reminder that, for the Swede, Old Rimrock is America, in all of its Revolutionary inheritance and its postwar promise. However, walking into the kitchen at the wrong time, the Swede finds out that Bill has not only been working for them as the architect for their new house but has also become Dawn's lover. As he glimpses the possibility of Merry's returning to the family, he discovers the family itself is in jeopardy.

The danger to the family and their way of life comes, for Zuckerman in the last chapter of his fictional creation, not just from the descendants of Revolutionary America but from the disintegration of American culture. The topic of conversation at dinner alternates between Watergate and *Deep Throat*, which is being shown not just in adult theaters but in regular movie theaters, to the disdain of Lou, who expresses shock that no one seems inclined to protect children from the "degrading things" afloat in the culture, things that are "an affront to decency and to decent people" (358). Marcia Umanoff, a cynical literature professor, responds, "And what is so inexhaustibly interesting about decency. . . . Not the richest response to life I can think of" (359, 360). Challenged to name a response she would recommend, perhaps "the high road of transgression," Marcia defends herself against Lou's incredulity by referring to Genesis: "Isn't that what the Garden of Eden story is telling us. . . . Without transgression there is no knowledge." Lou responds that what they taught him in school was "that when God above tells you not to do something, you damn well don't do it—that's what. Do it and you pay the piper. Do it and you will suffer from it for the rest of your days" (360). The paradise that is lost for the Swede, that is finally crumbling before his eyes as he is teased with the impossible possibility of its restoration, is here debated by the champion of liberation and the champion of restraint. What these two characters are doing, as any Roth reader recognizes, is rehearsing the central argument of Roth's fiction, and they are doing it in the end-of-the-1960s moment that gave it so much of its urgency.

Zuckerman has the Swede question his faith in the holy American order he has believed in all of his life just as Jessie, Orcutt's alcoholic wife, responding to Lou's attempting to get her to try pie and milk instead of scotch and scotch, stabs him in the temple with a fork. Unable even to recognize what she has done, Jessie is tragic, a casualty, and the act an example of the disorder the Swede feels he is confronting. But Marcia, who revels in this disorder, is not tragic. Rather, Zuckerman presents her as guilty of not trying to stem the tide of the disintegration she only too clearly recognizes. She fills the chair Jessie has just been lifted out of, the demonic replacing the merely pathetic, and laughs. She is one of those who choose "to laugh and to relish, as some people, historically, always seem to do, how far the rampant disorder had spread, enjoying enormously the assailability, the frailty, the enfeeblement of supposedly robust things" (423). The enormous enjoyment Marcia feels at the sight of a man nearly losing an eye underlines the detachment of her attitude, the lack of humanity in her insistence on the value of liberation and nothing else.

Though the frame never reappears in *American Pastoral*, Zuckerman can be seen as quietly returning in the last moments of the novel, asking his question, reminding readers that all they have read since he slipped away has been not realist account but reverie. That he does not answer this question is not because the question is rhetorical. The whole novel has led up to it, has been thinking about it before it has been asked. And Roth, through Zuckerman, is asking something larger than Zuckerman could answer: he is asking about the bomb he himself set off in his own work. He is reconsidering the ramifications of *Portnoy's Complaint* and his own rejection of much of what he was brought up with.

Does he think he was wrong to have set off his own bomb? After the metafictional experiments of so many of his later novels, after the incendiary language of novels from *Portnoy's Complaint* to *Sabbath's Theater*, in *American Pastoral* Roth, writes in an earlier style, influenced by Flaubert and James, that he was once proud to have left behind. The wealth of detail provided in finely crafted, infinitely subordinated sentences and the calmer, relatively rant-free prose of this novel represent a return to literary roots for Roth. No pages-long footnotes containing phone-sex conversations here, as in *Sabbath's Theater*; rather, readers are given pages-long catalogs, in exquisite detail, of the process of manufacturing gloves. This is not a retrenchment or a rejection of Roth's entire career; instead, the way in which he writes this novel represents a renewed appreciation of the value of his earlier influences. In terms of the literary liberation Roth attempted in the late 1960s then, *American Pastoral* can be seen as a reconsideration of what was lost in that act of rejection. And, as any one of Jerry's speeches attests, it's still got the patented Rothian rants.

While he always recognized the literary rebellion, in *American Pastoral* Roth also seems to admit, looking back, that *Portnoy's Complaint* was also a social rebellion, even as it recognized the difficulty of such an act.[5] The bomb that Roth tossed into the library, attacking the old forms and subjects, was accompanied by a bomb thrown into the kitchen, attacking the old ways and beliefs. *American Pastoral* also seems to be admitting that, however valuable Roth's freeing himself from both literary and social tradition was, there were losses as a result of that earlier book, just as there were losses incurred as a result of the actions of a generation looking to establish their own American pastoral. While an underlying current of ambivalence ran through earlier works, from Alex's struggles in *Portnoy's Complaint* to the sadness of still-raging Mickey Sabbath's continued defiance of convention in a novel Morris Dickstein calls "the last novel of the 1960s" (*Leopards* 228), in *American Pastoral* Roth more fully considers the extent of the loss and refuses to balance the ledger. As Ross Posnock puts it, there remains in the novel "some knot of irreducible ambivalence, of revulsion and sympathy" (*Philip* 114).

In *Reading Myself and Others*, Roth called the 1960s "the demythologizing decade" (86). Demythologizing is the job of the kind of novelist Roth has always seen himself to be. Twenty years after he wrote this, Roth seems to see that demythologizing, novelistic or otherwise, is not a value-free activity; that is, it works from its own ideals, its own vision of perfection, and it can tear down more than it intends. What he explores in *American Pastoral* is the idea, again, that tearing things down and starting over itself partakes of the myth that such a thing is possible, that a new, innocent world can be made. Thus, the irony that Roth lays out in this novel: these two very different-seeming phenomena, the American Dream and the rebellion against it, are built on the same myth.

What does *American Pastoral* do with this paradox? In *The Counterlife*, Zuckerman watches a film on human reproduction. He comments on the point of view from which it is shot, inside a woman's reproductive organs:

> According to one school, it's where the pastoral genre that you speak of begins, those irrepressible yearnings by people beyond simplicity to be taken off to the perfectly safe, charmingly simple and satisfying environment that is desire's homeland. How moving and pathetic these pastorals are that cannot admit contradiction or conflict! (368)

This refusal to admit contradiction, to move beyond the simplicity of one's own belief and the surety with which others are rejected, is in *American Pastoral* the *Et in Arcadia ego*, the unnamed death that lurks in the heart of the liberations of the 1960s as well as in the American Dream. The irony that characterizes Roth's artistic credo—the insistence on admitting contradiction—allows *American Pastoral* to look beyond myth and see America for what it is, and has been.

CHAPTER 3

After Identity
Morrison and Genealogy

Memory, on which history draws and which it nourishes in
return, seeks to save the past in order to serve the present and
the future. Let us act in such a way that collective memory may
serve the liberation and not the enslavement of human beings.

Jacques LeGoff, *History and Memory*

One must look very low and very high for the complicities of
human affectivity in tune with the terror recorded by history.
... Let a riot flare up in the streets, let the country be declared
in danger, and something in me is touched off and springs
loose. . . . It is to be noted that these shrouded depths of consciousness resurge at the highest levels of consciousness: the
meaning of terror is also the meaning of ideology; suddenly
justice, law, truth take on capital letters in bearing arms and
in surrounding themselves with the splendor of morose pas-
sions. Languages and cultures are thrown into the blazing
mass of pathos; a monstrous totality is equipped for danger
and death; God himself is adduced: his name is on sword-
belts, in oaths, in the speech of helmeted crusaders.

Paul Ricoeur, *History and Truth*

Perhaps that was why she began to laugh. Lightly at first and
then heavily, her head thrown back as she sat at the table. Did
they really think they could keep this up?

Toni Morrison, *Paradise*

n late December, 1997, seven months after the appearance of Philip Roth's *American Pastoral*, Toni Morrison's *Paradise* was published by Knopf. It was Morrison's seventh novel, the latest in a career that had garnered her great acclaim (including a Nobel Prize four years earlier) and had exerted a great influence on American letters and culture. In becoming the most widely read African American novelist in the late 1970s and 1980s, she had brought Black women's writing (and experience) attention on a scale it had never received previously. Especially after her first two efforts, Morrison's novels had also brought attention to African American history in a way that perhaps only the miniseries *Roots* (1977) has been able to. So it was something of a surprise when, in the space of half a year, novels by Morrison and Roth appeared that were so remarkably similar that Louis Menand called their publication "one of the weirder coincidences in American literary history." The two novels focus on particular ethnic groups, are set in the same historical period, and, most importantly, use paradise as the central metaphor through which they write about the experience of the group during the period. The surprise comes, of course, from the fact that such similar books could come from two writers thought of as so different: Morrison and Roth, the best known working Jewish American novelist, were not, in Menand's words, "writers one ordinarily imagines walking hand in hand, as it were, among common themes and concerns" ("War" 80). Yet at very nearly the exact same time they produced books that look back in very similar ways on the same moment in their nation's history.

While the appearance of the two novels could be seen as a chance literary-historical occurrence, I believe it can also be explained in part by the contemporaneity of both the writers' lives and also their novels' writing. Roth and Morrison were born two years apart in the early 1930s, formed in their teens and early adulthood by postwar America, came into their own in their careers as writers in the 1960s and 1970s (writing about sexuality and race, two central issues of the times); in the years just after the end of the Cold War Roth and Morrison were also entering their sixties — and writing *Paradise* and *American Pastoral*. What at first might look like simple coincidence may instead be understood partly as what happens when writers reach an age and stage in their careers that leads them to look back — and do so at a time when the culture of which they are part also looks back.[1] The convergence of key junctures in their careers with the turn of the 1960s on the one hand and that of their individual retrospective moments with a national return to issues and tensions central to that earlier time on the other, then, inform these works. The ostensibly coincidental appearance of these two novels may also be understood as what happened in American letters after history didn't end.

Paradise has been read as a book about religion and as a book about gender. It is these things, certainly; Morrison herself has insisted at times that it is primarily a book about religion.[2] A recognition of the nearly contemporaneous publication of *Paradise* and *American Pastoral*, however, highlights the way in which *Paradise*, like *American Pastoral*, is about history. In *Paradise*, Morrison looks back at the intertwined history of her ethnic community, her nation, and her career from the vantage point of post–Cold War America. As Roth does in *American Pastoral*, in *Paradise* Morrison describes the late 1960s and early 1970s using the metaphors of Edens old and new, of the Fall, of paradises lost, regained, and lost again — and using them not for themselves but rather to investigate the effects of their use throughout American history. And, as Roth does in his novel, Morrison reconsiders not just the times but her own oeuvre, revisiting and continuing the history of her artistic engagement with the world.[3] Specifically, Morrison looks back, from the time of the resurgence of the culture wars, at a pivotal moment for the civil rights movement. In doing so, she not only rereads that time and her own earlier reading of it, she also rethinks the effect of that time (and her reading of it) on her later works.[4]

The historical climate of the 1990s did not turn Morrison toward history. She has always been a historically minded novelist. Even before her novels turned more explicitly to the investigation of the past, starting with *Song of Solomon* (1977), they always kept an eye on it. Her first, *The Bluest Eye* (1970), was set not in the 1960s, when she wrote it, but the 1940s. From *Song of Solomon* to *Jazz* (1992), her novels were set in the past. This past has included Reconstruction, the 1920s, the early 1960s, and has in each case been set against an even older past, from the time of slavery to more recent times, which she revisits with her characters as they try to make sense of themselves and their world. Race, and so genealogy, has always been central to the process through which her characters before *Paradise* made sense not just of the past but also of their own lives. When in *Song of Solomon* Milkman Dead traces his family history back through slavery to its roots in Africa, searching at first for gold but in the end finding his name and his ancestral past, he is both vehicle for and part of the historical novel's genealogy, the project of searching for understanding through excavation of family history. In each of Morrison's novels, the historical background allows us to understand that the conditions, the consciousness, and the fates of individual characters goes back, through genealogy, all the way to slavery and even the middle passage. This background is carried generationally, through the great migration that brings her characters up from the slavery- or postslavery-era South, north to New York or Ohio, away from but not escaping these defining moments in their family histories. Memories of this genealogical background may be forgotten or dimmed, but the background is not lost, and the task of many of Morrison's main characters becomes not just delving back into their own individual, often rejected pasts but recovering this familial, collective past, including the painful, perhaps long-suppressed events that eventually shape these individual lives.

Paradise, in first performing its own repetition of the genealogically informed racial history that forms the backbone of Morrison's earlier works and then rejecting this performance, offers an implicit criticism of the way in which those earlier works engaged with race and history.[5] The content of this critique might be even more surprising than the Roth connection and is due to some of the same causes. Morrison is thought of as one of the clearest and most insistent voices on the problem of racial discrimination in America; from her first novel, she has paid careful attention to this issue across history. It is possible that, in the wake of the end of the Cold War, looking back at the time that made her as a writer, Morrison saw that racial essentialism was at the root of the fundamental narrative and intellectual structure of her previous work—and it is possible that *Paradise* is the result. In repudiating genealogy in *Paradise*, Morrison repudiates not only a central component of her work and a fundamental aspect of the historical novel but also a central tenet in the history of thinking about race in America. In this novel, she addresses the power and problems of essentialist constructions of race, of the fiction of racial purity and essence that Ralph Ellison called "blood-magic and blood-thinking" (*Territory* 21). *Paradise*, then, amounts to a deconstruction of perhaps the most fundamental American binary, that of black and white. That it appears in the wake of the fall of another binary organization of the world—the Cold War—is not a coincidence.

Paradise begins, "They shoot the white girl first. With the rest they can take their time." We are not told, then or at any time in the novel, who the white girl is. Readers of Morrison's work, familiar with her many skeleton-plot openings and, more generally, her stated desire to make her readers work with her to complete her novels, might expect this blank to be filled in as the plot is fleshed out, perhaps with a little work on their part.[6] They would be wrong.

The rest of the first chapter tells the story of this murderous 1976 attack. The attack is made on the Convent, a former Catholic school for Indian girls in Oklahoma, home since the late 1960s to a group of mostly Black, unattached, sexually liberated women. The attack is carried out by a group of men from the nearby all-Black town of Ruby. The rest of the novel is organized into chapters that tell the stories of the Convent women and of the usually separate but at times intersecting stories of prosperous, exclusive Ruby. A large part of this latter story, in addition to the stories of the lives of its present-day inhabitants, is the town's long history, which comes in three parts. The first is the pre- and postslavery story of the current inhabitants' ancestors in the deep South, a story marked by emancipation, a rise to prominence, and then a fall in which they are purged from positions of local and statewide power. The second is the story of the long journey up from the deep South, a journey that is marked by their ancestors' rejection not just by whites and Indians and all-Black towns generally but by one particular Black town populated by lighter-skinned Blacks (an event they call "the Disallowing"). The journey ends in the founding of their own exclusionary town, Haven. The third part of this history is the voluntary exodus of the young from Haven after their bittersweet return from World War II to still-racist America and the subsequent establishment of the new town of Ruby based firmly on the same unspoken exclusionary principles, later unearthed by one of the town's women—principles based on maintaining the town's pure Black blood. The violent attack that begins and ends the novel is carried out in the name of this town's moral health, but the real motivation is this unspoken principle.

Through the course of telling all these stories, the novel does not reveal who the white girl is. This is not because *Paradise* is a difficult novel, though it is.[7] And although some have argued that the novel supplies enough information for readers to figure out the identity of the white girl, the mystery is at least very carefully maintained and at most unsolvable.[8] And the fact of the mystery leads to the question of its purpose: why does the novel not make clear who the white girl is? The answer is found in the project at its heart. Through its own highlighting of readers' expectation that racial markers will be provided by selectively refusing to provide them in a novel all about racial marking, *Paradise* goes beyond exploring the harmful effects of race-thinking on its characters to examine its effects on readers and its own author. Before showing more closely how the novel works in this regard, I will look briefly at why I think Morrison may have wanted it to.

The history of race-relations in the U.S. has been, of course, quite eventful and rocky, and the course of this history has inevitably affected the work of contemporary American novelists concerned with race. The novels of Morrison—who has periodically written about these concerns in nonfiction pieces such as "What the Black Woman Thinks of Woman's Lib," which appeared in the *New York Times Magazine* in 1971, and in her introductions to *Race-ing Justice, En-gendering Power*, a collection of essays on the 1991 confirmation hearings of Clarence Thomas, and *Birth of a Nation'hood*, a collection on the 1995 murder trial of O. J. Simpson—have been especially connected to this history, both in the early years of her career and in the years that led up to the publication of *Paradise*.

The 1980s saw a number of challenges to the legacy of the civil rights movement. Reagan's offensive against that legacy took the form of a number of fights against the legislation that had ostensibly cemented the social gains won for African Americans. The goal of this offensive was, in the words of one legal scholar, "hastening an end to the Second Reconstruction in America. Reagan not only succeeded in reducing the protection of specific laws; he transformed the federal judiciary, once the foremost champion of individual rights, into a threat to those laws" (Schwartz 130). Affirmative action was under attack, as were a number of social programs and legal remedies lumped together by opponents as overly race conscious.[9] As Reagan put it at his first press conference as president, "I'm old enough to remember when quotas existed in the U.S. for the purpose of discrimination, and I don't want to see that happen again" (qtd. in Terry Anderson 165). Future Supreme Court justice Thomas argued against affirmative action, not in terms of the alleged injustice of quotas, but rather in terms of effectiveness: "I think it's debatable whether affirmative action has resulted in any changes that wouldn't have occurred naturally. In the long run, I don't think the results are going to be so positive" (qtd. in Evan Thomas). The consolidation of civil rights gains became instead a defense. The culture wars of the 1980s, many battles of which were fought over multiculturalism, were stirred up by calls for legal and social recognition of and respect for racially and ethnically identified groups in part as a response to efforts to negate racial considerations in public policy. Many battles of the culture wars, as a result, were debates over whether multiculturalism recognized and celebrated the value of individual cultures or balkanized American culture.[10]

This climate prevailed into the early 1990s, when a number of events occurred that brought race to the fore in public discussion and contributed to a reconsideration not simply of racial and ethnic identification but also of the categories themselves. They included the Thomas hearings, in particular Anita Hill's testimony against him, and the 1992 riots in Los Angeles occasioned by the acquittal of the officers who beat Rodney King. These events raised questions about identity, history, and racial solidarity and so added to a growing discussion of the identity politics of multiculturalism, potentially unsettling ideas that had become accepted by many Americans, particularly by African American intellectuals.

In 1995, *Atlantic Monthly* ran an essay claiming that African American intellectuals were the new public intellectuals (as the New York Jews were decades before), in part, it argued, because a number of them had stopped thinking and writing only about African Americans as African Americans:

> Recently, several black intellectuals have been redirecting their attention from race-based politics to the importance of American citizenship for race relations. That is, they have thought less exclusively about the meaning of "blackness" and more inclusively about what it means to be an African-American. (Boynton 56)

This trend of the rethinking of African American identity intersected with a questioning of the intellectual focus on identity more generally. In 1992, Kwame Anthony Appiah and Henry Louis Gates, Jr., edited a special issue of *Critical Inquiry* entitled "Identities." In their introduction they questioned the academy's overly narrow focus on race, class, and gender. Calling these terms the "holy trinity of literary criticism," they argued that they would soon "become the regnant clichés of our critical discourse" ("Editor's Introduction" 8). While they called for a more complicated understanding of identity—one that recognizes the ways individuals are multiply identified—their criticism indicated a problem they had with the way identity was being thought of at the time that went beyond their sense that it was simplistic. With the 1992 publication of his *In My Father's House*, Appiah made explicit his argument that the concept of race is false. Based on bad nineteenth-century science, he argued, the classification of humans by race, even in terms of genetic variation, which does not correlate to racial classification, has no biological truth.[11] In both African American identity politics and the Pan-Africanist movement, a reliance on race-based identity, while serving certain political purposes, is as essentialist as white racism and as inaccurate. Gates, informed by postmodernism and earlier thinkers whose ideas have been adopted by postmodernism (such as Bakhtin), was also talking at the time about racial identity as social construct rather than intrinsic essence. In "Blackness without Blood," published in 1990 in a collection of essays about the 1980s in America, Gates explains what he believes African Americans had done in their thinking about race: "Recognizing that what had passed for 'the human' or for 'the universal' was in fact white essentialism, we substituted one sort of essentialism (that of 'blackness') for another" (115). As did many others, Gates still insisted on race's social reality: "To declare that race is a trope, however, is not to deny its palpable force in the life of every African American who tries to function every day in a still very racist America" (125).[12]

These are two of the time's many rejections of what Ross Posnock calls the "romance of identity" (*Color* 3). They can be understood as moves away from what Alain Locke called the "fetish of biological purity" and toward a cosmopolitanism similar to that which he believes was overlooked in the thought of W. E. B. DuBois, Locke, and others earlier in the century (qtd. in Posnock, *Color* 17). These later rejections of essentialism were part of a larger questioning of identity politics among intellectuals fueled in part by the poor fit between certain strands of postmodern

thought and multicultural or identity politics. The antiessential-
ist stance of much postmodern thought, together with a sense of
the subject that does not allow for the notion of the coherent self,
left little room for belief in the idea of authentic racial selfhood.
Just as postcolonial returns to ethnic identity clashed with postmodernism's constructed, interpellated, overdetermined subject,
so too did cultural pluralism.[13] In the late 1980s and early 1990s,
multiculturalism was attacked from one side for its reassertion
of a coherent self and from another for what was often termed its
balkanizing effect.[14] The impact of these challenges was still felt at
the end of the 1990s, as can be seen in the June 2000 special issue
of *American Literature* edited by Houston Baker, entitled "Unsettling Blackness." In between, Morrison wrote a novel difficult not
to read in the light of these challenges.

To understand the ways in which *Paradise* is part of this moment
in intellectual history, it helps to see how it constructs the histories of its own characters and of the two places in which readers
find them. The explanation for the central event, the attack on
the Convent, is revealed as the pasts of the town of Ruby and of
the Convent and of their inhabitants are themselves revealed. In a
book in which the past is increasingly shown to control the present, many chapters are devoted to the stories of the individual
residents of the Convent, to the details of their pasts and to what
they do with and to their pasts. Much of the difficulty of the novel
resides in the fragmented, nonlinear way in which these stories
are presented.

The first of these retold pasts belongs to Mavis, who arrives at
the Convent not long after the accidental death of her two young-
est children in the backseat of the hot car in which she left them
and after her subsequent escape from the house where her husband and remaining children were, she felt, plotting to kill her. At
the Convent she meets the mirrored sunglasses-wearing Connie
and the pale, frail woman upstairs surrounded by a ring of light
in a house without electricity, a woman Connie calls Mother and
of whom she says, in response to Mavis's confusion upon meet-

ing the white mother of this brown Connie: "She is my mother. Your mother too. Whose mother you?" (48). In this moment, the novel presents the Convent as grounded in the maternal and race-blind.

Mavis is the first of the women to arrive, years before the attack. She stays, off and on, until it happens, drawn by Mother and Connie and the chance to remake herself. The other three come one by one, running from their own pasts, landing at the Convent in various states of disrepair and disrepute or shame.

Consolata, or Connie, is there to meet each of these women in one way or another when they get there. By the time the last of them arrives, she is no longer the strong, kind woman who met Mavis, but instead, after Mary Magna's death, an increasingly angry and sad drunk who lives in the basement, hating the women who'd come to live in her house. Rescued from the streets of Rio de Janeiro as a girl by the Mother Superior and raised at the Convent, Consolata becomes unable to console herself over her losses—of her virginity at nine by rape, of love thirty years later, and of the nun who raised her and who she was unable ultimately to keep alive with her newly discovered supernatural power (hence the glow Mavis notes). She succumbs to the self-loathing that afflicts all of these women, outcasts of one kind or another. Her rebirth, as literal as it is figurative (as the women note, "She has the features of Dear Connie, but they are sculpted somehow" [262], as if she'd come through some kind of purifying fire), comes with a new kind of religion, the Afro-Brazilian syncretic Catholic Candomblé, which is of course old for her (Bouson 209, Leonard, "The Black Album" 25). Armed with this new old belief, she takes control of her Convent and initiates a new program.

The results appear not long before the attack on the Convent, which comes at the end of *Paradise*. At this point, before the attack, the novel shifts from revelations of the Convent women's pasts to their learning how to free themselves from these pasts. Much of the story of the town and people of Ruby has already been told—their official past, the difference between this story and the true story, and the difference between their official present and what is really happening in their town. And the stories of these two very different places—one run by women learning to escape from endlessly relived, retold pasts, race-blind; another run by men trapped in a raced, rigid story of the past—are wound around each other as the novel tells of the times when the Convent's short history has intersected with the recent history of Ruby. In doing so, the novel prepares the way for the final, violent intersection with which it begins and ends, an intersection that is more a blindsiding than a crossroads.

It is an intersection toward which Morrison's work could be seen to be leading from the very beginning. In fact, it could be argued that Morrison's own retrospective moment, encouraged by at least three major events of 1993—the October awarding of the Nobel in recognition of her entire oeuvre, her writing of a new afterword (dated November) for her reissued first novel, *The Bluest Eye*, and the burning of her house and loss of her manuscripts in December—led her to see this impending development herself. The return to *The Bluest Eye* in particular, I believe, may have led to the idea at the heart of *Paradise*.

In the afterword to *The Bluest Eye*, Morrison discusses what she was trying to do in the novel and the difficulties she ran into in the attempt. The afterword reveals a writer determined to talk about problems in her work of more than two decades earlier. It also reveals Morrison's take on her thinking, two decades earlier, about the issues confronting America, especially Black America. In it she writes, "One problem was centering: the weight of the novel's inquiry on so delicate and vulnerable a character could smash her and lead readers into the comfort of pitying her rather than into an interrogation of themselves for the smashing" (211). The character about whom Morrison speaks is Pecola Breedlove, daughter of Pauline and Cholly, southerners who'd joined the great northward migration and ended up in Ohio, where their lives came apart. Pecola's story is told mostly from the childhood perspective of the adult Claudia MacTeer, a neighborhood girl of similar circumstances whose family heroically manages to keep things together in the face of the institutionalized, internalized racism of America in the early 1940s. Pecola's story ends with her rape by her father, her resulting pregnancy, and her ultimate mental disintegration, culminating in her belief that she has gotten for herself the blue eyes she'd always envied in Shirley Temple and all the other pretty white girls staring up at her from candy wrappers and down at her from billboards. Claudia's telling makes this as much the story of her own awakening to the realities of racism and especially of internalized racism—what DuBois called "double-consciousness" (45)—as it is the story of Pecola's disintegration.

As Morrison writes in her afterword, one problem in the construction of the novel is that Pecola is overburdened, that her fate is overdetermined, and that as a result readers may pity her rather than look at their own complicity in her fate. She writes,

> A problem lies in the central chamber of the novel. The shattered world I built (to complement what is happening to Pecola), its pieces held together by seasons in childtime and commenting at every turn on the incompatible and barren white-family primer, does not in its present form handle effectively the silence at its center: the void that is Pecola's "unbeing." It should have had a shape—like the emptiness left by a boom or a cry. (214–15)

Richard Wright, in "How Bigger Was Born," his essay on the making of *Native Son*, discusses his earlier story collection, *Uncle Tom's Children*. "I found," he laments, "that I had written a book which even bankers' daughters could read and weep over and feel good about" (531). He resolves, with *Native Son*, not to make the same mistake again. Like Wright, Morrison wanted to write a book too tough to inspire mere pity. The interrogation she hoped to inspire was that of the readers themselves for contributing to internalized self-hatred like Pecola's. The problem is that the book may be too tough. The result can be seen in the flip side of Pecola's overburdening: the silence of Pecola herself at the center of this shattered world.

Of course, the absence of an authentic self is the point of Pecola; any possibility of its existing, Morrison seems to argue, was lost when her parents' selfhood was crushed by the weight of racism. The boom or cry she wishes she had incorporated would have mitigated the smashing of Pecola as a presence in the novel if not as a person, would have given her a voice, however muted, and so would have more effectively represented the silence where she should have been. Instead, because of the silence, readers may not be led to the self-interrogation Morrison desires. Instead, in DuBois's words concerning double-consciousness, we may "look on in amused contempt and pity"—a pairing which nearly equates the latter with the former (45). Feeling sorry for Pecola isn't enough; it's almost as bad as laughing at her. And as James Baldwin wrote of Richard Wright and Bigger Thomas, it is dangerous to write characters who fall so short of the mark the author herself sets; as Wright could imagine Bigger but Bigger couldn't imagine Wright, so could the same be said for Morrison and Pecola.

Morrison, in her afterword, sees her failure to give a satisfactory shape or sound to Pecola as one of technique; she writes, "It required sophistication unavailable to me" (215). As a first novel, she seems to be saying, it should not surprise that the technique is found to be sometimes lacking. Looking back from five novels later, Morrison sees *The Bluest Eye* as marred by flaws that are the fault of her rawness as a writer; she seems to think that Morrison the editor should have caught the errors of execution made by Morrison the writer.

I would argue that *Paradise* can be seen as the result of Morrison's recognizing that the flaws in *The Bluest Eye* were not due to artistic inexperience but rather to the ideas at its heart, ideas central to the decade during which Morrison wrote it. Chief among these ideas is the weight of race and gender in the fate of individuals. The twin (and interanimating) rises of race consciousness and gender consciousness, or race pride and feminism, can be seen to lead to the overburdening of Pecola. Morrison was inspired by and involved in the development and dissemination of these ideas early in her professional career. As an editor at Random House in the 1960s and 1970s, she promoted Black women's fiction, such as novels by Toni Cade Bambara and Gayl Jones, and Middleton A. Harris's *The Black Book* (1974), a groundbreaking project Morrison edited that collected primary texts about the African American people and events left out of American textbooks and, so, American history. The texts collected in *The Black Book* would go on to influence Morrison's own recovery of that history in her fiction, the chief example being an 1856 article about a mother who killed her children rather than allow them to be returned to slavery, which provided the inspiration for *Beloved* (McKay, "Introduction" 6).

The sense of the inescapability of Pecola's fate in *The Bluest Eye* carries an air of historical inevitability, almost of predestination.[15] When readers are provided her family history, they are not being given, as an explanation for her horrible fate, the peculiar set of circumstances that created her family. Instead, they are given the genealogy not just of the Breedloves but also of the MacTeers and everyone around them. They came Up North from Down South, as part of the Great Migration of African Americans from the post-Reconstruction former slaveholding states, and found a coldness that was the product of something more than climate. In leaving the South, they were trying to escape the white gaze, found not just inside themselves but outside in the fields and in the court-houses and the single trees out front of them, the white gaze first encountered, historically, on the western shores of Africa. However, it was up North too, and not just in the people they met there but also, still, inside themselves. Only with great effort will an individual, usually with a strong family—the very thing this climate works against—be able to escape its effects.

This history is embodied in the brief story of the Breedloves and informs the entire novel. It makes the creation of Pecola and other Pecolas seem inevitable, part of a historical pattern. *The Bluest Eye* is set in the early 1940s to provide a historical grounding for a discussion of double consciousness inspired by what Morrison calls "the reclamation of racial beauty" (*Bluest* 210). This time represents, for Morrison, a time before the ideas that inspire the novel were widely articulated, before the widespread discussion of the insidiousness of seemingly innocent scenes such as Shirley Temple dancing with Mr. Bojangles. Because of what Morrison was using this setting for, then, the idea of genealogical near inevitability of the kind that determines Pecola's fate made sense.

In her novels after *The Bluest Eye*, Morrison travels farther back into the past, using genealogy as a kind of roadmap. Traveling back through the time after slavery to the slavery years themselves and back farther into the murky memories and myths of the time before slavery, traveling routes marked by names encoded in rhymes and songs, Morrison details the ways in which history shapes the present. Morrison's novels are steeped in genealogy, in history as lived by forebears, from *Sula's* historical perspective on the neighborhood known as the Bottom, following three generations; to *Song of Solomon's* convergence with crucial moments not just in civil rights history but African American history back to the middle passage, following four generations; to the colonial history that haunts the islands in *Tar Baby* (1981); to the novel of Morrison's set farthest in the past, *Beloved*; to *Jazz's* look back from the Harlem of the Renaissance to the beginnings of African American life under slavery.[16] *Song of Solomon* appeared at a time when the recollection of slavery and the return to African roots had a strong hold on the African American imagination, as shown by the phenomenon of Alex Haley's television miniseries *Roots* (1977). Through Milkman's genealogical quest, *Song of Solomon* links the distant slavery and preslavery past to the civil rights movement's late struggles, which are, by the fact of the temporal gap between the novel's mid-1960s ending and mid-1970s appearance, elided (and so, as John Brenkman has argued, emphasized ["Politics and Form"]). Like Haley, in *Song of Solomon* Morrison looked to the past for roots, for a sense of group identity in group history. The work that Sethe finds herself consumed by in *Beloved* is the work of "beating back the past" (73); she finds some measure of peace when she deals with her past, understands what led her to murder her child. It is only when she understands her past that she can stop fighting it, can "lay it all down, sword and shield" (173).

An examination of *The Bluest Eye* reveals that both the ideas and the basic techniques of Morrison's novels were present in her work from the start; *Paradise* examines the connection between these ideas and the time that gave birth to them. In its setting during the years formative to Morrison's writing and the years following her beginnings as a writer, years contemporary to the full flowering of the civil rights movement and to its decline, it reconsiders the effect of those times on those who lived through them, as any historical novel does, but it also reconsiders the genealogical inevitability expressed in her earlier works. What it finds is that the Black Power movement, which challenged the integrationist philosophy of the civil rights movement with its own separatism, was not a solution to this inevitability but rather reinforcement. Pride in race as essence, as inborn and pure, as in-the-blood, *Paradise* suggests, repeats the mistake made by white supremacist thinking. The determinism of *The Bluest Eye*, seen in the light of what Morrison and many others were coming to believe about race toward the end of the twentieth century, only made it seem, in the last words of the novel, "much, much, much too late" (206). At this late date, *Paradise* wonders, maybe it isn't.

As the secret pasts of Ruby are separate from yet intertwined with the story of the nearby yet so different Convent, dividing the novel in two, so Ruby's stories are themselves filled with doubling and divisions, with distinctions drawn between things and people close but not identical. Ruby's public and private histories as well as its present secrets are filled with twins and doubles, with sides taken and lines drawn, with parallels noticed and unnoticed. The ending of the part of Ruby's continuing history that includes the Convent, which provides a coda and a culmination to all that we have learned about it, comes out of this doubleness and division, this sameness and difference. This ending—the attack—is prepared for and presented by the novel in a way that reveals all the manifestations of this structural tendency and points out its roots in a history that goes back much farther than the history Ruby tells itself about itself.

The histories of Ruby, official and otherwise, can be pieced together by readers only as they make their way through *Paradise*. The official story, as retold by Deacon and Steward Morgan, the twin brothers who effectively run the town, begins in 1890 with the Old Fathers. This group of ancestors had been in Louisiana since the 1750s, as slaves, and after Emancipation had helped govern the state for a short time, until Reconstruction ended. Unhappy in a South in which they were again field labor, they began a long trek to the Oklahoma territory, where they hoped to settle and work their own land. What they found instead was rejection, not just from poor whites and Indians but also from the all-Black towns that had begun to pop up, on the grounds that they didn't have enough money, at first, but later because of the color of their skin. Described as "8-rock" after the darkest coal found deep in mines, these ancestors were turned away from the town of Fairly, Oklahoma, because they were too dark.

The secret of Ruby comes from this distinction drawn between them and those they wanted to join; it was so fine and yet so final, and the shame attendant to it so great, that they not only never forgot it, they based their future on it. When Deacon and Steward's grandfather Zechariah and the other patriarchs founded Ruby's predecessor town, Haven, they build a communal oven bearing a large iron plate reading, "Beware the Furrow of His Brow." Ostensibly religious in meaning—befitting the religiosity of the founding families, who saw their wanderings and establishment of Haven very much as an exodus in the Old Testament sense—the plaque was taken to urge obedience to a strict and demanding God. A second sense of the words on the Oven, though, betrays the inscription of their rejection on the hearts of Haven, a sense "in which the 'You' (understood), vocative case, was not a command to the believers but a threat to those who had disallowed them" (195). On their most central symbol of their trials they commemorate the one that hurt the most. The story behind Haven's founding, then, illustrates "the importance of shame and pride in the formation of racial and cultural identity" (Bouson 193). Haven outlasts the all-Black towns that had rejected it, through hard work and solidarity and, according to some, divine protection. That this survival is in large part due to wounds inflicted upon its people is not part of the common understanding.

In the other understood "You" in the Oven's message, the flip side of the miracle of Ruby is evident. This you, it turns out, is the resident who chooses not to follow the unspoken rule of the community, the blood rule. What the Old Fathers took from the Disallowing and passed on to the New Fathers was a determination not just to withdraw and protect but also to keep pure.

The 8-rock blood, the sign of purity that had become a stain, is recaptured as not just a source of pride but a covenant, a promise to keep Ruby 8-rock by allowing marriage only between the families or to outsiders also blue-black dark. Patricia Best, who has been compiling folders and notebooks documenting family trees as well as her own increasing discomfort with what her research uncovers, discovers this covenant and much more.[17] Pat uncovers the truth of the blood rule through investigation of, among other cases, her own: she connects to the blood rule not only the death of her mother in childbirth and the refusal of the men of Ruby to help but also the hatred directed at her and her father.

When Pat discovers that the reason for gaps and crossings-out in her trees is the blood rule and retaliation against those who break it, she burns her files and notebooks:

> She felt clean. Perhaps that was why she began to laugh. Lightly at first and then heavily, her head thrown back as she sat at the table. Did they really think they could keep this up? The numbers, the bloodlines, the who fucks who? All those generations of 8-rocks kept going, just to end up narrow as bale wire? (217)

Who fucks who becomes not merely a moral question but a survival question in the minds of these men, and what threatens that survival is woman, only one of two who's, but apparently the one that can go wrong.

There is a long recent history of the Convent helping the women of Ruby—helping them to go wrong, in the eyes of the New Fathers. This secret succor, to Arnette, who has been trying to abort her baby by K.D., nephew and lone male descendant of the twins, and to Sweetie, who has been trying not to walk out on her sickly children, is given freely but is turned by Ruby's men into reason to be rid of the Convent. Even Deacon's long-ago affair with Consolata becomes occasion for blaming the Convent women. Their behavior, so unlike the proper and protected behavior of the Ruby women, is sign of their evil, of the threat they pose. And so they are blamed for the thing that most needs to be blamed on someone, the turning of Ruby's young people against the old ways.

Reverend Richard Misner, an outsider who comes to minister

to Ruby, observes this turn, as seen in the disintegration or exit of some and the rebellion of others. He also takes part in it, bringing the ideas of the civil rights movement to a town that has somehow remained oblivious to it or, more exactly, has chosen to ignore it as one more thing from which to separate itself. Misner's ideas crystallize around the words on the Oven. The official story's "Beware the Furrow of His Brow" is in dispute, as the first word was lost when the Oven was dismantled and moved from Haven, and the young people argue that the "Beware" was in fact "Be," that the Old Fathers did not mean that their people should fear God's hand but that they should act as God's hands, bringing change to the world. This is taken as blasphemy by the New Fathers and by their minister, Reverend Pulliam, with whom Misner struggles for the future of Ruby. The Black Power fist that gets painted on the Oven illustrates the clash between generations and ideals that comes even, eventually, to Ruby; the younger generation's desire to change the world is at odds with the separatist ethos of Ruby tradition, of avoiding trouble by keeping away from whites. And their social behavior, reflecting the trend of out there, is becoming more liberal, a change of which the Ruby men, who like their women under control, cannot be in favor.

So armed with the rightness of protection by God and protection of womanhood, family, and the future of their town, the men of Ruby prepare to rid themselves of their problem. As Morrison shows us their preparations, leading us slowly to the final intersection between these two stories, she also shows us the turnaround at the Convent. Consolata's rebirth is followed by the establishment of a ceremony that forever changes the Convent women, allowing them to come to an understanding of their pasts, which in one way or another continue to mutilate them. The ceremony makes it possible for the women to tell their stories and for the others to relive them and, in doing so, allows all the Convent women to free themselves from endlessly repeating the past. "Unlike some people in Ruby," it might occur to a visiting friend, "the Convent women were no longer haunted" (266). They begin to establish a kind of earthly paradise.

Because Ruby is still haunted, because they are imploding under the weight of their exclusionary, other world Paradise-directed covenant, the men grab their "clean, handsome guns" (3) and head for the Convent. The novel's first chapter begins with the shooting of the white girl, leads us through the Convent with the searching men to their discovery of the other women out back, running, and ends, "God at their side, the men take aim. For Ruby" (18). The penultimate chapter shows the women fighting back before they run and shows the shooting of Consolata by Steward, which Deacon tries to stop and which the men's wives witness. The others go down in the backyard. People from Ruby race to the Convent, and the fitting of this latest episode into the official story of Ruby begins, but not without trouble. Steward points to the perverseness he thinks he has discovered in the house, but Deacon resists, saying, "My brother is lying. This is our doing. Ours alone. And we bear the responsibility" (291). And Deacon is not alone. Driving away, they are beset by doubts about Ruby's wholeness and health: "How hard they had worked for this place; how far away they once were from the terribleness they have just witnessed. How could so clean and blessed a mission devour itself and become the world they had escaped?" (292).

The answer, as Pat Best has discovered, lies not in change or in circumstance but in the very roots of Ruby's founding, in reacting to exclusion by further excluding, in the telling of their story as the tale of the exodus and nation founding of a chosen people who must keep themselves pure and separate if they want to endure and make it to Paradise. The rigidifying of this story against all other versions, against all others, makes for a narrow path, divergence from which becomes impossible, in spite of the pressures of the fast-changing outside world. The official version of the attack is contested, but things in Ruby seem to return almost to normal. The convenient disappearance of all the bodies helps this process along. What keeps things from returning completely to normal is the change in Deacon, who cannot go along: "It was Deacon Morgan who had changed the most. It was as though he had looked in his brother's face and did not like himself anymore" (300).

What he doesn't like comes out in a conversation he has with an unlikely new friend, the new minister. He realizes, he tells him, that his remorse for his affair with Consolata was not so much the adultery, though he felt awful about that, but the way in which he ended it. His remorse was for "having become what the Old Fathers cursed: the kind of man who set himself up to judge, rout and destroy the needy, the defenseless, the different" (302). He had judged and rejected the light-skinned, green-eyed, unconventional Consolata in a way that echoed for him the way the needy, defenseless, different people of Haven had originally been rejected and, now, the way Ruby had rejected the Convent. In his brother's face he sees the judge in himself.

Ignoring Misner's request for him to identify the woman, Deacon, without transition, tells another story. He returns to one of Ruby's originary moments of doubleness and difference, telling Misner the truth about Zechariah, their grandfather, the Old Father who was patriarch of the clan and about whose lost twin brother Pat Best had wondered. Coffee, his name before he rechristened himself, took a bullet in the foot rather than dance before a group of taunting whites, while his twin, Tea, danced. Deacon is unsure of the rightness of the silence with which Coffee shut out Tea and which he imposed on others who might speak about him, "not because he was ashamed of his twin, but because the shame was in himself" (303). Misner responds, "To lose a brother is a hard thing. To choose to lose one, well, that's worse than the original shame, wouldn't you say?" (303).

The brothers they have rejected as a response to the original shame of their own rejection are a loss to them. These brothers, on this reading, are the lighter-skinned blacks who turned them away. But in the context of the times and Morrison's reflection on them, they are also, I would argue, whites as well, and, of course, they are also sisters. The worlds the men of Ruby shut themselves away from are not just different in shade and color but gender, too. The exclusion of the difference they so fear, the shame and resulting anger they feel about themselves and toward everything that is not them, does not turn a blessed mission into something bad and wrong: it makes that mission wrong from the start. The lesson they learn from the Disallowing is the exact wrong one, Morrison seems to be saying. It is not their exclusion that is wrong: it is exclusion itself.

The ending of *Paradise* emphasizes Ruby's original error by pointing to the alternative possibility of inclusion. In mystical reappearances by the Convent women, perhaps resurrected by Consolata (she "steps into" the white girl, keeping her alive), perhaps never dead, and in the final, mysterious scene, the novel presents moments in which we see these women, alive or dead or somewhere between, coming to terms. The short final scene is a pietà, a woman "black as firewood" who could be Mary Magna, cradling in her lap the head of a woman with tea-colored hair and emerald eyes who must be Consolata, a gender- and color-crossing refiguring of the Virgin holding the dead Christ in her lap that alludes also to the Black Madonna (Bouson 214–15; Menand, "War" 82). In the image, Consolata is described: "All the colors of seashells—wheat rose, pearl—fuse in the younger woman's face." All the colors people come in are together in the faces of these women, as are love, in the company they share, and hope, in the boat that approaches the shore on which they sit. Filled with the lost and the saved, the boat comes to rest (as does the novel) "before shouldering the endless work they were created to do down here in Paradise" (318). Wherever this scene takes place, whatever the state of these figures, this happens down here, and there is work to be done. And it is Paradise. But not Ruby's Paradise. Morrison's insistence that the last word of the novel should not have been capitalized points to this last in a long line of differences.[18] This paradise is not up there and after, the novel's end seems to say, and it is not to be established by keeping others out there and admitting only those saved, only those similar. It is down here and now, and it does not exclude.

The small-p paradise glimpsed at the end of *Paradise* can also be seen in the opening authorial act of refusing to make race the most important thing we can know about a character. Identifying the first victim of the attack as "the white girl" calls attention to race right off the bat, of course; refusing to tell us which of the Convent women she is calls attention to our own desire to know. As Morrison has said of this choice, "Well, my point was to flag raise and

AFTER IDENTITY

then to erase it, and to have the reader believe—finally—after you know everything about these women, their interior lives, their past, their behavior, that the one piece of information you don't know, which is the race, may not, in fact, matter. And when you do know it, what do you know?" (Farnsworth).[19] In refusing to name the white girl, Morrison does what she has Pat Best do: she burns the notebooks and files of genealogy, as the fire that took Morrison's house destroyed her own genealogy-filled manuscripts.[20] These endless records have informed American thinking about race since the time they were first kept, even before the slave ships crossed the Atlantic, perhaps when the first settlers saw the natives. From these early moments, race was of primary importance in America. Setting the murderous attack that begins and ends the novel in July 1976, the time of the bicentennial, reminds us of this as well (Dalsgard 241). This need to divide, to see others as different and therefore to be excluded, has throughout American history been combined with and spurred on by Christianity and by an even broader Western tendency to see things in terms of twos, reductively—black and white, male and female, heaven and hell, innocence and experience, mind and body. Morrison's inclusion of Native Americans in the history of Ruby, from the Creek whose land Haven was founded on to the dispossessed Cherokee they encountered on their journey, echoes the treatment experienced by Native Americans at the time of European settlement and so reminds us of how central exclusion has been to the American story. The secret of Ruby—the blood rule—is one expression of a secret part of the Western tradition deemed not worth passing on.

In the early 1990s, Morrison also may have felt that this tradition was an assumption of her oeuvre that was not worth passing on. The rigidity of the history Ruby tells itself about itself is its downfall, or nearly. Morrison's first novel, again, was written during the time when she was making herself as a novelist and some Americans were trying to remake their nation into a fairer, more just society. Yet this novel was marked by a rigidity similar to that which Morrison sees in Ruby's self-told history, an insistence on racial essentialism and on the determinative power of race in America. Morrison's subsequent novels follow the pattern *The Blu-*

est Eye sets. *Paradise* was written during a much different time in her life and in the life of America. In it she is looking back, after her Nobel, during a later stage of her career and during a time not of uncertain, turbulent remaking but rather of endings and reconsiderations.

In *The Shape of the Signifier: 1967 to the End of History*, Walter Benn Michaels accuses Morrison (among others, including Stephen Greenblatt) of turning away from what he believes is true historical understanding and toward what he calls "posthistoricist identitarianism." He writes, "Where the conventional historian may be happy to settle for knowledge, Morrison and Greenblatt are more interested in experiencing the past (if only by talking about it) than they are in having true beliefs about it." (140) There are many problems with Michaels's argument about Morrison, not the least of which is that it is part of a larger, flawed argument. One flaw is that his central thesis—that the contemporary novel, contemporary identity politics, and contemporary literary theory share the same disabling refusal of ideology—is built on the use of structural similarity to argue historical causation. This deployment of the synchronic to make diachronic claims is an intellectual move developed and sometimes criticized in his earlier work, particularly *Our America*.[21] When Michaels in *The Shape of the Signifier* writes, "the end of history is just another name for the end of interpretation" (81), he is not just making a grand claim to see a deep underlying connection between cultural politics and trends in literary theory; he is asking that we join him in making both a category mistake and a logical error.[22]

This claim has the added disadvantage of not being true. The "novel at the end of history," as Michaels argues, is marked, or disfigured, or has the same shape as the literary and social theory and the politics of the time, namely, a refusal of logic, meaning, and interpretation, and an embrace of experience, of subject position (*Shape* 80). The shape of the times, then, is echoed in the shape of the novels. This means that in the period many more novels than not should follow the pattern he sees in Bret Easton Ellis's *American Psycho* (1991) or Morrison's *Beloved*; that is, they should be concerned not with making and finding meaning but rather with reinforcing identity. But this is not the case. The novels that are the subject of this book are very much concerned with the finding and construction of meaning. As I am attempting to show, these novels can be seen as responses to the triumphalist reception of the end of the Cold War, responses that take the shape of a renewed interest in history and a use of the resources of imaginative writing to reinterpret the past, often for the very purpose of thinking about the role of ideology in the way stories are told about it. Many of these post–Cold War novels seem intent not on respecting group identity and its rootedness in the past but rather on having arguments with themselves and others about what to think about these things.

If we do not buy Michaels's take on the shape of the literature of the times, then we may also, following his argument, have trouble accepting that the same fate has befallen the academy and public discourse. As I argued in my introduction, the discussions of identity that took place in the 1990s were if anything encouraged by the end of the Cold War, in that many Cold Warriors became Culture Warriors. These discussions were not about identity or subject position to the exclusion of ideology, as Michaels would have it; while the lines I have already quoted from Pat Buchanan's holy war speech—"It is about who we are. It is about what we believe"—might seem to collapse ideology into identity, they can also serve as reminders that the Cold War wasn't simply about ideology. Weren't containment policy and the domestic Red Scare at least as much about identity—us against them—as they were about ideas, not to mention power and money?[23]

Michaels's use of Morrison as an avatar of posthistoricism is based on his reading of *Beloved*. As Timothy Parrish has ably shown, Michaels gets Morrison's book wrong, "trivializes" it (*From the Civil War* 120) by reducing it to an attempt to bolster racial pride on an illegitimate claim to historical roots in slavery. It is one of a number of novels of the time that, for Michaels, "not only repeat the privileging of experience over beliefs but seek to extend it to the possibility of our experiencing (rather than learning about) something that never happened to us" (*Shape* 14). *Beloved* is not posthistoricist, concerned with the past only as a thing to be experienced. Rather, it is devoted to the exploration of the costs of "beating back the past." Sethe cannot "lay it all down, sword and shield" until she gets past reexperiencing her own past—being haunted by it—by working to understand it, to learn about it.

One cannot know why a critic writes about one book and not another, but *Paradise* would have, of course, caused even more problems for Michaels's argument. In turning on the moment when an authorially sanctioned character repudiates genealogy, *Paradise* rejects what Michaels would see as a foundation of identitarian thought. Like Roth, another target of Michaels,[24] Morrison —even in *Beloved*, before she confronts the implications of her ways of thinking about race and the past—is interested precisely in the problematic nature of the "true beliefs" people carry with them from the past into the present. In fact, she, like Roth, is concerned with the very notion of true belief and the dangers attendant to the holding too tightly to beliefs too rigid. Repeating the past's errors in attempting to reject them—the essential insight about their communities, their nation, and themselves that Roth and Morrison offer in *American Pastoral* and *Paradise*—is what happens when beliefs come to be seen as truths, beyond reconsideration. Reconsidering the past and the stories told about it is one thing that historical fiction can do; in the wake of the triumphalism that washed over the nation after the end of the Cold War, revivifying the culture wars and feeding a nostalgia for a victorious America that never was, it was for some writers the most important thing.

CHAPTER 4

How to Tell a True Cold War Story

O'Brien, Didion, and Closure

The collapse of the Soviet Empire in Eastern Europe is in large measure a result of the postwar strength and determination of the alliance of Western democracies.

Richard Perle

Let's by all means grieve together. But let's not be stupid together. A few shreds of historical awareness might help us understand what has just happened, and what may continue to happen.

Susan Sontag

We tell ourselves stories in order to live.

Joan Didion, *The White Album*

eorge Kennan, author of the famous 1946 cable known as the "Long Telegram" and the article that was its descendant, "The Sources of Soviet Conduct," published in 1947 in *Foreign Affairs* under the pseudonym "X," died in March of 2005 at the age of 101. These two pieces of writing are two of the most important texts in American foreign policy history: they established the central strategy of the Cold War, the policy of containment, which was at the heart of U.S. diplomatic, intelligence, covert, and military activity for most of the second half of the twentieth century. In Kennan's obituary in the *New York Times*, John Lewis Gaddis was quoted as saying, "He'll be remembered as a diplomatist and a grand strategist. . . . But he saw himself as a literary figure. He would have loved to have been a poet, a novelist" (qtd. in Weiner and Crossette).

As Gaddis and others have attested, Kennan's writing ability was the source of his influence on foreign policy. His "Long Telegram" is widely credited as the source of the Truman Doctrine, and the *Foreign Affairs* article's persuasive statement of an approach for dealing with what he saw as the fear-driven expansionist tendencies of the Soviet Union shaped the way containment went from policy to strategy. As he put it in the latter document: "Soviet pressure against the free institutions of the Western world is something that can be contained by the adroit and vigilant application of counterforce at a series of constantly shifting geographical and political points, corresponding to the shifts and manoeuvres of Soviet policy, but which cannot be charmed or talked out of existence" (575–76). Other than NSC-68 (which Kennan did not approve of, as he did not approve of other interpretations of the Soviet Union as actively working to take over the world), this statement of the way the U.S. should confront the Soviet threat—by application of a variety of countermoves, anywhere in the world—was the most influential of its kind.

The passing of one of the century's great political storytellers, a man who saw himself as a literary figure, is occasion for reflecting on the role his writing played in shaping U.S. conduct during the Cold War and also, more generally, on the role narrative plays in shaping the conduct of nations. Kennan constructed a powerful narrative that affected the way two generations of Americans saw themselves in the world, as a nation and as individuals. The decision to view relations between the two great postwar superpowers as best managed by "the logic of force," as he put it in the "Long Telegram," resulted in forty years of military, political, and economic interventions. The collapse of the Soviet Union was seen by many as the end of this story, as vindication and closure for Kennan's tale of two superpowers. Others have argued that even if the Soviet Union collapsed as a result of containment policy (and that conclusion is not undisputed), that end does not justify the half-century's worth of means, the wars, assassination plots, redirection of funds, secret training of soldiers, and Constitution-defying domestic and foreign conduct. The most significant index of the power of the story of containment is that it was able to motivate much of this activity (along with other, nonideological motivations). Also significant, though, has been its power to shape the larger story of American history. It is only by reading outside this story that it becomes possible to see that geopolitical events since the Cold War's end do not belong to a new, entirely different story, that in fact the ramifications of American conduct in the Cold War extend beyond that moment of closure and that its roots can be found in a story far older than that of the Cold War.

This chapter considers two novels that tell their own Cold War stories: Tim O'Brien's 1994 *In the Lake of the Woods* and Joan Didion's 1996 *The Last Thing He Wanted*. While both are thrillers, building up suspense carefully and self-consciously, they are not formulaic. Nor do they provide straightforward accounts of the key Cold War moments that are their subjects—for O'Brien, the war in Vietnam, for Didion, covert activity in Central America. Rather, they construct narratives that bend back on themselves in time, forcing connections between past and present. They also deviate from traditional narrative by questioning the act of storytelling itself. Both novels foreground the question of factuality, of how successfully narratives can capture the truth of past events, and the question of closure, of how valid and useful it is to attempt to assign final coherence and meaning. As they construct fictional narratives about the power of national narratives, they also question their own construction, exposing their inner workings and examining their own ability to represent reality and find meaning. And they place these national narratives under this same scrutiny.

In the Lake of the Woods and The Last Thing He Wanted, then, are both concerned with the facts of Cold War history, but they are also just as concerned with the way contemporary Americans think and talk about that history. They do more than history: they reflect historically on the making of historical narrative, on how Americans understand and represent the past at the particular historical moment after the Cold War ends. So in thinking historically about these novels and other similar novels of the mid-1990's, such as Pynchon's, Roth's, and Morrison's, we are doing what in one sense they are already self-consciously doing themselves. That this is so is, as I have argued, indicative not only of the historical-mindedness of the 1990s but also of the resistance inspired by triumphalist responses to the end of the Cold War. O'Brien's and Didion's post–Cold War Cold War novels don't simply look back, nor do they look back simply to tell different, contradictory stories; instead, they also look back at the act of looking back. They examine the way Americans constructed historical narratives during the Cold War and, carefully self-situated in the mid-1990s, they examine the way Americans continue to think about the Cold War after its end. In doing so, they suggest that endings obscure the role the present plays in the way Americans understand their past and, conversely but not paradoxically, the role understanding of the past plays in the way they act in the present. The stories people tell themselves about themselves as individuals and members of communities aren't just stories; insofar as they are listened to and accepted, they are also scripts. In drawing readers to recognize their attractions to the consolations of closure, *In the Lake of the Woods* and *The Last Thing He Wanted* urge them to keep their eyes open to the ways the hard lines drawn between past, present, and future are fictions and to the dangers of pretending otherwise.

―――――――――――――

On December 14, 2004, George W. Bush awarded Presidential Medals of Freedom to General Tommy Franks, commander of the war in Iraq, L. Paul Bremer III, former chief administrator of the American occupation, and George Tenet, former director of central intelligence. In his remarks at the ceremony, Bush said, "Today this honor goes to three men who have played pivotal roles in great events, and whose efforts have made our country more secure and advanced the cause of human liberty" (Sanger). The next day, the *New York Times* ran a story that cited an Army study on American troops who served in Iraq, veterans' advocates, and mental health care professionals, arguing that the number of soldiers returning from the war with serious psychological problems would over-whelm the health care system for veterans. In the story, the executive director of a veterans advocacy group is quoted as saying, "There's a train coming that's packed with people who are going to need help for the next thirty-five years" (Shane). That night, *Nightline* devoted its half hour to the topic of post-traumatic stress disorder in veterans of the Iraq war (Koppel).

The coincidence of these moments highlights the fact that much of the discourse surrounding the war in Iraq belonged to one of two different ways of understanding and representing war. These two different narratives—the triumphalist and the traumatic—are not just different but incommensurate, the latter informed by a recognition of the lasting psychological effects of violence not just on its victims but also on those who witness and commit it, the former built on a refusal to recognize the latter because it contradicts our official national story of innocence, virtue, and victory. Trauma and triumphalism, then, are both, in different ways, about the past and our memory of it. They are central not simply to our understanding of the importance of memory in the way we talk and think about our role in the world since September 2001 but also to our understanding of postwar America. This centrality, I would argue, makes them a necessary focus of any historicization of contemporary American fiction; I hope to demonstrate this by showing that Tim O'Brien's *In the Lake of the Woods* can be profitably read for the ways in which it is interested in these two central contemporary American narratives.[1]

In the Lake of the Woods tells the story of John Wade, a deeply traumatized veteran of the war in Vietnam, who is also the victim of an abusive childhood and may or may not be, in the novel's mid-1990s present, suffering the effects of the trauma of having murdered his wife Kathy during a stay at a cabin in the Lake of the Woods after the loss of his run for the Senate. Wade, it turns out, was involved in the massacre at what came to be known as My Lai and covered it up, a cover-up that came apart during the campaign. This story is told by a narrator who is himself a traumatized veteran. In the course of his telling, the narrator tries to figure out whether Wade killed his wife and, in doing so, links Wade's experience to his own, trying to come to grips with his own time in Vietnam. He also links Wade's story to America's experience not just of that war but of similar events in its past such as the American Revolution and the Indian wars. The narrator connects Wade's experiences to America's by highlighting the importance of forgetting—both to the response of individuals to traumatic events and also to the maintenance of the triumphalist narrative.

As Timothy Melley notes in his excellent essay on O'Brien's novel, there are contradictions in what appears to be its project. It seems to warn of the dangers of national amnesia, of forgetting events like those in My Lai, and to do this through the story of an individual's amnesiac response to trauma. This latter story, however, is ultimately unresolved: because of Wade's amnesia and our narrator's distance from the event, we never know whether Wade murdered his wife. In Melley's words, "O'Brien develops a profoundly amnesic character to critique the collective forgetting that has erased My Lai and other massacres from American historical consciousness" (112). The lack of resolution to Wade's story makes it an odd analogue to our amnesiac national narrative, as the analogy assumes that we are able to achieve some kind of resolution by recovering the truth of the past, of events like My Lai, and by representing them as a corrective to their having been forgotten.

Melley reads this paradox as expressive of the internal contradictions of the traumatic experience as elaborated by trauma studies, particularly those between trauma as repressed and as recoverable, which he identifies with fiction and history, respectively. O'Brien's novel, according to Melley, is torn between fiction's repression of the past and history's recovery of it:

> If Wade's narrative depicts posttraumatic *repression*, the battle to convert shame, guilt, and uncontrollable repetition into something more tolerable, then the narrator's story of recovery represents the equally frustrating attempt to *recover* the traumatic experience, to convert it from trauma to history. Insofar as fiction can be distinguished from history, the two narrative strands of the novel represent the fictional and the historical, respectively. (126)

This contradiction, Melley argues, is expressive of the historiographical and more general representational skepticism of our times and, like this skepticism, remains unresolved in O'Brien's novel. While I balk at Melley's surprising assertion of an opposition between fiction and history (that is, the writing of history) and his linking of fiction and repression—surprising given all that has been said about history's fictionality and fiction's ambivalent but undeniable purchase on the real as well as the obvious role imaginative representation can play in recovery—the crucial thing to assert here is that O'Brien's novel can be read as more than an expression of the contradictions inherent in the ways in which we think about the past and about representation.

A look at the novel's formal qualities will help us here. As has been noted by many readers, it is structured in an extraordinarily self-negating way.[2] It consists of two very different kinds of chapters: one kind contains more or less straightforward narrative, while the other consists of chapters in which the truth of the situation is much more in question. The more straightforward chapters can themselves be divided into two kinds: those that tell the story of John Wade and his wife Kathy's lives prior to the novel's present, with titles such as "The Nature of Love" and "The Nature of the Spirit," and those that tell the story of their week at the Lake of the Woods, with titles such as "What He Did Next" and "What Was Found." The more open-ended, less traditional chapters include those titled "Hypothesis," which offer different possible narratives of Kathy's disappearance, and those titled "Evidence," which are structured as lists of collected information, complete with footnotes and sources.

The stories of Wade's past and of the narrator's efforts to solve the mystery of Kathy's disappearance, separated in this systematic fashion, become increasingly intertwined over the course of the novel and at the same time begin to unravel. The evidentiary net is cast wider, across all of American history: notes in the "Evidence" chapters begin to refer not just to Wade's past or to the massacre at My Lai but to events as historically distant as the massacres of the Indian wars, Custer's last stand, and the slaughter of noncombatants by British soldiers at the battles at Lexington and Concord. Self-reflexive footnotes appear in late chapters (foreshadowed by a single early note warning readers that the narrator is working on little more than "supposition and possibility" [30]), including such nonevidentiary narratorial reflections as, "The human desire for certainty collides with our love of enigma. And so I lose sleep over mute facts and frayed ends and missing witnesses" (269), and, after reflecting on his own past,

> All these years later, like John Wade, I cannot remember much, I cannot feel much. Maybe erasure is necessary. Maybe the human spirit defends itself as the body does, attacking infection, enveloping and destroying those malignancies that would otherwise consume us. Still, it's odd. On occasion, especially when I'm alone, I find myself wondering if these old tattered memories weren't lifted from someone else's life, or from a piece of fiction I once read or once heard about. My own war does not belong to me. (301)

Here, the narrator's sense of the difficulty of determining the truth of his subject's past shades into reflection on the unreality of his own memories, almost into doubt about whether the past even happened, at least to him.

Similarly, the hypothetical chapters take on the self-reflexive cast of these footnotes. The last of the "Hypothesis" chapters (which is also, significantly, the last chapter in the novel) begins, "If all is supposition, if ending is air, then why not happiness?" (302). The chapter proposes one hypothesis and quickly turns to another, unlike earlier hypothesis chapters, which each presented single, uncontested explanations. Footnotes also appear for the first time outside of an "Evidence" chapter, beginning with "Even this is conjecture, but what else is there?" and pausing to weigh alternatives with "Finally, it's a matter of taste, or aesthetics," before ending, in the final footnote, with the word "maybe" (302 n. 131, 303 n. 134, 304 n. 136). Echoing this last, most tentative of footnotes is the final sentence of the novel, which ends with a question mark.

Certainly, the novel's form illustrates the impossibility of faithfully representing the past, particularly the traumatic past. And Wade's amnesia and the narrator's failure are expressive of the aporia, literally the impassibility, in attempts to bridge the gaps between present and past and between consciousness and experience, word and thing. However, the absence of resolution in the novel—to the story of Kathy's disappearance and to the story of the efforts of the narrator both to solve the case and also to deal with his own past—does not have to be read, as Melley has done, as an intentional failure and, as such, as an expression of postmodern radical skepticism about the possibility of understanding and representing trauma and the past more generally. Rather, in its careful formal eliciting of this reading, the novel can be understood to call attention to the persistence of our desire to close these gaps, to capture the truth about the past and to move on. In causing readers to recognize their need to close the gaps between evidence and hypothesis, fact and narrative, and to focus on their frustration at the novel's refusal to allow them to do so, the novel historicizes the way we historicize.

At the root of the historicization of our historicization in *In the Lake of the Woods* is its assertion that the way we think about traumatic narrative is haunted by the same desire for closure that characterizes triumphalist narrative. That influence, then—of triumphalism on trauma thinking—should be traceable to the times in which that narrative is retold. While the study of trauma can be traced to Freud's work in *Studies in Hysteria, Beyond the Plea-*

sure Principle, and *Moses and Monotheism*, the contemporary life of trauma studies can be said to have begun with the 1991 special issues of *American Imago* that became the 1995 *Trauma: Explorations in Memory*, edited by Cathy Caruth. Most of the important work in the field, such as Caruth's (including also *Unclaimed Experience: Trauma, Narrative, and History* [1996]), Shoshana Felman and Dori Laub's *Testimony: Crises of Witnessing in Literature, Psychoanalysis, and History* (1992), Judith Herman's *Trauma and Recovery* (1992), Dominick LaCapra's *Representing the Holocaust: History, Theory, Trauma* (1994) and *History and Memory after Auschwitz* (1998), was produced in the 1990s.

Contemporary trauma studies was inspired in part by the growth of Holocaust studies, as seen in the work of Saul Friedlander, LaCapra, Geoffrey Hartman, and others, as well as the 1980 recognition by the American Psychiatric Association of post-traumatic stress syndrome, following the war in Vietnam and the work of Robert Jay Lifton on the psychology of survivors and others connected to historical trauma.[3] However, it is equally important, I would argue, that trauma studies was born in the wake of the Cold War's end, the time of the triumphant declaration of the end of history and of the greeting of the golden anniversaries of mid-century events with assertions of a seamless history encompassing U.S. victory in WWII and what was claimed to be U.S. victory in the Cold War, culminating in the recent victory in the Gulf War. During ceremonies held in Pearl Harbor on December 7, 1991, the fiftieth anniversary of the Japanese attack, President George H. W. Bush made such an assertion: "To those who have defended our country from the shores of Guadalcanal to the hills of Korea, and the jungles of Vietnam to the sands of Kuwait, I say this: we will always remember" (qtd. in Engelhardt, "Victors" 215). Speaking further of the Gulf War, ended just months before, Bush said, "Once the war for Kuwait began, we pulled together . . . we were confident, and when it was over we rejoiced in exactly the same way that we did in 1945 . . . and what a feeling! Fifty years had passed but let me tell you—the American spirit is as young and fresh as ever" (qtd. in Engelhardt, "Victors" 211). The end of history was at the same time being triumphantly declared by Francis

Fukuyama, who made one of the earliest and most influential arguments for understanding the dissolution of the Soviet Union as the victory of the U.S. in the Cold War and, ultimately, as a victory for capitalism.[4]

Evident in the arguments of Bush and Fukuyama is the historical orientation of the nineties. What is also evident is the shape that this historical thought often took. As one historian argues of the triumphalist historical accounts written by Fukuyama, Samuel Huntington, and others, "History just happened to culminate in the reigning orthodoxy of our era, the neoliberalism of Thatcher and Reagan" (Cumings 79). History, just as in the nation-founding narratives on which classical epics were built, followed the course it did to bring us to our glorious, victorious present. When envisioned in this way, history is a closed book, and there can be great comfort in that. While trauma studies can be seen to be motivated by recognition of the triumphalist elision of the traumas of military loss and the loss of national innocence and righteousness central to the triumphalist narrative, I think it can also be seen as haunted by the same deep desire for the comfort of closure inspiring the Fukuyaman declaration and the triumphalist reading of history upon which it was based.

The psychoanalytic genesis of the concept of trauma (as expressed in the term's root sense, wound) contributes to healing being the assumed desideratum of narratives of historical trauma. Trauma theory tends to think of representations of historical trauma on the psychoanalytic model, in terms of recovering repressed memories, recognizing acting out, and working through the effects of the trauma in order to avoid further effects. However, in looking for a final, true version of historical trauma—believing, as Caruth and others do, that the lost event paradoxically exists in some raw form beyond or deep within memory that, once recovered, supplies the truth of the past—trauma theory can become another version of the end of history. The traumatic event, too powerful and extreme to be dealt with when it happens, is thought by some to be available for later retrieval and, upon retrieval, to afford a healing that in some way entails its transformation or erasure. Paradoxically, then, the desire to confront the past becomes a desire to be rid of it—to dig it up, deal with it, and then bury it once again. In drawing our attention to our desire for resolution in its protagonists' story, O'Brien's novel, set and written in the early 1990s, points to the influence of the triumphalist reception of the end of the Cold War even on narratives that do not elide trauma. Our desire for endings, happy or not, is strong, and we look to narrative to give us what Frank Kermode called "the sense of an ending."[5] If one way in which narratives of historical trauma can be useful is the way they interrupt the triumphalist narrative, forestall the end of history, then *ending* stories of historical trauma's long-term effects—in effect, curtailing their power to interrupt—robs them of their value.

Historicizing theory is a tricky business. In *A Mirror in the Roadway*, Morris Dickstein argues this, noting that even the widely accepted notion that the Cold War was one cause of the rise of the New Criticism is difficult not just to prove but to explain: "Nowadays, politically minded scholars tend too readily to think of the shift from the old historical approach to a new formal approach after 1945 as a function of the Cold War. . . . Yet no one has convincingly shown how the Cold War *caused* any of these changes, though it may have coincided with them" (250). It is easier to note similarities between disparate elements of culture than to persuasively demonstrate causal relationships, though if the historical moment is distant enough and the similarities are noted often enough, these relationships may come to be accepted as true.

Historicizing more recent theory, like historicizing contemporary fiction, is arguably trickier. That people like Jeffrey Williams, Peter Herman, and many others are doing so says something not just about the generation of scholars that has been called "post-theory" and the related growth of the history of criticism and theory as a field but also about the intensity of both our interest in understanding things historically and also our interest in how we do so.[6] Loren Glass's essay "The End of Culture," in exploring the connection between the ostensible resurgence of attention to history in Walter Benn Michaels's New Historicism and the Reagan era, usefully suggests the importance of further thinking about the ways in which our searches for usable pasts are shaped by the nature of the use our present wants to make of them. If, as Glass and others have noted, the synchronic homologies of much New Historicist work are essentially structuralist and so do not really help us understand culture historically and if that kind of ahistorical reading can be said to reflect a certain refusal to engage history characteristic of its times, then there would seem to be call for examination of the connection between trauma theory's ambivalence about historical closure and the ambivalence of the 1990s about the end of the Cold War.[7] In his 1999 *After the End*, James Berger writes that Freud's ambivalence about the event—about whether the historical cause or the structural condition should dominate our understanding of trauma—is echoed in theory's ambivalence toward historical specificity generally, an ambivalence he traces to the postwar experience of trauma and, most recently, to the Reagan era's triumph-restoring amnesia. Similarly, again, if this historical analysis of the way theory thinks about history has value, we should extend it into the 1990s and beyond.

Ultimately, we should think about the way we look at the past today, after September 2001. Trauma has been brought home, and we are reminded of the uses to which this kind of event can be put, how the instant histories produced shape our memories of the event, how the subsequent traumas are justified, elided, and effaced, closing the open wound and opening new ones.[8] We are reminded of the ways in which the past can be dragged out into the light by the events of the present; likewise, we are reminded of the ways in which new events become episodes to be shoehorned into old stories. Wolfgang Schivelbusch, in his 2003 *The Culture of Defeat*, writes,

> The Vietnam debate was never settled; rather it was buried under the Reagan-era defense buildup, the double victories of the Cold War and the Gulf War, and the reestablishment of America's universally acknowledged military, commercial, and cultural hegemony over the rest of the world. But earthquakes and aerial bombardments often reveal what lies beneath—for instance, the ruins of earlier, fallen cities—and it is possible that the destruction of September 11 uncovered the suppressed remains of Vietnam. (293)

While Schivelbusch is referring here to the debate over whether the war in Vietnam was a loss for the U.S. or merely a failure to win, the uncovered remains also must include debates over the conduct of the war and over the rightness of the war itself. Especially in this light, a historical understanding of ways in which Americans understand their nation's place in the world in the past, present, and future would recognize that it is not only or not even primarily the destruction of September 11 that did the uncovering. Rather, I believe, it must be understood that it was the U.S. response to that destruction that revealed the persistence of the triumphalist narrative and the desire to see new events in its light. As Schivelbusch puts it,

> Thus the United States responded by taking action against Afghanistan, much as thirty years earlier when, tired of fruitlessly battling the Vietcong guerrillas, the United States trained its sights on North Vietnam. Indeed, the Bush doctrine of preventive military strikes eerily resembles the anti-Communist domino theory, that earlier expression of the horror of falling. Could it be . . . that America's post–September 11 war fever is really a response to an earlier and unresolved defeat? (294)

Again, while Schivelbusch's focus is on the way nations deal with defeat, in this case it is not only the story of victory or hegemony that is challenged but also the sense of righteousness and of what an appropriate response to attack might be. What Schivelbusch calls war fever is only one aspect of a more complicated and much longer-running story, as O'Brien's references to Indian wars demonstrate. The terrorist attacks of 2001 have been seen by those in power (and by those in think tanks and in journalism who have written in support of the war in Iraq) as another installment in the drama of America under attack, and the administration has responded accordingly. That this is so — that it is seen this way by some — is illustrated by the frequency with which reference has been made to the Indian wars in discussions of the wars in Iraq and Afghanistan. As one supporter of the war in Iraq put it,

> The red Indian metaphor is one with which a liberal policy nomenklatura may be uncomfortable, but Army and Marine field officers have em-

braced it because it captures perfectly the combat challenge of the early 21st century. But they don't mean it as a slight against the Native North Americans. The fact that radio call signs so often employ Indian names is an indication of the troops' reverence for them. (Robert Kaplan)

It is not immaterial that this analysis is framed by a culturally tone-deaf pseudo-apology. The racial cast of the triumphalist narrative allows ample room for the Huntingtonian clash of civilizations. The resurfacing of racism and assumptions of cultural (and, of course, religious) superiority in American responses to 9/11 demonstrates that the wounds of the past, whether ignored entirely or prematurely healed over in historical narratives, are still open. That a quagmire is a quagmire and Haditha could become this war's My Lai only further support this argument.

But is Kathy Wade's disappearance another My Lai for John Wade? What if the novel provided closure to that question? It is, as noted earlier, carefully set up to encourage our desire for that closure. It begins, "In September, after the primary, they rented an old yellow cottage in the timber at the edge of the lake of the Woods" (1). Within two pages, we learn that, in the present time of the narration, Kathy has already disappeared: "In less than thirty-six hours she would be gone" (3). Two pages after that we get a glimpse of the violence inside her husband, "real depravity" (5). By the second chapter, the first of the "Evidence" chapters, we see interviews that refer to John and Kathy in the past tense, descriptions of objects titled "Exhibit," and, in a footnote, a "Missing Persons Declaration File" about the now-ended search for Kathy (8, 9). The third-to-last entry in this chapter quotes from one interview: "The guy offed her" (12). From the very beginning, then, the novel is set up to confirm the suspicion that John killed Kathy and to do so with the empirical certainty that comes from the marshaling of facts and carefully tested hypotheses. Much of its narrative drive comes from the expectation that such a confirmation will be coming at its end. What we get instead of a last chapter titled "Conclusion," however, is a final "Evidence" chapter and a final "Hypothesis" chapter. The "Evidence" chapter offers evidence in the form of interviews that suggests that it is perfectly plausible to think John and Kathy arranged their joint disappearance; even the comments by one interviewee who insists on Wade's guilt note the absence of evidence to prove it. The final "Hypothesis" chapter, as noted, is the only "Hypothesis" chapter to offer competing hypotheses or to include footnotes. This is part of a larger movement in which the chapter and the book as a whole spin apart, centrifugally, the single narrative line that is expected to lead to confirmation—the line we began in the novel's first pages—instead splitting and fragmenting until no conclusion is possible. So the expectation that drives the narrative from the beginning is frustrated. This final chapter represents the end of an investigation not just of the disappearances but of a past that stretches farther back to contain John and Kathy's whole history, John's entire life, from boyhood to Vietnam to Washington, and even the national history contemporary with that life and running back to the nation's origins. And it ends drowning in questions marks, conditionals, hypotheticals, and other expressions of uncertainty.[9]

This observation, fittingly, brings us back to a question: What if the novel let us know that John did kill his wife? It could be argued that such closure would hardly be triumphalist; the darkness at the heart of American culture, it might be said, is illustrated by Wade's act. But such closure, I believe, would undercut the novel's insistence on mystery, on unknowability; more importantly, it would undercut the frustration readers share with O'Brien's narrator as he finds himself unable to construct a coherent narrative of the past. As he writes in the final footnote, after proposing a happy-ending hypothesis:

> My heart tells me to stop right here, to offer some quiet benediction and call it the end. But truth won't allow it. Because there is no end, happy or otherwise. Nothing is fixed, nothing is solved. The facts, such as they are, finally spin off into the void of things missing, the inconclusiveness of conclusion. Mystery finally claims us. . . . One way or another, it seems, we all perform vanishing tricks, effacing history, locking up our lives and slipping day by day into the graying shadows. Our whereabouts are uncertain. All secrets lead to the dark, and beyond the dark there is only maybe. (304 n. 136)

Where there is only maybe, there can never be certainty. But while certainty would feel like a blessing, a "benediction," there is no speaking well of the past that does not carry a danger.

Near the end of "How to Tell a True War Story," from the 1990 *The Things They Carried*, O'Brien reflects on the questions of truth and possibility. Of the story of the soldier diving on a grenade to save three other soldiers, he writes,

> Is it true?
> The answer matters.
> You'd feel cheated if it never happened. Without the grounding reality, it's just a trite bit of puffery, pure Hollywood, untrue in the way all such stories are untrue. Yet even if it did happen—and maybe it did, anything's possible—even then you know it can't be true, because a true war story does not depend upon that kind of truth. Absolute occurrence is irrelevant. A thing may happen and be a total lie; another thing may not happen and be truer than the truth. (89)

In *The Things They Carried* and *Going After Cacciato* (1978), a tension exists between actuality and truth. War stories—art—may relate events that did not occur, but the idea is that narrative art has different, perhaps higher goals in mind: providing art's special pleasures, that is, finding beauty even in horror, and also reaching or at least approaching deeper truths, truths not about individual events but about larger conditions. And there is a further tension within this second goal. As O'Brien insists a little earlier in "How to Tell a True War Story," these kinds of truths are not moral. A true war story "does not instruct, nor encourage virtue, nor suggest models of proper human behavior, nor restrain men from doing the things men have always done. If a story seems moral, do not believe it." These truths available through art are not affirmative truths; rather, they pledge, as O'Brien puts it, "absolute and uncompromising allegiance to obscenity and evil" (76). *In the Lake of the Woods* goes farther, however, by pledging allegiance to nothing—not to the everyday truth of actuality, certainly, and not to the higher truths of moral uplift—but it also rejects even the truth of evil. As in his earlier works, whether things happened is not important, and education and the possibility of virtue are not to be found; but here even the cold comfort of a confirmation of the existence and perhaps some understanding of evil is absent. Knowing with any certainty that John killed Kathy would make some sense out of the mystery; and O'Brien, it seems, is now determined not to provide even that closure to their story or, by the extension made repeatedly in the novel, to U.S. history. Trying to plumb the darkness in Wade's heart and in America's, to understand the underlying causes that make Wade and the nation act the way they do, is the continuous working through that's needed. Knowing the answers, however, is neither possible nor desirable. It is not possible because the future is always unfolding, and so these stories can never end; and it is not desirable because our understanding of the past must be continually revised if it is to be more than a false magic act of illusory closure.

O'Brien's narrator, in a footnote, writes, "In any case, Kathy Wade is forever missing, and if you require solutions, you will have to look beyond these pages" (30 n. 21). We want solutions, in our murder mysteries, our psychotherapy, and our world. However, there are times, O'Brien's novel can be read to say, when trauma is preferable to triumph, an open wound more useful than one that has healed over. Working from LaCapra's view, first articulated in *Representing the Holocaust*, that trauma narratives are always stuck between acting out and working through, we might consider the usefulness of a trauma narrative and a trauma theory that act out and work, but not *through*. This reimagination of the way we theorize trauma could address the failures of current models for constructing narratives about the past.[10] Pasts that never stop happening, to paraphrase DeLillo on the return of repressed trauma in *Underworld*, histories that are not resolved not so much because they are sublimely ungraspable but rather because they are never finished—these allow us to continually revise the stories with which we try to understand the past in our own time. (201)

It is this knowledge, a kind of negative knowledge, that allows *In the Lake of the Woods* to seem prescient about the fallout of 9/11. It seems to know how to think about 9/11—or to help its readers know how to think about it—because it forces us to enact the drive for closure that has animated the way so many Americans have thought about the nation's long history of Indian wars of one kind or another, from the Massachusetts Bay colony to the Communist Reds, finding new enemies to fit into this old storyline. One place where these stories can be retold and reexamined, turned inside out and seen in the context of the times in which they are told and retold, is the printed page, a place, "these pages," as O'Brien's narrator implies, that does not require the imposition of solutions.

If *In The Lake of the Woods* can be read to enact covertly a particular narrative form in order to implicitly suggest an analogous approach to the construction of national history, Joan Didion's *The Last Thing He Wanted* is explicit in its focus on the connections between narrative form and the structures of national histories. It pays close attention to the formal aspect of narrative, its own and others', and in doing so points its readers' attention both to the ramifications of the different models on which they choose to shape their personal and national stories and also to the persistent desires those shapes seem to satisfy. Leading readers to recognize their desire for closure, as O'Brien's novel does, *The Last Thing He Wanted* explores how one of the things most wanted in stories—satisfying closure—is also one of the most dangerous things stories can supply, not only for understanding the past but for living in the present.

The Last Thing He Wanted turns out to be—that is, gradually reveals itself to be—a book about the United States' mid-1980s adventures in Central and South America, specifically our involvement in the internal politics of Nicaragua and in particular the adventure that led to the arms-for-hostages scandal known as Iran-Contra. Looking back at this moment from after the Cold War's end, Didion's novel reflects on the way the past can be explained away or ignored if it serves the interests of triumphalist narrative to do so. It also reflects on the attraction of these stories to those not directly involved. It does so not simply by telling a story with that theme at its center; instead, like *In the Lake of the Woods*, it makes use of and subverts narrative convention in order to display these acts of constructing, performing the processes by which narratives both national and personal capture and—sometimes unintentionally and sometimes quite intentionally—fail to capture the past.

The Last Thing He Wanted is the story of Elena McMahon, former Los Angeles socialite/celebrity wife, who took her daughter and walked away from life with her powerful husband and remade herself as a political reporter for the *Washington Post*. The events of the novel are set off by her decision to walk off the 1984 presidential campaign she is covering. She gets caught up in an arms deal of her father's that goes wrong not because of unhappy accident but because of much larger deals, namely, American adventurism to the south generally and the scandal that would become known as Iran-Contra in particular. McMahon, through no fault of her own exactly, goes from living an apolitical life, to following the domestic political horse race, to facing up to geopolitical reality: she gets caught up in the Cold War. Though much of this happens to her rather than because of her, her willed ignorance of her father's business and, by extension, of her nation's, does not help. The shadowy world of arms dealers, covert intelligence operations, and politics is the wrong one for McMahon to begin anew again in; it is a place she has just enough worldly experience and knowledge to stumble into but not nearly enough to get out of alive. In spite of her quasi romance with a State Department fixer named Treat Morrison, she is murdered as part of a political assassination plot (itself intended to influence a congressional vote) that included her father's deal, set up to make him the fall guy. Much of the action involves the main character's gradual (but too-late) coming-to-awareness of the conspiracy into which she has been drawn, as she is drawn further into it; much of the action of the reading, of the novel's plot, involves following the narrator's after-the-fact reconstruction of these events.

This reconstruction is carried out by an unnamed journalist-novelist, who tells what she claims is a true Cold War story about a woman she knew and about the domestic politics and geopolitical forces behind her fate. She writes this story a decade after it happens, and though the telling is laden with facts, from the material and real estate requirements necessary to build a landing strip in the middle of a Central American jungle to the larger sweep and finer details of Iran-Contra, its facticity is also significantly undermined by its use of the kind of techniques common in many of Didion's novels and essays, including the metafictionally unreliable narrator-author. Reconstructing events not just from her memories but through research (interviews, transcripts of hearings) collected, we might imagine, in the stack of file folders pictured on the first edition's cover, the "not quite omniscient" narrator tells a story that, to borrow a favorite locution of the novel, "does and does not" feel true (5). As important as the question of truth raised by this reconstruction is the question of closure, of how the story ends but especially of what it all adds up to in the end. As with *In the Lake of the Woods*, the question of factuality in *The Last Thing He Wanted* is related to the question of meaning. The narrator's investment here in documentation and knowability, then, and the concomitant question connecting what can be known to the different and some would say larger question of what can be said, what can be concluded, are as important to this novel as they are to O'Brien's.

The Last Thing He Wanted, then, is a novel whose form is central to its meaning, which makes sense given that Didion has been concerned with the workings and meaning of narrative form in both her fiction and her reporting since early in her career.[11] A brief look at some of her earlier uses of form will help us to more closely examine her use of form in *The Last Thing He Wanted*.

Didion's 1968 collection, *Slouching Towards Bethlehem*, contains essays written mostly in the three years prior to its publication, essays exploring from many different angles Didion's response to the changing scene around her. Its title essay, written about Haight-Ashbury, begins by making its allusion to Yeats explicit: "The center was not holding" (84). Her reflections on the early and mid-1960s illustrate this observation, detailing the ways in which the culture had loosed itself from whatever moorings might have held it together and had begun to fly apart. In describing local examples of the superficiality, hypocrisy, mindlessness, and anomie she encounters from the Haight to Hollywood to Hawaii, Didion mounts an indictment of mid-1960s America. The cultural fragmentation that Didion saw—what she calls in the preface "atomization"—

she tried to reflect in the form of these essays (xiii). The title essay, divided up into sections that are often unconnected or are connected only by implicit transitions readers must supply, reflects this. The technique, essentially modernist, employs a fragmentation that is not so total, I would argue, that connections cannot be made. Though Didion argues that the Yeats reference occurred to her because it provided "the only images against which much of what I was seeing and hearing and thinking seemed to make any pattern," because "the world as I had understood it no longer existed" (xiii–iv), she is still a reporter in these pieces, one who, though she sometimes includes herself, still is trying to provide accounts that make sense of the world. The title essay's famous moment—when Didion sees a five-year-old girl high on acid—is powerful precisely because its author and its assumed readership share a sense that this is not how things should be. So it is not too much to say that she is shoring these fragments against her ruins or that, like Eliot in *Prufrock* or *The Waste Land*, she gives a sense of a world that, though it is fast changing and sometimes frightening, is still intelligible in its changes.

In *The White Album*, which appeared a decade later (1979), Didion also spends a good deal of time reporting on the centrifugal disintegration of what she and many of the 1950s generation with which she identified herself had seen as a flawed but still comprehensible America. However, she is no longer standing in the middle of the decade in which this disintegration happened, mirroring its fragmentation; rather, these essays are written mostly in the 1970s, the decade that was in many ways other than the obvious the aftermath of the 1960s. They began, of course, when the 1960s ended, which happened for Didion on the day after the murder of Sharon Tate and others by the Manson family. Written outside of and after that disintegration, looking back on it, after the Summer of Love had been followed by the summer of Manson and (for the most part) after the falls of Saigon and Nixon, many of these essays express disintegration in more radical form than do those collected in *Slouching*.

Early in the essay "The White Album," which opens the collection, Didion reprints an excerpt of a psychiatric evaluation. The report summarizes an unnamed patient's Rorschach test, which it says "*is interpreted as describing a personality in process of deterioration with abundant signs of failing defenses and increasing inability of the ego to mediate the world of reality and to cope with normal stress*" (14, italics in original). She begins the single paragraph of commentary following this page-long italicized excerpt: "The patient to whom this psychiatric report refers is me." Didion thus dramatizes the notion that her reportage refuses, in a more radical way than her previous work, the pose of objectivity. What saves these essays from being seen as unreliable accounts interesting only for what they say about their author is the connection named at the same paragraph's end: "By way of comment I offer only that an attack of vertigo and nausea does not now seem to me an inappropriate response to the summer of 1968" (15). Thus the connection between Didion's inner disintegration and that of her surroundings (which, it is suggested, are producing more than the "normal stress") makes the style in which she expresses her inner inability to construct intelligible narratives more than what one critic has called "a rearguard action against the composition of the self" but rather also a way of saying something about the world (Carlton 47).

Writing the essays in *The White Album* after "the tension broke" in August 1969, Didion stands in a different relationship to the turmoil of the decade, one which allows her to see (and so, incorporate into her writing) not just her own reflected turmoil but also and especially her resulting suspicion of traditional narrative, of the stories through which we try to domesticate chaos or pretend it doesn't exist. As the first sentence of the book claims, "We tell ourselves stories in order to live"; as Didion makes plain at the bottom of the first page, the 1960s were "a time when I began to doubt the premises of all the stories I had ever told myself," which she admits is "a common condition but one I found troubling" (11). These stories, personal and national, no longer seemed to be working. Her writing here works in part by refusing authorial objectivity and the traditional gestures of storytelling more fully than the writing collected in *Slouching Towards Bethlehem* does. Yet even here it is still an attempt to capture reality, part of which is our experience of it, in particular our experience of the difficulty (but not, ultimately, impossibility) of understanding it. It is in the retention of this irony that we see Didion still holding on to the ideal of intelligibility, of being able to tell stories that work, that explain the world.[12]

This tension also animates Didion's novels (after her first, more traditional novel, *Run River* [1963]) from 1970's *Play It as It Lays* on. Elizabeth Hardwick writes that the latter is "the first of the digressive, elusive novels, typical in style and organization of the challenging signature of a Joan Didion work. Shadowy motivation, disruptive or absent context in a paragraph, or pages here and there, are not properly to be read as indecision or compositional falterings." Instead, Hardwick argues, "the author is in control of the invention" ("In the Wasteland"). Like *Democracy* (1984), which has as its setting 1975, around the time of (and including) the fall of Saigon, *The Last Thing He Wanted* was published a decade after the time of the story it tells. Also like *Democracy*, it focuses on an important moment in the Cold War and does so through a use of fictional technique informed by Didion's subversion of conventional expectations in her journalism, which in both novels is informed by the sense that the traditional narratives are no longer working to describe reality. However, in a relationship analogous to that between *Slouching Towards Bethlehem* and *The White Album*, the degree of formal and thematic suspicion of traditional narrative is greater in *The Last Thing He Wanted* than in *Democracy*. This is so, in part, because of its different temporal relationship to the times that are its subject. In this case, the temporal difference is not the distance from the specific time of the stories, which is roughly equal for both *Democracy* and *The Last Thing He Wanted*, but in the distance of the later book from the larger historical era that contains the settings of both books as well as from the time of the writing of the earlier novel—the Cold War. While both are historical novels written ten years after the fact, just as *The White Album* is shaped by the end of the 1960s, the end of the Cold War helps to make *The Last Thing He Wanted* a more long-viewed and more radically open-ended examination of that time and of the ways in which narratives constructed it then and thereafter. A brief comparison can demonstrate this difference.

Democracy is a colonial novel set mostly in Hawaii but also in other postcolonial locales such as Indonesia, South Vietnam, and Kuala Lumpur. It tells the story of the twice aptly surnamed Inez Victor, née Christian, wife of a senator and failed presidential hopeful and daughter of an old money father, who murders her sister Janet and Janet's local Hawaiian congressman lover. Inez becomes romantically entangled with Jack Lovett, the exact details of whose employment remain murky but are somehow connected both to national security and also to the covert commerce often intertwined with it. Returning to Honolulu after the murder, Inez is forced to confront her personal, familial, and historical past and in the process takes control of her life, leaving her husband and, after Lovett dies saving Inez's daughter from an ill-advised visit to a falling Saigon, ending up alone in Kuala Lumpur, working with refugees. Much of the reading experience of *Democracy* consists of untangling the causes of the murder and coming to an understanding of the larger geopolitical forces at play.

This story is narrated by journalist-novelist Joan Didion, explicitly named, who says she worked some years before with the main character and has seen many of the characters in the news, but who begins her story by admitting that the novel readers have in their hands was preceded by a different false start. While the claim to fact and the admission of artistic creation do not logically clash, the effect is the invocation of two contradictory sets of generic expectations, such that readers are unsure whether the characters are actual people and also whether the author is one, or at least that she is one they can trust. Though she introduces herself to her readers six pages into the novel with the claim, "Cards on the table," the promised laying bare of conventional narrative devices and the sharing of authorial motivation do not serve simply to make what is read seem more real (17). They also cause readers to mistrust both the usual devices fiction uses to give the sense of verisimilitude and also their own instincts, their own ability to know what's true.

The similarities between *Democracy* and *The Last Thing He Wanted* should be obvious. They share colonial settings, Cold War intrigue, similarly detached heroines who leave husbands and have troubled relationships with daughters, and national-security-apparatus-connected love interests. Hawaii, in *Democracy*, is in some ways still a colonial outpost, though its grandeur is past and its stewards are killing each other. On the unnamed Caribbean island where Elena finds herself in *The Last Thing He Wanted*, she is taken to Hotel Colonial, whose outward appearance, with its "impressive glass porte cochere and polished brass letters," belies its lobby's "industrial fluorescent light" and "stained velour upholstery of the single chair" (86). The two novels share a reportorial fascination with the workings of covert operations; they also share a disgust that this kind of activity and the motivations behind it ultimately render hollow the democracy the Cold War was supposed to have been about spreading or at least protecting. As Alan Nadel writes of *Democracy*, "the novel is profoundly elegiac, marking as it does not the story of *democracy* but its loss" (277, italics in original). These two novels are about what in "the rhetoric of the time in question" in *The Last Thing He Wanted* is described as "*trying to create a context for democracy and maybe getting your hands a little dirty in the process*" (13, italics in original). (One critic even argued in a 1990 article that *Democracy* in fact "anticipated many of the details and the central dilemma raised by the Iran-Contra scandal. That dilemma of whether to curtail democracy to further foreign policy goals" [Tager 173].) They also would seem to share narrators, a style in which half-told reconstructed stories somehow still manage to create suspense, and a suspicion that past and present are difficult if not impossible to understand, let alone represent.

In both novels, the Cold War context is supplied through documents and other kinds of research—as are many of the details of the individuals affected by this context, as the national and personal plots in these books cross. The family at the center of *Democracy*, one "in which the colonial impulse had marked every member" (26), is seen in photos in *Fortune* and read about in the *New York Times*. In *The Last Thing He Wanted*, Elena's fate, the larger conspiracy, and, most generally, "life on the far frontiers of the Monroe Doctrine" are pieced together in part from FBI interviews and transcripts of select committee hearings (10). In both novels, as in O'Brien's novel, the feeling of facticity that results is both reinforced and undercut by the narrators' refusal to pretend certainty. An example, from *The Last Thing He Wanted*:

> There was for example the airline that operated out of St. Lucia but had its headquarters in Frankfurt (Volume VII, Chapter 4, "Implementing the Decision to Take Policy Underground") and either was or was not (conflicting testimony on this) ninety-nine percent owned by a former Air West flight attendant who either did or did not live on St. Lucia. There was for example the team of unidentified men (Volume X, Chapter 2, "Supplemental Material on the Diversion") who either did or did not (more conflicting testimony) arrive on the northern Costa Rican border to burn the bodies of the crew of the unmarked DC-3 that at the time it crashed appeared to be registered to the airline that was or was not ninety-nine percent owned by the former Sky West flight attendant who did or did not live on St. Lucia. (10–11)

These repeated gestures can be read to work in a number of ways. Certainly the *was* or *was nots* and *did* or *did nots* can be seen as accurate reflections of the difficulty of establishing the truth when it can only be gotten at through the testimony of people not unanimously committed to telling it. On the other hand, we read these accounts in stories about fictional characters; though these stories are filled with actual facts and are, on one important level, about actual events or historical moments, Elena and Inez (and Treat and Jack and others) do not actually exist. So the things readers read about did and did not happen. The epistemological difficulty, then, meets what is almost an ontological difficulty, a generic one that is characteristic of novels that mix fact and fiction and central to those that do so in pursuit of larger historical truths. When readers can't know what is real, when real and not-real are cheek-by-jowl, what sort of conclusions are they supposed to draw about the relationship between these stories and the real world? And if the people telling these stories seem to refuse to make meaning out of the real and not-real events they recount, are readers then unable to make meaning out of the world somehow related to them?

The answers to these questions are different for the two novels, and the reason for this is both formal and historical. Specifically, the difference lies in the nature of narrative form in each book, form that reflects the different times in which they were written. *Democracy*'s narrator tells a story with a foregone conclusion: a murder is committed, and the book works backward, and forward, to reveal not who did it but why. That the book has narrative pull at all—and it actually has a great deal of it—is due to the skill with which the narrator pieces together the story and draws us into the main character's reactions. "This is a hard story to tell," she comments early on; it is, in part, because its telling is so intricate and in many ways nonlinear, because it doesn't follow simple chronology and draw us inevitably to a dramatic, conclusive event (15). But the narrator knows how things end and is interested in explaining them, a task that is hard, but not impossible. The narrator of *The Last Thing He Wanted*, on the other hand, does not lay all her cards on the table, as it were, from the start; and though what happens to Elena is known by the narrator from the start, it is only revealed at the end. Further, the novel's sense of how things will turn out in the end in a larger sense, in the future, is murkier. Closure, perhaps paradoxically for a novel ending with the main character's death, is more problematic here.

The nature of narrative closure is foregrounded from the start in *The Last Thing He Wanted*—in particular, the way it is about learning how things turn out and what they mean as well as the feeling of learning those things. This dual nature of closure is highlighted by the narrative structure of the novel. We know early on that something very bad happens to Elena:

> I thought she got caught in the pipeline, swept into the conduits.
>
> I thought the water was over her head.
>
> I thought she realized what she had been set up to do only in however many elongated seconds there were between the time she registered the presence of the man on the bluff and the time it happened. (12)

But we don't know exactly what that bad thing is until the end, the end of (to use Shklovsky's terms) the *fabula*, Elena's story in chronological order, and the end of the *sjuzhet*, the novel's reordered narration of those events, which meet at the end of the novel. And they intersect at dramatic points throughout the novel, often through the use of the free indirect Didion employs when she wants to blur the line between Elena, finding out what is and has been happening to her, and the narrator, reconstructing the same after the fact. An example is the moment when it becomes clear that a contact who had appeared to Elena to be helping her get back home is not actually doing so. The sickening sound of the puzzle pieces clicking into place is heard in the phrase "of course," when she realizes that the false passport that has been prepared for her contains a photo of herself that she'd left behind in her father's house:

> At some point recently on this campaign . . . she had stuck the five or six remaining prints in a pocket of her computer bag.
> Why wouldn't she have?
> Of course she did.
> Of course her computer bag was in a closet at the house in Sweetwater.
> *By the way, I saw your dad. He says hi. I'm keeping him in the picture.*
> (98)

This repeated line of dialogue, originally spoken by the man she'd thought was helping her, is the last of the chapter. The next chapter begins,

> Of course Dick McMahon was by then dead.
> Of course he had died under circumstances that would not appear in the least out of order. (99)

While readers are, of course, meant to share in the sickening feeling, Didion's narrator makes this sharing explicit when she reflects on the psychic costs of Elena's ignoring just what it was her arms-dealer father did for a living and connects the deal Elena is finishing for her father with a name from her childhood. It had cost something, the narrator says,

> To keep the name of her father's friend just outside the frame of what she remembered.
> Of course the name of her father's friend was Max Epperson. You knew it was. (155)

Readers may hear the puzzle pieces click and feel they had seen the connection before they were told, or they may simply enjoy the feeling of the connection being made. And the narrator, perhaps flattering, perhaps sure of the strength of her design, addresses readers directly and says she knows this about them.

One part of the meaning of the form here, then, is in the clicking, or in the wanting to hear the clicking, in the desire for pattern, meaning, closure. The phenomenological here is as important, or maybe even more important, than the intellectual, in that readers seem meant not just to receive knowledge but to experience its reception. And this experience, as in *In The Lake of the Woods*, leads to another moment that is important as both experience and knowledge: the moment when readers realize they want the experience. In other words, as in O'Brien's novel, the narrative is structured not only to lead readers toward knowledge but to make them notice the leading and, more importantly, to notice their desire to arrive at closure. The recognition of this desire becomes, then, in both novels, a kind of knowledge. Elizabeth Hardwick, in her review of the novel, writes, "Joan Didion's novels are not consoling, nor are they particularly attuned to the reader's expectations" ("In the Wasteland"). On the contrary, I would argue that what appears to Hardwick as a lack of feel for or interest in reader expectations is in fact Didion's way of reminding readers of them and that *The Last Thing He Wanted* especially is interested in the consolations of form, in particular those of closure. It is interested in the consolations of closure because it is a Cold War novel written after the end of the Cold War: it is a historical narrative, written after the period whose last gasp it chronicles, about how historical narratives can depend, dangerously, on the idea that the past *is* past.

In the Lake of the Woods never arrives at the truth of the central event it tries to reconstruct, of what really happened; *Democracy* begins with its central event and proceeds to find out why it happened. *The Last Thing He Wanted* ends with the intersection of what happened and why, with the death of the protagonist and an understanding of the plot that led to it; what it does not supply, in the end, is the end of the history it reconstructs. Toward the culmination of the novel's coming together, of the meeting of fabula and sjuzhet, during which the pace of event and revelation perceptibly pick up, there is a short chapter among the shortening chapters—the one directly before the one in which Elena's death occurs, in fact—set at the time of the novel's writing. In the chapter the narrator interviews Mark Berquist, a key political operative in the plot, now a junior senator in a young class of junior senators (clearly the Republican Revolution, Contract-with-America class of 1994). Relating the story of the interview, the narrator writes,

> I said that I was trying to get as much perspective as possible on a certain incident that had occurred in 1984.
> Mark Berquist's eyes flickered suspiciously. Nineteen eighty-four had ended for him with the conclusion of that year's legislative session, and was as distant now as the Continental Congress. To bring up 1984 implied that the past had consequences, which *in situ* was not seen as a useful approach. (211)

Through another skillful use of the free indirect, the narrator has Berquist voice an approach to reality and to the past that the novel sees as central to the construction of plots like that which ends in Elena's death, of Cold War foreign policy, and of triumphalist history. In working to resupply the contras—the activity, outlawed by the 1982 Boland Amendment, that led the Reagan administration to look for funds elsewhere—the belief that America can do no wrong and will emerge victorious and righteous in its defense is central. Also important is the belief that whatever means lead to a triumphant end are justified and that those consequences are the only important ones. Most important is the sense that the ultimate victory to which Cold War activity such as that chronicled in this novel contributed is the winning of the Cold War and that, with the fall of the Berlin Wall and the dissolution of the Soviet Union, the story of a nation trying to spread democracy and getting its hands a little dirty in doing so is over. It's the end of history.

Like *In the Lake of the Woods*, it is in the expression of the falseness of this triumphalist closure, of its attractiveness and danger, that *The Last Thing He Wanted* can be seen as a response to the end of the Cold War. It is also in these ideas that Didion's novel can be seen to speak to more recent events. If the events of September 11, 2001, can be understood only in the context of American foreign policy in the Middle East and that policy can be understood only in the context of the Cold War, then history—the past policies and actions that continue to have repercussions—is not over. If the Bush administration's response to 9/11 can be understood only in the contexts of past approaches to foreign policy—both containment policy and colonialist and imperialist designs going back to the Monroe doctrine and even earlier—then it is hard to argue that the Cold War represented the closure of any truthful narrative of American history.

Two moments in the novel illustrate this historical continuity that the novel seems to argue should not be ignored and do so in ways Didion could not have predicted but cannot have been surprised by. The third chapter begins with a list of names of people involved in Iran-Contra (without ever naming the scandal explicitly). Among those named is Elliot Abrams, who pleaded guilty to two counts of withholding information from Congress in its investigation of Iran-Contra, but who is also known for his part in the cover-up of the El Mozote massacre in El Salvador and other contemporary Central American atrocities carried out by forces the administration supported. A seeming relic of the late Cold War, Abrams was resurrected by the second Bush's administration and, in its second term, was promoted to Deputy National Security Advisor, where he advised Secretary of State Condoleezza Rice on Middle East affairs and, as reported by Didion herself in a 2006 essay in the *New York Review of Books*, was one of those pushing for a war in Iraq before September 2001 ("Cheney").

Another small moment in the novel linking the Cold War to the wars in Afghanistan and Iraq comes later, when Elena's visit to the American embassy during a Fourth of July picnic deepens her involvement in the preexisting conspiracy. When an aide interrupts a conversation during the picnic to run a background check on Elena, he is talking with a "Brown & Root project manager who had just arrived to supervise the hardening of the perimeter around the residence" (123). An old Texas company, Brown and Root had connections to Lyndon Johnson going back to government contracts he steered their way in the 1930s, connections that funded his campaigns and led to contracts building warships in WWII and doing much of the Army's construction work during the war in Vietnam. More recently, as KBR (formerly Kellogg, Brown, and Root), a subsidiary of Halliburton, it was awarded a number of large contracts for construction of infrastructure and the restoration of oil fields in Afghanistan and Iraq. The vice-president for both terms of the second Bush's administration, Dick Cheney, was chairman and CEO of Halliburton from 1995 to 2000.

Didion, of course, is no soothsayer. But the names she names do more than place Iran-Contra in a long history of Cold War foreign policy misadventures fueled by the intertwining of ideology, power, and capital from the Far East to Central America. They also connect this long history to events in the Middle East that occurred not only after the end of the Cold War but after the writing of the novel, thus demonstrating the power of her novel's vision of American conduct in the world and of the kinds of narratives that make such misadventures possible. In *Fixed Ideas: America Since 9/11* (the May 2003 separately published version of an essay that appeared in the *New York Review of Books* four months earlier), Didion displays not only her prescience in seeing where the Bush administration's fixed idea of an imperial nation was headed but also the roots of that prescience in an understanding of history. The book ends,

> In the early 1980s I happened to attend, at a Conservative Political Action conference in Washington, a session called "Rolling Back the Soviet Empire." One of the speakers that day was a kind of adventurer-slash-ideologue named Jack Wheeler, who was very much of the moment because he had always just come back from spending time with our freedom fighters in Afghanistan, also known as the Mujahideen. I recall that he received a standing ovation after urging that copies of the Koran be smuggled into the Soviet Union to "stimulate an Islamic revival" and the subsequent "death of a thousand cuts." We all saw that idea come home. (43–44)

The elision of moments like this and like the one on which Didion focuses in *The Last Thing He Wanted*—when, in the rhetoric of the times, the humanitarian resupply becomes known as "the lethal, as opposed to the humanitarian, resupply" (44)—makes possible the continuation of the triumphalist American narrative and so makes possible the repetition of those moments. That under the banner of spreading democracy American foreign policy has led to another endless war, that Cold War figures became leading members of the second Bush administration, and that, two decades after Iran-Contra, Oliver North had a television show—on a news channel—require the survival of this narrative.

An early chapter in *The Last Thing He Wanted* ends with the narrator's description of her project: "You could call this a reconstruction. A corrective, if you will. . . . A revisionist view of a time and a place and an incident about which, ultimately, most people preferred not to know" (13). Regardless of their feelings about the activities of this or other such times and places, the description assumes, "most people" feel that what's past is past; what few want are reconstructions of such moments, especially ones that refuse to treat them as over, as unconnected to the present. *In the Lake of the Woods* and *The Last Thing He Wanted* tell true Cold War stories because they are about pasts that, to again borrow from DeLillo, seem never to stop happening.

CHAPTER 5

History Is What Heals

9/11 and Narrative in Eugenides and Lethem

I'm not even sure I'll live long enough for
cigarettes to kill me.
Art Spiegelman, *In the Shadow of No Towers*

A place of my own—it's great!
Superman

The future is stupid.
Jenny Holzer

During a ceremony held in Pearl Harbor on December 7, 1991, the fiftieth anniversary of the Japanese attack, President George Bush put the end of the Cold War into what he saw as its proper context: "Now we stand triumphant," he said, "for a third time this century, this time in the wake of the Cold War. As in 1919 and 1945, we face no enemy menacing our security" (qtd. in Engelhardt, "Victors" 214). The dissolution of the Soviet Union, for Bush, fit easily into the seamless narrative of America's history as world power. Looking back from this latest "victory," Bush saw a succession of victorious moments such as the one in which he now believed himself to be living.

I am arguing in this book that a number of historical novels of the 1990s can be seen as responses to this reading of the Cold War's end, which reinvigorated the triumphalist narrative of American history. For some, the events of September 11, 2001, which I see as bookending the 1990s as a period in American cultural life, posed surprisingly little challenge to this narrative. Instead, they were seen to introduce a new enemy to America's superior way of life in the amorphous and shape-shifting form of Terror (or Al Qaeda, or Islamic Fundamentalism, or, in a leaden summer 2005 test balloon, Extremism). Again, just as in the early 1990s many Cold Warriors found a new fight in the Culture Wars, seeing the American Left as the greatest threat to America, many Cold and Culture Warriors found a new fight after 9/11. But for others, awareness of other kinds of narratives was encouraged by 9/11. From many of the subsequent reactions of the U.S. government, including military action, there emerged a story of divergence from righteousness, not to mention victory. Bush the father's characterization of America as without enemies threatening its shores did not describe the state of the nation under the son's administration; the present moment did not, for many, fit into the father's triumphalist narrative. In addition to this resistance to a continuation of post–Cold War triumphalism in the triumphalist response to Terror, there also emerged a story about a different kind of terror—the terror caused by the recognition of contingency. This recognition informs a view of the course of human events as not chartable along the upward line of humankind's inexorable progress toward liberal democracy but rather as heavily featuring randomness and vulnerability and, therefore, not assuming an ever better future.

The formal phenomenon of closure is closely linked in the literature and thought of the second half of the twentieth century to the existential phenomenon of contingency. A major assumption of this book is that the shapes fictional narratives take (especially those about the past) are affected by the historical imagination of their times. It follows from this assumption that the way these stories end—the way their narratives come to a close, the kind and degree of closure they reach—is especially affected, since ends are especially important to the ways in which people understand the past and connect it to their own times. The felt relation of a time, a writer, or a particular kind of historical imagination to the fact of contingency, then, informs the way stories are told, in particular the nature of their endings (and not just in the recent past, as Frank Kermode has shown). Postmodernism, though, has been especially invested in the connection between closure and contingency. In an early (1972) statement of postmodern doctrine made in the first issue of *boundary 2*, the postmodern journal he cofounded, William Spanos describes the relationship between closure and contingency after midcentury:

> Only after the existentialist philosophers revealed that the perception of the universe as a well-made fiction, obsessive to the Western consciousness, is in reality a self-deceptive effort to evade the anxiety of contingent existence by objectifying and taking hold of "it," did it become clear to the modern writer that the ending-as-solution is the literary agency of this evasive objectification. (152)

The distrust of closure is widely articulated in postmodern thought, early (as in statements by Leslie Fiedler, Ihab Hassan, John Barth) and late (Linda Hutcheon, Fredric Jameson, Brian McHale). I think, however, that it is worth it to examine the changing nature of that distrust in recent years. What endings mean and why writers embrace them or avoid them depend in part on how particular pasts are felt to connect or not connect to the present that looks back on them, as I argued in my readings of *In the Lake of the Woods* and *The Last Thing He Wanted*. What endings mean also depends in part on how contingent existence feels and how public discourse and constructions of history deal with that feeling. As a result, events that reawaken a sense of contingency and challenge already constructed narratives—in particular, historical traumas—can affect the shape of literary endings. This is especially the case, I will argue, for historical literature, work whose focus is explicitly on the past and always implicitly, as a result, on the way that history "ends"—on the way the past leads to the precarious present and, ultimately, the future.

Jeffrey Eugenides's 2002 *Middlesex* and Jonathan Lethem's 2003 *The Fortress of Solitude* are two post-9/11 novels with an interest in the past. As historical novels, they depend on a set of notions about the relationship between past, present, and future and about the possibilities and problems that attempts to understand and represent the past entail. Both are particularly concerned with the importance of dealing with the wounds of the past, of confronting the hurts that befall us in order to then be able to live happy lives. As a result, endings are important to them: how the stories of the past conclude can indicate, formally and thematically, the success of this project of narrating and processing the events of that past. How *Middlesex* and *The Fortress of Solitude* end, then, can tell us something about the ways their times, particularly the years after 9/11, thought about the course of history.

Middlesex has been praised as an expansive, epic portrait of the American twentieth century from its immigrant roots to the present.[1] It takes its readers from a Turkish village in the 1920s to the race riots of the late 1960s, following a Greek and then Greek American family across time and the world, spinning an interestingly twisted yarn in the voice of the family's latest product, whose gender identity, complicated by a genetically inherited hermaphroditism, is at the center of his story and is said to be resolved at novel's end. While it is no longer common in current critical discourse to discuss works in terms of aesthetic failure or success, I believe that *Middlesex* fails aesthetically and that it is important to talk about it in these terms because how it fails says something about its historical imagination and the historical imagination of its times. At the root of its failure, I'll argue, is the way it imposes a false closure on its narrative of the main character's gender crisis. This closure represents something other than a poor aesthetic choice. Rather, its falseness—the unearned, unwarranted character of the novel's ending—is unintended, and so it represents a failure that is especially indicative of the unconscious effect of its historical imagination.

The Fortress of Solitude, while its chronological sweep encompasses a smaller part of the twentieth century, also centers on the project of understanding an individual's past in the context of family and community history. Lethem's novel tells the story of a white boy growing up in Brooklyn during the earliest stages of gentrification in the 1970s, one of very few white children in his neighborhood; it then jumps to the late 1990s, following its protagonist into his thirties as he confronts the effects of his formative encounters with racial and class politics—as he deals with the way he dealt with being that white boy years before. *The Fortress of Solitude* is different in many ways from *Middlesex*, from its setting to its themes, but it is also significantly similar. Like *Middlesex*, it is a bildungsroman; like *Middlesex*, it features a protagonist who, around the turn of the twenty-first century, finds himself facing up to his past, in particular with crucial events that happened decades before but that continue to haunt him; like *Middlesex*, the success of a romantic relationship and the future happiness of the protagonist depend on that past being successfully confronted. So, like *Middlesex*, it sets up expectations of closure: the boy will become a man, the past will be dealt with, the relationship will be fixed, the future will be happy. Unlike *Middlesex*, though, *The Fortress of Solitude*, while attracted to the same kind of closure, resists it, thus avoiding the aesthetic failure that marks Eugenides's novel. While *Middlesex* allows its protagonist to narrate his past in a way that enables him to move forward, *The Fortress of Solitude* is less clear about its protagonist's success at what amounts to the same task; and the questions the novel has at the start—about race and class, about the fluidity of cultural identity and the permeability of social barriers, about the responsibilities individuals do or don't have to others—remain unanswered at novel's end.

As I argued in my discussion of *In the Lake of the Woods* and *The Last Thing He Wanted*, the adoption of the trauma model for national narratives has been motivated in part by the sense that there have been and continue to be disastrous consequences when historical narratives leave out certain kinds of events or ignore their importance. As James Berger (*After the End*), Dominick LaCapra (*History in Transit*), and others have argued, however, relying on the medical model inherited from Freud can make the traumatic narrative too quick to heal the wounds it uncovers. One cause of this shortcoming in some trauma narratives may be the same as that which revitalized the triumphalist narrative in the 1980s and 1990s—namely, the end of the Cold War, which provided a model of narrative closure difficult to resist. A history whose tragic losses and dark secrets can be uncovered and healed is not as opposed as it might seem to a history in which those things stay hidden, a history that's all about victory and righteousness, a history where everything turns out all right for America in the end. The events of 9/11, which some have found a fit for a narrative of America as innocent victim (and then righteous avenger), have been for others a model of an open wound that needs healing—or closing. In what follows, I will demonstrate first how Eugenides's *Middlesex* imposes healing closure on what begins as a more open-ended story, making things, even traumatic things, turn out all right in the end and in doing so displays a desire for closure I believe is common to many aspects of American culture after 9/11. Then I will show how Lethem's *The Fortress of Solitude* avoids such an error, thus demonstrating a continuing resistance to this strain of historical wishfulness.

If after the end of the Cold War a discussion ensued about the course of the nation and its very nature in light of its ostensible geopolitical victory, after 9/11 there were questions about the possibility of understanding the past and moving forward from it at all. When the world suddenly feels like a very dangerous place again, when the future seems less of a sure bet, closing the book on the past becomes even more fraught.

Middlesex is a long historical yarn spun by Cal Stephanides, an American of Greek descent born to first-generation Greek American parents, who pass down to him a rare genetic mutation that results in his being raised as Calliope. His hermaphroditism goes undiscovered until his teens. Before the discovery, he leads a mostly happy life as a girl; after the discovery, he decides against the surgery his doctor proposes to make his body conform to his rearing, and he cuts his hair and begins to live as a boy. We are told this story by Cal more than two decades after his decision, in the very detailed context of another story spanning three generations and two continents. This larger story is held together not just by the thread of Cal's genealogy (tangled, as it were, by a number of incestuous pairings) but also of his genetics: the mutation responsible for his hermaphroditism is in some sense the hero of this story, what the narrator calls "this roller-coaster ride of a single gene through time," as it survives atrocity, displacement, and war (2).

In the telling of this story, *Middlesex* sets itself up to make a brief for free will against the determining effects of both biology and society. Eugenides's handling of the gender issue, however, undercuts this brief because he resolves his hero's conflict too quickly and too neatly. Calliope decides he is a boy, cuts off the ends of his name and his hair, and because he decides it, readers seem meant to accept it. This exercise of free will, however, strains plausibility. While there is some acknowledgment of the difficulty entailed in changing one's gender identification and presentation and a small part of the novel details Cal's immediate post-Callie life, this section of the novel is rushed and haphazardly plotted, and the ideas that animate the story earlier are lost. The questions raised in the book thus do not survive the novel's paired resolutions, Calliope's decision in the mid-1970s and the beginning of Cal's first real romantic relationship with a woman, which is made possible by his 2001/2002 telling of the story of his past. While there is much to be said about the novel's treatment of gender and sexuality, what I will focus on here is the fact that its exploration of these issues and the part they play in its hero's life is foreclosed.

Middlesex opens, "I was born twice: first, as a baby girl, on a remarkably smogless Detroit day in January of 1960; and then again, as a teenage boy, in an emergency room near Petoskey, Michigan, in August of 1974" (3). On the next page, after this unconventional twist on a conventional bildungsroman beginning, another generic side of the book is introduced with the phrase, "Three months before I was born." While telling the story of the family situation immediately prior to the main character's birth is not unusual for a bildungsroman, what is initiated here is a plunge backward into a family history that occupies almost the first half of the novel. This story is played out against a backdrop of historical events and settings such as the 1922 Turkish massacre of Greeks at Smyrna, Prohibition, Henry Ford–era Detroit, and the 1967 Detroit riots. And while *Middlesex* does tell a family story over several generations, it wants to be more than family saga: it intends to engage national history, showing not just a family across time but a family buffeted by historical change.

Because of its present-day frame, *Middlesex* might not appear to be a historical novel. Eugenides himself doesn't identify it as such; he has said, "The book is not conceived as an historical novel. I always think an historical novel continuously remains in the past. This book tries to explain the past and comes up to the present day" (Interview). While the historical novel need not be set in the past entirely or at all, at least according to Lukács's claims for the novel after Balzac,[2] what is more important here is that *Middlesex* does not exactly come up to the present. Its main action is split between the Stephanides family history, which runs from the early 1920s to the late 1950s, and the life of its narrator from birth until the mid-1970s. Its present time frame, set in the early years of the twenty-first century, contains the quasi-metafictional story of the narrator's writing of these other two stories—of the novel *Middlesex*, or most of it—and the concurrent story of his courtship of Julie. But there is a quarter-century gap between the end of the story our narrator tells of his past and the present of the frame. This gap provides a clue, I believe, to the specific nature of this novel's historical imagination.

The gap is not important because it establishes that the novel is set safely in the past and so really is a historical novel. Nor is it important because it highlights what for many postmodern historical novels has become a staple: the recognition that present concerns impinge on reconstructions of the past. The "truth" of past events is not just ultimately uncapturable, these novels assume, but attempts to capture it are always colored by present-day needs. The present-day frame of *Middlesex* is enough to point that out even without the gap: Cal needs to tell the story of his past in order to function in the present, as his happy second chance reunion with Julie at the end of the novel illustrates. The narrator's frequent metafictional admissions that he is taking liberties as he writes a fiction "based on real events," as they say in the police procedurals, reinforce this truth. His history of himself is motivated by particular concerns, as are all histories.

The central importance of the gap for understanding the novel's historical sense lies instead in the nature of the historical events that take place during it. Historical events of the years that *are* narrated by Cal are crucial to the story of the Stephanides family. The immigrant experience of the family; the impact of the Detroit riots on their fortunes; the national malaise, felt before Jimmy Carter named it—their lives in America are touched by historical convulsions and shifts in mood. Very early in the novel, the narrator discusses his father's faith in his ability to influence his planned child's gender through carefully timed conception:

> I can only explain the scientific mania that overtook my father during the spring of '59 as a symptom of the belief in progress that was infecting everyone back then. Remember, *Sputnik* had been launched only two years earlier. Polio, which had kept my parents quarantined indoors during the summers of their childhood, had been conquered by the Salk vaccine. . . . In that optimistic, postwar America, which I caught the tail end of, everybody was the master of his own destiny, so it only followed that my father would try to be the master of his. (9–10)

Milton Stephanides lived in an America that seemed able to exercise its will freely and so encouraged individuals (some, anyway, as the section on the riots points out) to think they could successfully exercise their own. His story, however, is told in a different time, after Watergate and the loss in Vietnam, during an economic crisis in which America's dependence on Middle East oil illustrated the distance between its self-sufficient superpower dreams and the world's interdependent reality. At the end of the late chapter in which his father's death is retold, Eugenides writes,

> Milton got out before many of the things that I will not include in this story, because they are the common tragedies of American life, and as such do not fit into this singular and uncommon record. He got out before the Cold War ended, before missile shields and global warming and September 11 and a second President with only one vowel in his name. (512)

Eugenides is careful at these crucial points of his novel, the beginning and the end, to highlight national events and reflect on national moods, and so to alert readers to the connections between these factors and his characters' stories. As Milton got out before the events of the last thirty years, though, so too does *Middlesex*, raising the question of the elided history's connection to the narrator's present. Between 1975 and 2002, a number of events occurred that were important to America's identity and sense of place in the world, including not just the events of the 1970s but also the heating up of the Cold War — in rhetoric and in Afghanistan and Central and South America — the end of the Cold War, and the events of September 11. In other words, the influence of the significant historical "things" that happen between Cal's return home on the occasion of his father's death and his telling of his story — especially, in my view, the fall of the Wall and the fall of the Towers — must inform the way he tells it. But the book won't tell us how.

One way to think about this novel's relation to history is to examine its imagination of the future and to do so with reference to the concept of the future anterior as developed mainly by Derrida and also, somewhat differently, by Lacan and Lyotard. Derrida first uses this unusual verb tense in the exergue to *Of Grammatology* for the sense of time it opens up to think about speech acts and writing, the interpretation of literature, and the construction of history:

> The future can only be anticipated in the form of an absolute danger. It is that which breaks absolutely with constituted normality and can only be proclaimed, *presented*, as a sort of monstrosity. For that future world and for that within it which will have put into question the values of sign, word, and writing, for that which guides our future anterior, there is as yet no exergue. (5, italics in original)

Derrida is here proposing that this dangerous monstrosity is nonetheless a positive possibility; he calls it "a way of thinking that is faithful and attentive to the ineluctable world of the future which proclaims itself at present, beyond the closure of knowledge" (4). Of the Derridean future anterior, Tony Thwaites writes,

> Grammatically, the "will have been" of the future anterior is not at all a matter of "a future determined by what preceded it": that would be a possible—but certainly not even then a necessary—use of the simple future, the "will be." The future anterior is a much stranger tense, of a future which has not yet arrived and is itself yet to be determined, but which determines retrospectively, in its turn, the past which *will have been* for that future. Invoking a past which has itself not yet arrived, or is always in the process of arriving, the future anterior not only describes the empirical delays attendant on any historicity, but also, in its complex textual folding, the very structure of historicity as perpetually renewed wager. (par. 12h)

The future anterior's "that which will have been" points to the past that will exist only once the future arrives. Lyotard and Lacan both adopted it because they wanted to make use of its counterintuitive yet (or, and so) revealing sense of the passage of time, Lacan for the light it can shed on the psyche, Lyotard for his construction of cultural history, in particular of the postmodern. Lyotard defines the postmodern as what happens when "the artist and the writer . . . are working without rules in order to formulate the rules of what *will have been done*" (81). Lacan describes the future anterior this way: "What is realized in my history is not the past definite of what was, since it is no more, or even the present perfect of what has been in what I am, but the future anterior of what I shall have been for what I am in the process of becoming" (63). In both cases, we are, as in Derrida, beyond the closure of knowledge.

In his 1976 lecture "Declarations of Independence," Derrida makes use of his concept of the future anterior when he considers the American Declaration of Independence as an example of the dual power of language to describe and perform: it is, Beardsworth writes, "both a *description,* by its representatives, of the prior fact of the American people and their representatives and the very *performance* of this people and its representative signatories" (par. 6). This performance, Derrida says, is an act of invention, carried out through what he calls a "fabulous retroactivity" by which the American people claim to be a people before they have become one: looking back from the future, it is claimed, they *will have become* a people (*Negotiations* 50). The future anterior here resides especially, for Derrida, in this passage:

> We, therefore, the Representatives of the United States of America, in General Congress, assembled, appealing to the Supreme Judge of the world for the rectitude of our intentions, do, in the Name, and by the authority of the good people of these Colonies, solemnly publish and declare, that these United Colonies are, and of right ought to be, free and independent states.

The last line conveys the sense of description of the present and desire for the future: the colonies "are" free and also "of right ought to be" free. Saying it, in a sense, made it so, in that saying it was so enabled action based on the idea that it would be so.

Cal's moment of self-determination—the moment when he turns his back on his past and proclaims himself male—is a moment that depends on the future anterior. So too does that moment's twin at the end of the novel, when Cal has reached the end of the retelling of the story of his youth and is at the beginning of a relationship with Julie, a relationship that after a false start earlier in the novel now promises to last because Cal has worked through the traumas of the past. These two moments belong to the future anterior because they are constructions of history—Cal's personal history—that claim to describe a present but really construct a past built upon a wish for the future. Though Callie becomes Cal when she tells her mother and father (in writing) that she is a boy, she is a boy only because she decides to reject her rearing and selectively interpret her ambiguous physiognomy. She cuts her hair, walks like a boy, and names herself with a boy's name. In the moment that she declares herself male, she begins the process of constructing a history of her life that leads up to the present she imagines for herself. We see the future anterior in Cal's response to his mother's question "Don't you think it would have been easier just to stay the way you were?": "This is the way I was" (520). Likewise, Cal's intimation at the end of the novel that he has begun a sustainable relationship—that he has come to grips with who he is through the telling of his life story and as a result is able in the present to lead a healthy, shared life—is really a statement less of fact than of hope. And it similarly constructs a past that in the future, it is hoped, will be seen to have prepared the way for present happiness confirmed by future happiness.

If that future is happy. Whether the future will be happy is, in all cases, unknowable because of the contingent nature of existence. What the idea of the future anterior reminds us is that we do not simply write our histories so that they lead happily to the present in which we find ourselves. That present, in actuality, is similarly unknowable, so we try to see the past leading to how we hope the present will turn out—in the future. As Tony Jackson has remarked concerning the future anterior as it appears in Lacan,

> Is it possible to think of ourselves absolutely now, exclusive of some expected direction into the future? So the sense of now emerges from a sense towards the yet to be. So when we recall the past, we are actually projecting, of course upon some more or less noumenal core of the real, an image of what will need to have been in order to bring about who we expect to be.

The book Cal writes tells the story of who he needs to have been in order to bring about the well-adjusted, happy man he expects to be but certainly does not know he will be. The book Eugenides writes does not seem to question Cal's shaping of his narrative; there is no detectable ironic distance between the two.

Cal's too quick, too neat resolution of his gender story and of the issue of hermaphroditism is, then, *Middlesex*'s own, and it is the result of its historical imagination, one that falls prey to the anxieties attendant on our living, to use Frank Kermode's phrase, in "the middest" (7), unable to know the future and often unwilling to deal with the traumatic past—or too willing to tell its story and declare its wounds healed. The ending is rushed, especially for a novel of more than five hundred pages, and simplistic; it happens very quickly and insists too much on its not being such a big deal: "After I returned from San Francisco and started living as a male, my family found that, contrary to popular opinion, gender was not all that important. My change from girl to boy was far less dramatic than the distance anybody travels from infancy to adulthood" (520). However, this girl-becomes-boy bildungsroman *does* portray a change more dramatic than adolescence and often seems to know it, as in its fleeting recognitions of Cal's difficulties in San Francisco, including getting beaten up in Golden Gate Park and working as Hermaphroditus in an underwater peep show. But it downplays the significance of this change.[3] And it is followed by plot machinations that creak and grind, often implausibly, as in the scheme engineered by Cal's priest uncle (and one-time spurned suitor of his mother) to fake Calliope's kidnapping after she runs off to become Cal and her father's resulting death in, of all things, a car chase. On a bridge. And it oversimplifies what had been a complex and nuanced exploration of what makes gender and of the history both of the argument between nature and nurture and also of the ways medicine has dealt with hermaphroditism. In the end, the "middle" of its title, which it had so promisingly staked out as its territory early on, is abandoned.

Just as Cal's autobiography and Eugenides's novel tell stories of the past built on the image of a desired yet-to-be, so Americans, ever since before the Declaration, have been telling stories of their national past built on what they believe their nation to be at present, which itself has been only what they have hoped for its future.

The telling of these stories requires that the traumas of the past be either elided or confronted. The danger of the confrontation lies in its emphasis on working through. Motivated in cases of historical trauma by a desire to uncover past losses or atrocities that have been elided, the remembering of which is thought to have potential future value not just in national healing but in directing future action, working through can be performed in such a way that the useful historical reminder is dealt with and then put away. The traumatized subject is able, on this view, to domesticate the past through an exercise of free will, to escape its power to determine the future—as *Middlesex* believes Cal does. The problem is that, with the reforgetting of the traumatic event, its potential to remind is lost. Healing the wound, on this view, might be less valuable than leaving it open. But the need to imagine a happy future is powerful; and the constructions of the past that result can seek what might be called closure in their future-oriented motivation: whether the past is seen as free of trauma or full of it, the result can be a view of the past as a closed book, as that which leads to the happy ending that is the present.

As I've suggested, the trauma that announced the end of the 1990s occurred in September 2001. American optimism and faith in self-determination, in the ability to write one's own destiny, were shaken by these attacks, so unforeseen and close to home. The happy future assumed to be around the bend after the U.S. found itself the only superpower was harder to assume in such a radically contingent-feeling present. The history that needed to be written to lead from the past to that happy future was going to be hard to write.

But again, people are eager to heal their wounds. The trauma of 9/11 provoked repression, vengefulness, and self-recrimination; most reactions save the last were eager to move past it or use it as motivation for military action. The closure such thinking provides is far more comforting than the alternatives. The attempt to deny the anxiety of contingency that is central to triumphalist narrative—as well as to a traumatic narrative too keen on healing

—enables reconstructions of the past that lead to rosy futures, right past uncertain presents. This kind of historical imagination drives *Middlesex*. Eugenides's description of the book as explaining the past and coming up to the present reveals a desire for a past whose traumas can be healed over (in this case, by the working through that literary representation, a kind of written talking-cure, seems to offer) and can be shown to have made possible a happy future. "History is what hurts," Jameson wrote twenty-five years ago (*Political Unconscious* 102); history, for Jameson, is an absent cause that can only be seen in its limiting effects. For Eugenides and other contemporary novelists influenced by the strain of trauma thinking too keen on closure, history is what *heals*: it is marked by deeply wounding limit events, whose hurts are healed through narrative.

Seeing history as something to be healed has an effect on how one represents it. In the case of *Middlesex*, it has formal effects that identify it not simply as a postmodern historical novel but as a post-9/11 historical novel. At one point in his account of his early life, Cal writes,

> Aside from their blinding brightness, there was another odd thing about Milton's home movies: like Hitchcock, he always appeared in them. The only way to check the amount of film left in the camera was by reading the counter inside the lens. In the middle of Christmas scenes or birthday parties there always came a moment when Milton's eye would fill the screen. So that now, as I quickly try to sketch my early years, what comes back most clearly is just that: the brown orb of my father's sleepy, bearish eye. A postmodern touch in our domestic cinema, pointing up artifice, calling attention to mechanics. (And bequeathing me my aesthetic.) (225)

The metafictional touches in *Middlesex* are there to remind us that a creative intelligence is behind its construction of history. As much postmodern fiction has shown, there is always an eye behind the viewfinder and a hand pointing the lens. As the contemporary history of these techniques enters another century though, the early connections between postmodern techniques and radical epistemological skepticism are less clear. As Hutcheon puts it in her discussion of what she calls the "historiographic metafiction" of the 1960s, 1970s, and 1980s, "Postmodern fiction suggests that to re-write or to re-present the past in fiction and in history is, in both cases, to open it up to the present, to prevent it from being conclusive and teleological" (110). Many writers in the last ten or fifteen years have used metafictional techniques popularized by earlier novelists, and while the meanings of formal choices are always hard to pin down, it can be safely said that the radical tang of metafictional technique is not always what it once was.

Nor is it always intended to be. Eugenides does not feel that he is a postmodernist, though Cal claims postmodernism as his own aesthetic and Eugenides himself sees aspects of it in his work. In the interview with Bram van Moorhem he remarks on *Middlesex*'s combination of self-conscious narration and traditional novelistic storytelling and then makes clear that this does not make him postmodern:

> I don't want to constantly frustrate the reader by taking him down on dead ends, at the dead end of literature or something—that doesn't interest me. I want, in a way, a Classical shape to my books and a pleasing and elegant form to them, which is old-fashioned. But within that, I still have a lot of postmodern play without the continuing sense of relativism that . . . I got so tired of.

One of the dead ends of postmodern play that Eugenides is tired of concerns the literal end—the problematization of closure. While he enjoys the calling attention to mechanics, the pointing up of artifice, he favors what he calls classical shape and elegant form—things surely characterized by clean endings. But as I have argued, the choice to end or not to end has meaning. Again, the distrust of closure so closely identified with postmodernism is a response to the existential confrontation with contingency brought on by the horrors of midcentury; one formal aspect of that response is a refusal of closure, a radical open-endedness. In contemporary fiction, especially fiction written after the end of the Cold War, that distrust is often specifically informed by the resurgence of the triumphalist narrative inspired by what is taken as American victory. The formal response often takes the shape of reopenings of historical narratives previously closed, in particular unearthings of repressed pasts. This response can sometimes result in an inadvertent repetition of the very failing that inspired it in the first place—the welcoming of closure in the form of the healing that is the goal of working through, which manifests itself in the hasty, foreclosing, elision-enabled ending. Reading *Middlesex* in this light further suggests that this repetition of the compulsion toward closure modeled by the end-of-history claims following the end of the Cold War is in recent years intensified by the desire to heal the new wound of 9/11. In the end, Eugenides's novel is chock full of closure. And this closure is not simply a formal tying up of loose ends but also foreclosure: the meaning of the ambiguity of Cal's body, the undecided relative importance of different determining forces on the question of his gender, the ramifications of his choice to exercise his free will—these issues are dropped. The "middle" of the book's title, that place between genders and other neat distinctions, that place where things aren't always clear and settled, is abandoned in the end.

If *Middlesex* serves here as an example of a novel succumbing to the desire for closure in the face of contingency, Jonathan Lethem's *The Fortress of Solitude*, also a turn of the century bildungsroman in which a young protagonist confronts the wounds of his past in order to try to move forward, serves as a counterexample. Setting itself up for a happy ending, in accordance with the desire for closure common to much narrative (but in contemporary times especially attractive because especially hard to come by), *The Fortress of Solitude* offers a different kind of end.

Lethem's novel, about a white boy growing up in pregentrified 1970s Brooklyn, follows the boy to the early 1980s, then jumps to the late 1990s when, after leaving Brooklyn for Vermont and then Berkeley, he tries to come to grips with what happened during his childhood. The protagonist, Dylan Ebdus, lives in Gowanus, a neighborhood destined to be transformed, through the magic of gentrification, into Boerum Hill. Dylan's mother, Rachel, is committed to the idea of an integrated inner city and sees herself not as an agent of gentrification (which she calls a "Nixon word" [52]) but rather as someone committed to social change. At the heart of the novel is the story of Dylan's friendship with a just-older Black boy, Mingus Rude, with whom he forges a close and complicated relationship, one that shapes his conflicted sense of who he is (and is not) as a white, middle-class boy on a Puerto Rican and Black street next door to the projects. Over the course of his childhood and adolescence, Dylan deals with his mother's sending him to the public schools instead of one of the private schools where most of the white kids go, with his mother's suddenly running off, and with his own struggle to find a way to fit in on the street and in the larger world. At the center of Dylan's engagement with these worlds is his relationship to Mingus, who protects him and offers him access to street life that would have otherwise been unavailable to him, such as an early schoolyard hip-hop DJ face-off. At the center of his engagements with Dean Street and 1970s Brooklyn, then, is ambivalence: he is victimized, yet yearns to be a part of Black culture, a thing that even then he realizes is both real and a construction, and is both hampered and, in the end, saved by his whiteness. Dylan and Mingus's friendship is marked by things they share, including names inspired by musicians (Bob and Charles, respectively), absent mothers (Mingus's father was granted custody of him in a divorce settlement) and barely present fathers—Dylan's, Abraham, is upstairs in his art studio, making an art film by painstakingly painting individual frames, while Mingus's, Barrett, is upstairs, high, angry about the flameout of his career as a soul singer. The boys' time together is spent reading comics, tagging Brooklyn with graffiti, experimenting sexually, and (in a fantastic element much debated by readers) inventing and becoming, with the aid of a magical ring, a third-rate flying superhero named Aeroman. Their relationship is also marked by one significant thing that they don't share, their races, which will play a large role in the divergent courses their lives will take.

Part 1, which takes up two-thirds of the book, tells these stories of Dylan's youth, including his leaving Mingus first by attending not the local high school but Stuyvesant, a competitive public school in Manhattan, and then by preparing to go off to college in Vermont. It ends in 1981 with a violent confrontation between Barrett and his fallen preacher father, outraged at his son's lifestyle, a confrontation that appears at first to be a version of a famous incident of the early 1980s, singer Marvin Gaye's murder by his father. A brief (fifteen-page) part 2 consists entirely of the liner notes, written by the adult music writer Dylan, for a retrospective CD collection of Barrett Rude's music, in which readers learn that the shooting was not of Barrett by his father but of Barrett's father by Mingus, protecting his father from his grandfather. Part 3 is narrated (as part 1, in the third person, was not) by Dylan, in his midthirties in 1999, living in Berkeley with Abby, of whom Dylan says, "I loved having a black girlfriend" (312), thereby highlighting one of the difficulties in their relationship. In this last section of the novel, Dylan looks back and retells the events of the eighteen years since the shooting. He also narrates the action of the present, which includes his attempts to reconnect with the three most important missing people in his life—his runaway mother, his largely absent father, and his best friend, Mingus. In the end, he comes to some understanding of his father's choices and a new appreciation of his art. Dylan also learns, in a long section of the book given to us from Mingus's point of view, what the intervening years were like for Mingus, in the aftermath of the shooting and in the years since, which were largely spent moving between prisons and crack houses, some of the time with Dylan's erstwhile neighborhood nemesis, Robert Woolfolk. After this account, which we discover was delivered to the invisible Dylan (Aeroman's old magical ring now giving its wearer a new power) through the bars of his cell, Dylan tries to give Mingus the ring but is told to slip it to Woolfolk in his cell; Woolfolk dies trying to fly from a gun tower. Finally, Dylan fails to find his mother but learns that she regretted and was ashamed of having left her family.

Early readings of *The Fortress of Solitude* were marked by praise for one element of the book and criticism of two others. The praise was earned for the evocative portrait of Dylan's childhood in part 1, which was almost universally appreciated for its vividness, accuracy, and depth of feeling. The criticism was aimed at the fantastic, superhero thread, which many readers seemed to have a hard time knowing what to do with in the context of an otherwise realistic book, and at the direction the book takes after part 1, in the short liner notes section and in the first-person account of Dylan's adult-hood in part 3, which many readers found to be a letdown. While readers have to decide what to do with the fantastic element, for my purposes the latter criticism is more significant. The closer look at *The Fortress of Solitude* that follows will show that what is perceived as a weakness of the latter parts of the novel is part of a larger design. Having a clear picture of that larger design is cru-cial to understanding not just how the novel works but also how it understands the relation between past and present differently than *Middlesex* does.

Part 3 of the novel, the part narrated by the adult Dylan, begins with an argument with his girlfriend. Abby has just discovered that Dylan is going from Berkeley to LA on a trip to see his father and has kept this information from her, and she is angry that he felt he couldn't tell her about it. Arguing about his depression and his failure to recognize it or talk to her about it, she throws CDs from his huge (mostly soul and rhythm and blues) music collec-tion to the ground, describing the wall of racks as "a wall of *de-pression*" (317). She tells him, "You're so busy feeling sorry for me and *whoever*, Sam Cooke, you conveniently ignore yourself," and adds, "I'm just the official mascot for all the shit you won't allow yourself to feel. A featured exhibit in the Ebdus collection of *sad black folks*" (316, 317). His musical tastes amount, in her words, to "a million whining moaning singers, ten million depressed songs" and an excuse not to think about what's bothering him, about why he lives in the past, why, as Abby says to him, "Your childhood is some privileged sanctuary you live in all the time, instead of here with me" (319). The question that has the greatest impact is why: "why are you so obsessed with your childhood?" (319). Dylan at first has trouble answering, thinking, "I truly wanted to answer, not only to appease her. I wanted to know it myself." The response he is finally able to make describes his predicament and sets him into motion for the rest of the novel's journey back into his past: "My childhood is the only part of my life that wasn't, uh, overwhelmed by my childhood" (319). He then reflects to himself, "Overwhelmed—or did I mean *ruined*?"

This moment in the novel provides the hinge between the time capsule of childhood in part 1 and the narrative of the present in part 3. Pinning the problems in their relationship on the unresolved issues of Dylan's youth, which are mostly unknown to her, Abby helps Dylan see that he needs to bring his past up into the light, to deal with what happened then and with its impact on him in the present. From the vantage point of the end of the century, Dylan looks back and tries to connect where he is in the present and where he started from. But Dylan's response to Abby—and his subsequent reflection on it—also provide both a key descriptive term for one often-criticized aspect of the experience of reading this novel and also a way to understand it not as authorial failure but as part of an intentional design.

The term is "overwhelmed": what readers have reported, again, is a feeling that the vivid, powerful part 1 overwhelms the rest of the novel, making the experience of reading parts 2 and 3 less gripping and involving and more distancing, even off-putting. "The book's structure begins to creak and break apart," one reviewer wrote, adding, "the novel never regains the breathtaking verve of its childhood section" (Charles). Another argued, "The first section could be a book on its own. The second half lacks its originality," and added that she found the Dylan of part 3 "less compelling" (O'Rourke). John Leonard wrote that "everything goes wrong about two thirds of the way through" ("Welcome"). We are less captured by the scenes—instead of scenes such as those in part 1 in which the kids on the block play skully or stoopball or in which Dylan is "yoked," the name for the daily occurrence of Dylan's being put in a headlock and having his money taken from his pockets, we have in part 3 many interior moments of self-analysis and self-doubt and a number of events less dramatic and less dramatically rendered than those from Dylan's childhood. As a result we may identify less strongly with Dylan. It is understandable that readers feel let down by this development, as it seems to be a movement away from the thing for which fiction is often most valued—the engrossing reading experience that is the effect of the sometimes-invisible workings of point of view, free indirect discourse, narrative drive. It is understandable that readers feel not only that the rest of the book is overwhelmed by part 1, as Dylan feels the rest of his life has been overwhelmed by his childhood, but that it is also, in his other term, ruined.

I would argue that this feeling is exactly the point. Lethem himself has said as much:

> I always knew I was going to do it, and I always felt it was the big risk the book had to take, that I knew was dictated by the material. They had to grow up, and it was in some ways an expulsion from the garden of childhood. The book had to change radically to reflect the way in which, however difficult it may be, childhood experience is this magical zone, and then adulthood is much more paltry in a lot of ways. It feels risky to me, because I know that Dylan is a bit of a shit in the second half of the book. He's not really that fun to get to know when you first meet that new voice, and it feels like a loss. ("Out of Brooklyn")

Some reviewers also have seen how the structural split in the novel might serve it thematically, expressing the idea that the past can live powerfully in our psyches, making the present seem colorless, a letdown itself, by fictionally representing life in the present less powerfully. As John Leonard (who nonetheless, as quoted earlier, sees "everything going wrong" in the second half) put it, "What if nothing else for the rest of your life will ever be as meaningful as how you felt in the seventh grade, being beaten up on your way home from school?" ("Welcome"). Peter Kurth wrote on *Salon*, "When the narrative shifts, midway through, from Lethem's voice to Dylan's, it comes as a violent shock. But that's adulthood, after all, when the mixed and melted images of youth get stuck in the fixations of a fully formed personality." And it is not only the power of the past and the relative rigidity of adulthood that are illustrated. In the words that open the chapter in part 3 in which Dylan first narrates events from the years immediately after the shooting, he is "a fierce rocket of denial" (382), shooting away from Brooklyn and the aftermath of events to go off to college in Vermont. Eighteen years later, haunted by his past, Dylan still won't deal with it, resulting in the present's seeming always less real, less present, paradoxically, than the past.

But it is not just the power of the past in general or even the important fact of Dylan's refusal to deal with it that the disparity between the two main sections of the book serves to illustrate. As a brief comparison to *Middlesex* will help show, it is what lies between these two sections that provides the key to what the structure of *The Fortress of Solitude* expresses about the novel's historical imagination.

Central to my understanding of *Middlesex* is the importance of the twenty-five-year gap between the story of the main character's past and the present of the frame, because it allows the novel to treat that past as something distant and disconnected. While the novel sets things up so that this past must be dealt with in order for the main character to live happily in the present, the historical chasm of those years, ignored by the narrative, has nothing to do with that central dynamic, thus rendering it suspect. Because the novel can treat the past as something distant and disconnected, in other words, it can neatly dispense with it, but the chronological and narrative leap that makes that neatness possible also makes it untenable. Too much is left out. *The Fortress of Solitude* at first appears to be similarly structured. A gap nearly as long as that in *Middlesex* lies between the 1981 shooting that ends part 1 (and, in a way, Dylan's childhood) and the 1999 of part 3. The difference is that we learn what happens in between, because although part 3 is set much later, significant portions of it are devoted to filling in the gap.

Most of this is about Dylan's life. There is sharp satire of Camden College, a Bennington-like college (in fact, it is modeled on Lethem's experience at Bennington), once a noble educational experiment, now a place where mostly wealthy, mostly white young people do things other than studying. There is also sharp satire of Dylan's use of his Brooklyn roots, smoking Kool menthols, wearing a Kangol cap long before it was cool for white kids to do so. "I'd throw Brooklyn down like a dare," he says, adding, "Basically, I turned myself into a cartoon of Mingus" (389). There is Dylan's expulsion for drug dealing. There is, in California, Dylan's learning the arts of radio DJing and liner notes writing. There is a return trip to Dean Street, during which Dylan learns about the effects of gentrification in the years since he'd left and feels, meeting up with Marilla, his first friend on the block, "astonishment at my own denial of this place" (433).

A significant part of the gap-filling work done in part 3, however, is not about Dylan but instead about Mingus—which, of course, makes it also very much about Dylan. More than his abandonment by his mother, more than his race and class guilt and cross-racial and cross-class identification, more than the combination of anger at the situation his mother placed him in (as the whiteboy who would single-handedly integrate his neighborhood by getting put in headlocks) and guilt (he is even accused by would-be yokers of being a racist), he is haunted by his guilt at having left behind Mingus, whom he calls "the rejected idol of my entire youth, my best friend, my lover" (443). In two powerfully affecting chapters, the story of Mingus's life since the shooting is presented from his own point of view. It is a personal history shaped in part by the interrelated histories of New York City and drugs and prisons and the lives of urban Black youth in the 1980s and 1990s, when what has been called "urban decay" and the crack epidemic and Rockefeller drug laws emptied streets and swelled prisons. But it is a personal history first, the story of a motherless boy whose father is sunk low in depression and rage and is awash in money and drugs to which the young man has too-ready access; it is the story of a charismatic, gifted street artist, who becomes a seventy-pound petty thief, in his words, "nothing but a booster and a crackhead" (477).

And it is a history that is part of Dylan's history, a fact he realizes he needs to confront. Like his own life since leaving for college, Mingus's life continued after 1981. Likewise the life of Dean Street, of Gowanus. Dylan's dilemmas—of racial and class identity, of responsibility to people and places, of reconciling the person he is in the present to the person, or people, he has been—are harder to resolve if he figures in all of his life rather than just a distant, severed past. While *Middlesex*'s past effectively ends in the mid-1970s, allowing Cal to look back on a past wound and a past moment of self-determination and declare them finished, understood, and so no longer affecting him in the present, in part 3 of *The Fortress of Solitude*, Dylan stops jumping the gap and begins to suture his life back together. He stops leaving things out. Doing this allows him to begin to understand how past flows into present, how it is not a faraway thing but everything up until a second ago and not something one can deny or be done with.

Not being done with the past makes writing history—personal or community, biographical or national—a less neat but ultimately more valuable task. Seeing people and places as fixed becomes more difficult, as does declaring the ends of things. These difficulties, though, are valuable. Looking back not just on his childhood but also on the years after means that Dylan can't close the book on his past, even when confronting it; he can't scrutinize it, trapped in amber, decide what it was and what it meant, and move on. Life continues, like people do, and always changes. And change is ultimately what Dylan must deal with and what *The Fortress of Solitude* is about. From its opening images of two little white girls in their nightgowns roller-skating on Dean Street as dusk falls, blond hair streaming in the pink light, heralds of gentrification, the novel foregrounds change. The abandoned and run-down brownstones of the neighborhood become tin-ceilinged bistros with exposed old brick and new hardwood floors, like "the set for an idealized movie" (433). Nerdy high school boys become drug dealers. Charismatic leaders become small-time criminals. People change for any number of reasons: other people leave them, or historical shifts change their circumstances, or time passes. What Dylan learns, looking back not just on how things were but on all the ways they've been, is this. In the narrator's words in part 1, "Dylan never met anyone who wasn't about to change immediately into someone else" (232); in his own words, "Life's eternal lesson: people return in new guises" (479). The lesson of this lesson—the lesson this novel takes from seeing the past as ever changing and, in my view, from reckoning with its own historical moment, after the Cold War and especially after 9/11—is the existence and importance of contingency. Things change, in unforeseen ways, and they always will.

Trying to understand all the ways in which his life, Mingus's life, and his world have changed, Dylan comes to recognize that the task Abby pushes him toward and he then sets for himself is as much about the future as it is the past. In Derrida's terms, *The Fortress of Solitude* isn't just aware of contingency: it's aware of the hidden centrality of the future, and its unknowability, to the way we see the past. We construct our narratives of the past to lead not to where we are, which can't really be known either, but to the particular future we hope will arrive someday.

Dylan's recognition of this view of history develops over a few moments in the last third of the novel. He goes to see Abraham in LA because Abraham is being honored at a science fiction convention for his long career painting sci fi novel cover illustrations, which have paid the rent for the decades during which he has devoted his real energy to the painstaking process of painting the individual frames of his film. At the convention, Abraham shows two sections of the film to an audience that includes Dylan. The more recent section of the two is taken by Dylan to be significant:

> a green triangle with blunted corners, one trying and failing to fall sideways against the phantasmic, blurred horizon. . . . It trembled, tipped a degree, nearly kissed earth, jumped back. Progress was illusion: two steps forward, two steps back. Impossible, though, not to root for it. To feel it groping like a foot for purchase. Daring, hesitating, failing. (362)

The audience is, in Dylan's words, "unexpectedly moved" by what Abraham calls the triangle's "struggle" (362). Someone asks, "Will it ever—?" (362). A chapter later, Dylan thinks he has a lesson from this moment in his father's film: "I was halted in a motion half-completed," he says, and thinks he must complete it, must, with a music critic nod to the Beatles, "get back to where I once belonged" (380, 381).

The real lesson, though, is closer to what Dylan provides as the book's final image. It is prepared for by his closing reflections on what he calls "the middle spaces," the places of integration between and across divisions, the places he describes, referring to the commune his mother landed at in Indiana after fleeing Brooklyn, as "wrested from the world before the makers of highways wrested it back." Camden College, he wonders, might have been like this once too, a middle space, but "a middle space opened and closed like a glance, you'd miss it if you blinked." Likening Camden's spirit to that of his integrationist mother, he criticizes them as he admires them; he claims, "I'd been pushed out like a blind finger, to probe a nonexistent space, a whiteboy integrating public schools which were just then being abandoned, which were becoming rehearsals only for prison" (510). Things change. He reflects on her dream of changing Gowanus, of integrating it in a way that wouldn't alter its essential nature, wouldn't gentrify it, and sees in this dream something of what Derrida sees in the Declaration:

> Her mistake was so beautiful, so stupid, so American. It terrified my small mind, it always had. Abraham had the better idea, to try to carve the middle space on a daily basis, alone in his room. If the green triangle never fell to earth before he died and left the film unfinished, it would never have fallen—wasn't that so? Wasn't it? (510–11)

The final image echoes this meditation on closure and continues its correction of Dylan's taking his recognition of himself as "halted in a motion half-completed" as motivation to find closure. Dylan is remembering the drive home from a trip to Camden to pick up his things after his expulsion. Abraham had driven him up from Brooklyn, and they were returning home through a blizzard. Silent, they were headed back to Dean Street, but they, especially Dylan, didn't know what else they were headed toward, didn't know what the future held. By chance, or contingency, he'd been caught and kicked out of college, and what lay before him was unknown, as it sometimes seems not to be but always is:

> Abraham and I let ourselves be swept through the blurred tunnel, beyond rescue but calm for an instant, settled in our task, a father driving a son home to Dean Street. . . . We were in a middle space then, in a cone of white, father and son moving forward at a certain speed. Side by side, not truly quiet but quiescent, two gnarls of human scribble, human cipher, human dream. (511)

The motion half-completed is here not something to be completed but rather what all motion through time is—not something to be finished, as if that were possible, but something that continues on-ward, turning present into past, heading blindly into the future.

"The better idea," then, is to see the task as moving forward slowly, on a daily basis, at a certain speed. The beautiful American mistake of trying to claim the future—to integrate or to gentrify, to leave things behind, to remake oneself into some final version—is a mistake because it tries to deny contingency. Trying either to elide the past or to heal over its wounds is not just futile but, in Dylan's word, stupid.

At the end of *The Fortress of Solitude*, the expected happy ending has still not materialized. More than once, Dylan has said he needs to call Abby and explain everything to her—just not quite yet. The epiphany, the moment of healing, the closure, the glimpse of the happy future that this trip back into the past will provide—this book does not provide them. The problems of gentrification, integration, racialized identity are not magically solved by novel's end. It does not hold that kind of view of history. That view is quietly evoked by the historical reference with which the second chapter of part 3 opens: "It was September 1999, a season of fear—in three months the collapse of the worldwide computer grid was going to bring the century's long party to a finish" (321). The irony, of course, is that this didn't happen, that the imagined apocalypse of Y2K amounted to very little. This irony is available because it appears in a book completed four years later. History didn't end at the close of the twentieth century and the second millennium, just as it didn't end at the end of the Cold War, or during a September two years later, or at the end of this book. History continues at a certain speed, this novel seems to be saying, and we can best understand our lives and the lives of our nations if we see history that way, if we fill in the gaps, if we mind the connections, remain skeptical of sudden metamorphoses and neat closure, and try to stay in the middle—in the middle of half-completed motions and in the middle between confusion and certainty.

At the end of *The Fortress of Solitude*, Dylan doesn't know how to solve the insoluble problems of race and class and the complex, contradictory ways in which they define him; he doesn't know how to feel about Mingus's protection of him, his abandonment of Mingus, and the privileges of being white and middle class; he doesn't know whether his connection to Black culture is identification or appropriation, whether there really is a difference between gentrification and integration, whether he can have a Black girlfriend and love her for reasons other than that she's his Black girlfriend. He does know, however, that there's no magic ring that can make him Black (as he wondered at the school-yard battle where he was the only white boy and nobody bothered him) or make him understand all these things. He knows what is possible, and that is, in Abraham's father's words about the triangle in his film, "the daily task. A refusal to speculate, only encounter. Only understand" (362).

In addition, as the final image also shows, it is possible to move forward, to encounter, not in a fortress of solitude but with someone else. *Middlesex* is in many ways a very solitary novel; Cal grapples with his past alone and, though he tells us that he will have a happy future with Julie, the novel closes with the image of Cal alone, in a doorway, thinking about the future. In contrast, *The Fortress of Solitude*, like *Mason & Dixon*, ends with an image of two characters together, not in happy resolution, but together, having overcome the forces of division enough to hold on to each other and to a vision of a world of unfixed positions, of possibility. As Mason and Dixon have learned to live in between, in the middle, "before a ceaseless spectacle of transition" (713), so Dylan and Abraham, in this image—Abraham in his art and Dylan in the novel's present—learn to accept change, to recognize the fact of contingency and reject false closure. Mingus and Dylan, the real buddy-story pair of this book, are irrevocably split. It is impossible to picture them together in a car driving anywhere in the novel's present. So *The Fortress of Solitude* remains, in one reviewer's words, "a heartbroken book" (Scott, "When"). But it is not a book without hope for the future and for the possibility of life outside of the fortresses of solitude life builds for us.

Writing a historical novel that asserts the possibility of self-determination after 9/11 can be seen as making a certain kind of sense. A reassertion of American optimism in this context is the understandable result both of the old American ability to construct, from a hoped-for future, a past that leads to it and also of the contemporary American tendency, especially prevalent after 9/11, to read the hurts of history as available for healing. It is, in the end, an attempt to achieve closure. This closure allows the past to be constructed optimistically, as it is when Eugenides ends his novel with young Cal standing in the doorway of his childhood home, losing track of time, weeping for his father and his past but looking outward and "thinking about what was next." Of course, this optimism relies on the teller's already knowing what is next (as we do, from the frame story). Such construction, as I've tried to suggest in the case of *Middlesex*, can be inadequate. A more useful if less comforting alternative is suggested by Derrida in a dialogue in the 2003 *Philosophy in a Time of Terror*, where he argues that the world will be traumatized by 9/11

> not in the present or from the memory of what will have been the past present . . . [but] from the unrepresentable future, from the open threat of an aggression capable one day of striking—for you never know—the *head* of the sovereign state par excellence. (Borradori, Derrida, and Habermas 98)

The significance of the event here is in the awareness of contingency it brings and in the resistance to healing closure it encourages. The medical model, which sometimes leads trauma theory to uncritically valorize working through, might be the wrong one here. Instead, perhaps especially in light of the figure of autoimmunity that Derrida develops in this dialogue and elsewhere to discuss what he sees as empire's death drive, it might be more useful to mind not the event of wounding but rather the self-wounding repetitions, such as elective war or domestic surveillance. At a time when what will come next seems increasingly unimaginable, American stories that acknowledge the terror of the future and resist imposing closure on the past are becoming increasingly important. *The Fortress of Solitude* is such a story.

Writing the kind of novel that Eugenides wrote after 9/11 doesn't only make a certain kind of sense; it may also characterize a moment in literary history after postmodernism. If I'm right that the nature of the distrust of closure changes after the end of the Cold War and that this modulation of postmodernism's distrust is further spun by the events of 9/11, then the formal evidence offered by *Middlesex* and *The Fortress of Solitude* can help point to one defining characteristic of a new moment in American fiction, one in which the stakes of the decision of whether or not to end the old-fashioned way are raised. How high they are raised and what shape historical narratives will take only the future, of course, will tell.

AFTERWORD

DeLillo and the Anticipation
of Retrospection

We're in between two historical periods, the Cold War and
whatever it is that follows it. I'm not sure that this is what follows it. This may just be the interim. I think we're just beginning to wonder what happened, and what didn't happen.
Don DeLillo, 1998 interview

We don't want the smoking gun to be a mushroom cloud.
Condoleezza Rice

"We're all gonna die!"
Don DeLillo, *Underworld*

n his epilogue to the 2000 reissued edition of *The Sense of an Ending*, Frank Kermode reflects on the time when his study of fiction and apocalypticism first appeared:

In the autumn of 1965, when I gave the lectures which make up *The Sense of an Ending*, the end of the present millennium still seemed far in the future; but no one could ignore the imminence of events that could without too much exaggeration be characterized as apocalyptic. The Cuban missile crisis and the assassination of President Kennedy were quite recent events, the Cold War remained very cold, and words like "megadeath" were common currency. . . . It seemed more than merely possible that there was a bad time coming, possibly a terminally bad time. (181–82)

As I discuss in my introduction, the sense of this kind of apocalyptic ending weakened nearer the millennium, after the end of the Cold War. Kermode himself notes that when the second edition of the *Oxford English Dictionary* appeared in 1989, the word "megadeath" was nowhere to be found: its absence, he writes, "may hint at a change of mood, a lessening, however temporary, of apocalyptic anxiety after that time" (181). This undeniable lessening of anxiety created a climate in which the post–Cold War historical conversation that is my subject could take place. With immediate fears receding, it was a time to look back in triumph, anger, or wonder; to look back at the Cold War and the longer sweep of American history; to look back at particular events, the narratives constructed of those events, and the larger models of history on which these narratives are built; to look back through historiography, literary and social criticism, and fiction. The novels I read here and the work of the thinkers and popular narratives to which they talk back all have as conditions of possibility not only the end of the Cold War but also the easing of the sense that a terminally bad time, in Kermode's phrase, might be just around the corner.

This sense of the war being over, of the threat of nuclear apocalypse no longer hanging over the nation's head, thus makes possible not only these books but this book about them. However, just as many of the novels I read ask readers to reconsider a variety of end-of-history narratives, reasserting the continuities and connections that exist across American history, so too this book, at its end, has to question its own end-oriented periodizing narrative. In particular, I would like to revisit a historical assertion on which the book's larger argument rests, that is, that nuclear fear was not as significant a factor in American life after the end of the Cold War as it was during it. To do so, I will read Don DeLillo's 1997 novel *Underworld* as revelatory of the latent persistence of nuclear fear in the 1990s. First, though, I will argue for the resurgence of nuclear fear after 9/11 through a brief look at Sid Jacobson and Ernie Colón's *The 9/11 Report: A Graphic Adaptation* (2006) and the work of the White House Iraq Group in 2002. I do this first because the manifestations of nuclear fear evident in these two phenomena indicate that we should look back at the 1990s to see whether there was a more significant presence of nuclear fear than had been supposed. What is evident in *Underworld*, perhaps the most significant fictional account of the Cold War in the 1990s, is that there *was*—nuclear fear continued to play a role in the American historical imagination after the end of the Cold War. What this finding indicates, in turn, is that the effects of this fear on the way the past is reconstructed and the future imagined deserve further scrutiny.

My first text, *The 9/11 Report: A Graphic Adaptation*, offers the opportunity to examine one dominant public response to the events of 9/11, as the larger public narrative informed and was in turn influenced by the *9/11 Commission Report* on which it is based. Faithfully adapted from the words of the *Commission Report* by two veteran comic book artists, Sid Jacobson and Ernie Colón, the *Adaptation* fits the text to its format by condensing the Report's words and dramatizing its scenes in illustrations; the result is that the main features of the *Commission Report* are displayed in high relief. For my purposes, what is significantly made more pronounced in the *Adaptation* are the factors that led to the failure of the *Commission Report*; one of these factors, I believe, was a historical imagination still driven by nuclear fear.

In their foreword to the *Adaptation*, Tom Kean and Lee Hamilton, chair and vice chair of the 9/11 Commission, say their purpose in the *Commission Report* was "not only to inform our fellow citizens about history but also to energize and engage them on behalf of reform and change, to make our country safer and more secure" (ix). The *Commission Report* did not do these things, in part because of White House resistance and political pressures that led to a refusal, in Benjamin DeMott's words, to "call a liar a liar" (37) and so to a failure to clearly lay out the breakdowns and negligence that kept the U.S. from protecting itself from what happened on that day in 2001 or from the premeditated rush to war that followed.

Jacobson and Colón's *Adaptation* makes clear the role the contemporary American historical imagination played in the *Commission Report*'s failure. This role was twofold. First is the effect of the cowboys-and-Indians story of American might and right on the Commission's version of events: this influence is clear in the style with which the *Adaptation* is drawn, evident in images of a heroic George W. Bush with clenched fists, wearing a leather bomber jacket, issuing directives and standing over maps with generals.[1] Triumphalist narratives need heroes, of course, and villains (the *Adaptation* does not disappoint in that department either), and the line between the two must be crystal clear, as Susan Sontag and Bill Maher learned.[2] What is less obvious but equally important to the *Adaptation*, and so to the *Commission Report* and to the dominant popular understanding of 9/11, is the role played by the bomb. Near the end of the *Adaptation*, on a page in the future recommendations section devoted to the issue of Al Qaeda's attempts to acquire WMD, a drawing of skyscrapers with a dark cloud rising behind them is accompanied by text that reads, "An amount of plutonium the size of an orange could be fashioned into a nuclear device that could fit into a van like the one in the 1993 WTC bombing . . . and level lower Manhattan" (120). In this panel's imagining of a future attack with a combination of the image of a mushroom cloud and a reference to the World Trade Center bombing of the early 1990s (and the dramatic ellipsis near the end of the sentence), it is not hard to sense the motivating presence of nuclear fear. In one of a number of similar moments, the final image of the *Adaptation*, a drawing of the charred, smoking remains of the towers, echoes this calling up of the idea of the bomb in its illustration of the apocalyptic quality of the site's appearance—which led to its being quickly and widely referred to as Ground Zero, a term borrowed from Hiroshima.[3]

This surfacing of nuclear fear in the *Adaptation, Commission Report*, and the popular imagination has helped shape the construction of the narratives of these events, which have in turn shaped the course of events since. This has happened in two main ways. First, the official narrative account of the past chose not to tell the truth but rather to comfort, in the face of this fear. Second, the fear inspired heightened vigilance and a readiness to support military action. While other historical moments were invoked in responses to the attacks—Pearl Harbor especially springs to mind—it was the fear of the bomb that was especially available not only to those trying to describe events but also to those trying to influence public opinion in order to orchestrate official reaction to them.

The White House Iraq Group—a group of senior members of the administration, set up in August 2002 by Andrew Card and chaired by Karl Rove, whose purpose was to sell the upcoming invasion of Iraq to the American people—is one of the most significant examples of those trying to influence opinion. Their most important attempt depended on the fact that, more than a decade after the fall of the Berlin Wall and MAD (Mutually Assured Destruction), nuclear fear had not disappeared from the American historical imagination. Introducing the idea of the war a few days before the first anniversary of the attacks, members of the group repeatedly used the phrases "smoking gun" and "mushroom cloud" together to warn of the danger posed by the nuclear arms the administration was insisting were in Saddam Hussein's possession and to urge "preemptive" action.[4] Wanting the strongest possible launch of their "new product," as Card referred to the invasion, the administration used its best line, one whose effectiveness relied entirely on the assumption that nuclear fear was still a powerful button to be pushed.[5]

Nuclear fear's ostensibly incongruous currency early in this century is certainly part of the general terror concerning the future that characterizes the historical moment and that contributes to the desire for closure I see in fiction of the time. The awareness of contingency raised by these sudden, unforeseen attacks manifested, for some, in the form of the mushroom cloud. But while the contemporary availability for manipulation of fear of a nuclear apocalypse is significant for our understanding of this moment, it can also tell us something about the moment preceding it. Although the 1990s were felt to be relatively peaceful and prosperous, allowing for the retrospection in American culture of the time, the popular sense that the Cold War had been won and the notion that threats from afar were no longer to be feared had at least two other significant effects. One was that the attacks of 9/11 were met with shock: the possibility of this kind of event, of domestic, apocalyptic-seeming attack, had receded from the foreground of the popular imagination. Another significant effect of the peaceful surface of the post–Cold War 1990s is that it masked the continuing life of nuclear fear. That the attacks should be met not just with shock but with the imagery and language of nuclear apocalypse indicates that nuclear fear was not gone but instead lay just below the surface, a fact that can be seen (though often is not) in DeLillo's *Underworld*.

DeLillo's 1997 magnum opus has been hailed by many readers as the most important novel of the 1990s.[6] It is a history of the Cold War told from the 1990s, a historical novel that, after an opening set piece about a day when two shots were heard around the world (Bobby Thomson's famous pennant-winning ninth-inning home run and the test shot that confirmed that the Soviets had the bomb), tracks backward from the 1990s to the 1950s, with a final return to the mid-1990s in the epilogue. It is, at 827 pages, a book about many things, but as much as anything else, it is a book about the bomb, the threat it sees as at the center of the Cold

War world, the thing that haunted America's inner life. And it is about the 1990s' nuclear inheritance, the material and cultural fallout of the years lived under the bomb, figured in the novel as waste. It is a book, then, that appears to come *after*. Martin Amis, in his review in the *New York Times*, called it "DeLillo's wake for the cold war . . . an 827-page damage check." While this is true, I don't think it is the whole story of the book: rather, its look back is driven not simply by a desire to commemorate a bygone time or to understand the past and its effects, but also in significant part by anxiety about the future. And while it is true that all historical narrative could be said to be in some way motivated by future-oriented concerns (as I argue about the post-9/11 historical novels discussed in the last chapter), the specific concern of *Underworld* is the fear of nuclear apocalypse, which is a fear not so much about how the future will turn out but about whether there will be one at all.

A quick look at the narrative structure of *Underworld* shows that it is a book that comes after, that it looks at the specter of the bomb that hung over the Cold War as a thing entirely of the past. The prologue, "The Triumph of Death," begins at the beginning of this period, in 1951, at that game in the Polo Grounds, and it takes full advantage of the phenomenon common to narrative reconstructions of history, the feeling of inevitability, of knowing how things will turn out. The Cold War, just born, will be the cause of decades of arms and space races, overt warfare, covert action, and military-industrial complex influence and will die forty years after its birth. Thomson will hit Branca's pitch over the wall and the two shall remain famous, linked forever in triumph and shame. The famous attendees—Jackie Gleason, Frank Sinatra, J. Edgar Hoover—will each live out their lives in ways already known. And death, in all cases, will triumph, as attested to by the title, taken from the Brueghel painting whose reproduction is ripped out of *Life* magazine (of course) and floats down from the stadium's upper deck to Hoover, on the very day he learns that the Soviets have again successfully tested their bomb.

The novel proper also supports this reading of the book as a postmortem on the Cold War. The first section of the body of the novel jumps forward in time to 1992, where readers are introduced to Nick Shay, a waste-management executive from Phoenix who is the novel's protagonist, his family, and an older woman he somehow knows from his past. *Underworld* then starts its march back to the beginning of the Cold War and of Nick's adult life (punctuated by short sections involving the boy who ended up with Bobby Thomson's home run ball), moving in not-so-quick succession from a section set in the mid-1980s and early 1990s to one set in spring 1978, to another in summer 1974, to one scattered across the 1950s and 1960s, and finally to a section spanning a few months in late 1951 and early 1952. Along the way, secrets are revealed, connections are found, later events are shown to have had roots in earlier ones, lineages are traced, and history moves backward. The older woman from the first section turns out to be someone Nick had an affair with when he was a teenager in the Bronx and the wife of his brother's chess teacher. An affair Nick has later, when he is married, happens only after an affair his wife has with a coworker of his. Ownership of the home run ball, in Nick's possession in the 1990s, is traced back through time. The secret from Nick's past is that he murdered a man back in the Bronx when he was a teenager. Thomson and Branca are shown together in photos with, in order, George H. W. Bush, Ronald Reagan, Richard Nixon, John F. Kennedy, and Dwight Eisenhower. The Wall falls before Kennedy is assassinated, which happens before the Cuban missile crisis, which happens before the Russians have the bomb. This movement back toward the beginning of a period already ended culminates in the epilogue, which provides the other end of the novel's frame, returning it to the early 1990s and Phoenix (as well as Kazakhstan, former site of the Russian atomic testing program).

As the above suggests, there is in all this backward-looking the continued assertion that the period is seen to be marked by connections, that the different lives, the disparate events, the scattered places and eras of the Cold War are all connected, that there is an underworld beneath the visible world where historical forces order events above. Connections are everywhere, between different kinds and ideas of waste, between different senses of "underworld," between the lives and experiences of these characters. The idea is as present in the novel as the sense of loss is. This loss is felt with regard to many things, including the innocence of an earlier time, the texture of life before the bomb hung over it, but also the texture of life when it *did*, and especially the order life was given by it. There was, in DeLillo's words, "a sense of limits we don't have anymore" (qtd. in Knight). Post–Cold War life suffers from this loss, the book seems to say; these connections gave it a sense of order that is missed in the wreckage left after.

So the book seems to come *after*, then, both because it focuses on the differences between life during and after the period that it takes as its subject and also because its narrative structure is characterized by a movement deeper back into that period, one that uncovers connections, provides explanations, and, in moving backward toward a beginning, makes for a reading experience that provides a feeling of inevitability. As the novel moves back in time, the things that have already "happened" (in that they have already been read about) begin to feel as if they somehow had to, because the things that happen earlier (in the chronological sense), which the reading comes to later, gain an air of leading to the things that happen earlier in the reading and later in the chronology. In narratological terms, the order of the sjuzhet reinforces the order of the fabula—that is, the order in which the novel's plot structures readers' encountering of events lends a sense not only of causation but also of inevitability to the order in which events happened chronologically. The resulting coherence of the period—and the feeling of completion that beginning and ending the body of the novel with the moment after the period's end lends—makes *Underworld* feel like a book that's looking back on a period that unfolded, and ended, the way it had to. What comes after also feels final and inevitable: in the epilogue, Nick's trip to Kazakhstan to watch the destroying of nuclear waste by nuclear explosion feels like a bringing together of everything or, in the book's words, "the fusion of two streams of history, weapons and waste" (791).

Yet there is much about the novel that does not fit this description. *Underworld*, in conducting a damage check after the Cold

War, also shares the inclination of the novels by Roth, Morrison, O'Brien, and Didion to look back on different moments in the same period and question the triumphalist reading of the end of the Cold War. As David Noon puts it, "Writing against the dominant tendencies of popular historical memory in the 1990s, DeLillo refuses to identify the collapse of the Soviet Union as the clean and inevitable unfolding of history, devoting his attention instead to the ambiguous consequences of 'victory' for the United States" (85). We don't hold a wake for a victor, we throw a parade, and the march back in time that structures *Underworld* is not that kind of march. As Nick's guide at the Kazakh test site, Viktor, sums up the Cold War, "You won, we lost. You have to tell me how it feels. Big winner" (793). "Big winner" is surely ironic, but "how it feels" after the Cold War is what the book's 1990s-focused parts are about, just as how it *felt* is what the rest of the book is about. The change of tense is important. The bomb fear that made it feel the way it did is not what makes the "victors" feel the way they do after. So the inevitability in *Underworld* is not the inevitability of being on the right side of history. The question that needs to be answered, then, is why the novel creates a reading experience that would seem to contradict its understanding of history.

A return to narratology might help, adding another pair of terms, Barthes's proairetic and hermeneutic. For Barthes in *S/Z*, these are the two ways in which narratives pull readers along, making them want to find out, respectively, what is going to happen and why things happened as they did. The adventure story is typically driven by the proairetic: What will happen next? How will it end? The detective story, on the other hand, is typically driven by the hermeneutic: Who did it, or why did she do it, are the questions that need to be answered. *Underworld* would seem to be more invested in the hermeneutic than the proairetic; we know what happens in the Cold War and just want to know why and what it all meant. But *Underworld* is not a typical detective story, in which the sjuzhet or plot consists of finding out exactly what happened and why, through acts of discovery; rather, moving backward chronologically, it takes us back to see for ourselves the earlier causes of later events. That the acts of detection, as it were, happen not in analepses but in the course of an entirely reversed plot makes the nature of narrative suspense in *Underworld* different.

Peter Brooks's revision of Barthes can help make clear the nature of this difference. In *Reading for the Plot*, Brooks argues that plot "might best be thought of as an 'overcoding' of the proairetic by the hermeneutic, the latter structuring the discrete elements of the former into larger interpretive wholes, working out their play of meaning and significance" (18). We read to the end of a narrative hoping that the plot will tie everything together in the end. Rather than thinking of the two terms as naming separate functions, Brooks is saying, we should think about the order in which events are related as serving the unfolding of explanations and interpretation. It seems to me that we should really be talking about narrative suspense in three ways then: first, the proairetic drive to see what happens in the fabula or chronology that exists outside of plot; second, the hermeneutic drive to see what explains these events; and third, the drive to satisfy hermeneutic desire by getting to the end of the sjuzhet or narrative reordering of these events. At the end of a story then, this third kind of suspense has us: we want to be able to see how events were related to us in ways that explained them. As Brooks puts it, "Perhaps we would do best to speak of the *anticipation of retrospection* as our chief tool in making sense of narrative, the master trope of its strange logic" (23).

This phenomenon, the anticipation of retrospection, can both explain the effect of *Underworld's* plot and identify what motivates it. Reading *Underworld*, we are driven by the increasingly strong feeling as we move backward chronologically and forward through the novel that we will be able to look back over our experience of reading the novel and see how everything came to make sense. Hence the sense of inevitability that is the effect of reading *Underworld*: things had to be related the way they were in order to make sense. This doesn't mean that the U.S. had to "win" the Cold War, that things had to happen the way they did, only that they did.

That they did, and that they're done. It is this second effect—not that events did happen the way they did, but that they are done happening, that the chronological chain of events that constitutes the Cold War period is over—that I believe explains what ultimately motivates *Underworld*. It is important to the novel that the Cold War is done happening because of what the novel itself so powerfully shows was at the center of that time: the bomb. The anxiety created by nuclear fear is a thing the novel seems to desperately want to leave behind, to be able to look back on. The anticipation of retrospection here is a looking forward to looking back on nuclear fear. As the novel moves back in time to the beginning of the age of bomb fear, readers paradoxically move closer, with a feeling of inevitability, to the time when they no longer have to be afraid of the end.

Underworld, then, though it seems to be a novel about a time that is over and about the effects of that time on its present, is in fact a novel motivated by anxiety concerning something it can't tell the story of: the future. In asserting its interest in the historical phenomenon of nuclear fear and the now-completed period it had so great an effect on, *Underworld* betrays an anxiety that could be called proairetic, except that its object lies outside the text, after the end of the story. It is concerned not with how things will turn out but whether they will turn out at all, whether the story will continue. It could even be said that *Underworld* looks forward to looking back on its own time in a way entirely consistent with the future anterior, but with a nuclear twist: it constructs a history that leads not to how it hopes the future will be but rather to a future, period.

Whether a terminally bad time threatens immediately in the form of a suitcase bomb or farther off in the distance in the shape of global climate change or whether things will continue on indefinitely, contemporary novelists attuned to the historical seem destined to write under the sign of the future. Those of us who read their work and are similarly interested in the presence of history in literature and in the world will need to continue to pay attention to the way the past gets constructed, by our writers, our public servants, and ourselves, out of our national and personal hopes for and fears about the future. In *White Noise*, DeLillo writes, "All plots tend to move deathward" (26). As DeLillo, Brooks, and Freud argue, our desire for the end of the story can be seen as a desire for the end. The notion that the death drive animates our psyches and our literature is not a universally accepted one though; those who read trauma narratives as attempts to heal wounds in order to live more happily certainly disagree, and those who value Eros over Thanatos likewise prefer to see our stories as about more than death. Resisting historical narratives that declare ends and keeping a careful eye on the ways in which fears of the end shape the stories we tell ourselves about the past might even be ways to look away from the end and toward possibility. As Charles Mason's children at the end of *Mason & Dixon* imagine America as the place where "the Stars are so close you won't need a Telescope" and "the Fish jump into your Arms" (773), so a vision of America that is aware of its historical errors while remembering its greatest promise might animate our approach to its contemporary possibilities, literary and otherwise.

NOTES

Introduction

1. See Boyer (*By the Bomb's Early Light*) for a discussion of the immediate reactions to the use of the Bomb, as reflected in the widespread appearance of the language of awe, terror, and apocalypse; see also Lifton and Mitchell (*Hiroshima in America*), and Nadel (*Containment Culture*). For parallels in reactions to 9/11, see May, Judith Greenberg, Amy Kaplan, Young.

2. See Cumings, Kellner, Robin, Schrecker ("Cold War"), Willis.

3. A contrasting interpretation, in the words of Raymond Garthoff: "The West did not, as is widely believed, win the Cold War through geopolitical containment and military deterrence. Nor was the Cold War won by the Reagan military buildup and the Reagan Doctrine, as some have suggested. . . . [T]he Western and above all the American role in ending the Cold War was necessary but not primary" (128–31).

4. As Gaddis argued in December 1991 at the 90th Anniversary Nobel Jubilee Symposium "Beyond the Cold War: New Dimensions in International Relations," "The use of one or two nuclear weapons, in the post–Cold War World, would not end the world as we have known it. . . . Nuclear weapons have evolved from their initial status in our minds as the ultimate instrument of the Apocalypse to, first, a means of deterrence, and then a method of reassurance, and then an object for negotiation, and then an inconvenience to be circumvented, and finally an embarrassment of such magnitude that old Cold War antagonists now race to divest themselves of what they once raced each other so avidly to possess. From having worried about how nuclear weapons could destroy us we have progressed to worrying about how we can safely destroy them, and that is undeniably progress" ("The Cold War" 29).

5. Two signs of this trend are the attention garnered by Michael Hardt and Antonio Negri's *Empire* (2000) and the January 2001 special topic issue of *PMLA* entitled "Globalizing Literary Studies." See Baucom ("Globalit, Inc.") especially for discussion of these questions. See Baucom (*Specters of the Atlantic*), Bhabha, Edwards, Giles, and Gilroy for

examples of transnational literary and cultural study. See Bauman, Gray, Jameson and Miyoshi, and Stiglitz for criticisms of globalization.

6. Roth and Morrison, whose reading habits and critical interests are more available to scrutiny than Pynchon's, write novels that entertain national themes, but they maintain interest in literature from other parts of the world. Roth has championed and popularized a number of Eastern European writers; for twenty-five years, Roth edited the Penguin series *Writers from the Other Europe*; see also his 2002 *Shop Talk*, which collects interviews with Ivan Klima and Milan Kundera, among others. Morrison has written on literature from Africa; in a 2001 piece on the work of Guinean novelist Camara Laye in the *New York Review of Books*, Morrison writes, "[B]eing introduced in the early Sixties to the novels of Chinua Achebe, the work of Wole Soyinka, Ama Ata Aidoo, and Cyprian Ekwenski, to name a few, was more than a revelation—it was intellectually and aesthetically transforming" ("On 'The Radiance'" 18). And Didion and O'Brien write about Americans not just at home but abroad, stressing the importance of the American role in world politics to national identity, while Eugenides brings a first-generation perspective to his account of the American experience.

7. Barth, "The Literature of Exhaustion."

8. See Gardner for an influential statement of this view of metafiction.

9. In "My Three Stooges" (*Hooking*). Wolfe's criticisms of Updike, Mailer, and Irving are perhaps not so strange, given that each wrote a negative review of his 1998 novel *A Man in Full* (see Menand, "In a Strange Land," and Adair). See also Wolfe, "Stalking the Billion-Footed Beast."

10. For Althusser's rejection of mediation, see *Reading* (186–89). Jameson argues that what Althusser is really rejecting is not mediation but rather Goldmann's homology, a concept introduced in Goldmann's *The Hidden God* and applied to the novel in his later *Sociology of the Novel* (Jameson, *Political* 43).

11. See especially "Nostalgia for the Present" in *Postmodernism* (279–96).

12. See Lyotard for analysis of the loss of the *grands récits* or metanarratives by which he believes we have understood the world.

13. One example would be Hutcheon, as mentioned, who says that our concern should be not with the one truth getting told but rather with multiple truths being voiced; Dominick LaCapra, for another, in exploring the distinctions made between literature and history, maintains that both can be seen as shaped by the way narratives are constructed while still trying to truthfully represent the past: "It is common to distinguish

history from literature on the grounds that history is concerned with the realm of fact while literature moves in the realm of fiction. It is true that the historian may not invent his facts or references while the 'literary' writer may, and in this respect the latter has a greater margin of freedom in exploring relationships. But, on other levels, historians make use of heuristic fictions, counterfactuals, and models to orient their research into facts" (*Rethinking* 57).

14. See Schaub (*American*), especially his introduction, in which he presents Richard Chase's catalog of the "old mistakes" of liberalism, among which were "the facile ideas of progress and 'social realism,' the disinclination to examine human motives, the indulgence of wish-fulfilling rhetoric, the belief that historical reality is merely a question of economic or ethical values, the idea that literature should participate directly in the economic liberation of the masses, the equivocal relationship to communist totalitarian and power politics" (qtd. in Schaub 7).

15. For the part of his career represented by *The Theory of the Novel* (1920), Lukács held that the genre is shaped by a structural irony, an unstable irony in which authorial subjectivity, rather than presiding over the world it creates, instead is split between the narrating voice of the novel and the subjectivity of the main character, with the result that the character misunderstands the world and the author refuses to show us how the world "really" is. For Lukács, this irony reflects what he saw then as the most basic truth of modern life: that the subjective, inner world is irreconcilable with the objective, outer world, that we cannot fully understand that world. By the time of *The Historical Novel* (1937), Lukács had found Marx and so believed that we can understand the world—and its history—by understanding capital. In the time of *The Theory of the Novel*, though, he still believed that this kind of total understanding was impossible.

16. Barth's *The Sot-Weed Factor* (1960) and *Lost in the Funhouse* (1968) are examples of contemporary metafiction. Sterne's *Tristram Shandy* (1767) provides an example of the use of many of the same techniques hundreds of years earlier. Richardson uses letters in *Pamela* (1741); DeFoe uses the diary in *Moll Flanders* (1722) and the claim to present another's manuscript in *Robinson Crusoe* (1719).

17. Stendhal uses this statement as an epigraph in *Red and Black* and ascribes it to César de Saint-Réal, a seventeenth-century French historian, who may not have ever said it (Stendhal 60 n. 3).

18. Auerbach, in *Mimesis*, his study of the representation of reality from *The Odyssey* to *To the Lighthouse*, says this of Woolf's representation of multiple consciousnesses, but also argues that Woolf's attention to

real things at a time of historical upheaval asserts a human commonality, an assertion that he too seems to have found valuable when he wrote his study in the early 1940s in exile in Istanbul from Nazi Germany: "In this unprejudiced and exploratory type of representation we cannot but see to what extent—below the surface conflicts—the differences between men's ways of life and forms of thought have already lessened. . . . [I]t is still a long way to a common life of mankind on earth, but the goal begins to be visible" (551, 552).

One. After Enlightenment

1. For the accuracy of Pynchon's language, see Menand ("Entropology").

2. Some argue that *Vineland*, with its focus on family, is an exception; see Moody and also Berger ("Cultural Trauma"), who notes, "The novel ends with a family reunion; its final word is 'home'" (par. 3), though he gives more weight to the relationship between two other (unrelated) characters, Prairie and Weed (par. 45).

3. Ricciardi also sees a turn away from total resignation in *Mason & Dixon*. She cites Richard Rorty's argument in "Achieving Our Country," in which he argues that Pynchon's novels in general and *Vineland* in particular merely articulate a desperate pessimism unaccompanied by any impulse to outrage or protest and that they exemplify a "rueful acquiescence in the end of American hopes." Disagreeing, Ricciardi argues that "*Mason & Dixon* deviates from the sense of resignation that permeates Pynchon's earlier works insofar as the novel responds to an urgent consciousness of the need for historical witnessing" (1072). While failing to take issue with Rorty's overstatement or specify the content of this need, Ricciardi does identify the turn taken by Pynchon in *Mason & Dixon*.

4. For a description of a similar meaning in the representation of a single historical moment, the 1960s, in *Vineland*, see Berger ("Cultural Trauma"), who likens Pynchon's understanding of later interpretations of the 1960s to Walter Benjamin's *jeztzeit*, "the critical moment of historical, redemptive possibility which continues to erupt into the present even after many previous failures" (par. 5).

5. As David Cowart has pointed out, the connections between the 1960s and Pynchon's work have not been much explored by critics, a failure only slightly redressed by reactions to *Vineland* ("Pynchon" 12).

6. See Miller for the ways in which the 1960s have been reimagined by subsequent decades.

Two. After the Fall

1. *I Married a Communist* (1998) and *The Human Stain* (2000) complete the trilogy. Following 2001's *The Dying Animal*, *The Plot Against America* (2004), while not thematically part of the historical trilogy, certainly continues Roth's focus on U.S. history. See Royal, "Plotting," for an account of the naming of the original trilogy as such (114 n. 1).

2. For the fullest consideration of the relationship between Roth's work (through *Sabbath's Theater*) and his Jewishness, see Cooper.

3. Robert Greenberg, among many others, argues for the importance of intergenerational struggle to Roth's work, connecting it to a larger "cultural origin of transgression" (487). On the father-son conflict in Roth's work, see Rubin-Dorsky.

4. Mark Shechner also sees this novel as politically conservative, saying that Roth's sympathies now lie with the ideas of people such as anti-1960s neoconservative David Horowitz (mock-imagining Roth's internal monologue here, Shechner writes, "I shall henceforth be the David Horowitz of the novel"). He solves for himself the problem of the new Roth with this move, though he also guesses that parts of the novel were written many years earlier, which does not help explain the supposed Roth shift (163, 162).

5. As Debra Shostak notes, Umanoff's defense of transgression and Lou's condemnation of it offset each other, thus foreclosing a reading of the novel as squarely on the latter's side (putting aside for a moment the importance of the Zuckerman frame): "*American Pastoral*, then, by implication offers a much-delayed critique of *Portnoy's Complaint*, but without urging readers to condemn the impulse toward freedom and understanding represented by the earlier novel's breakthrough into speaking the unspeakable" (5).

Three. After Identity

1. Menand, it should be noted, does not make the argument that the similarity between the two novels is simply coincidental, connecting their writers through biography and history: "Roth, too, is a writer who was 'made' by the very cultural changes that his novel contemplates with ambivalence and regret" ("War" 81).

2. See Aguiar, Krumholz, Page ("Furrowing"), Romero, Stave, Terry, Yukins. Morrison herself has said that *Paradise* is the final book in a trilogy of novels about love, *Beloved* being about familial love, *Jazz* being about romantic love, *Paradise* being about religious love (Rose).

3. See Schur ("Dream") for a discussion of *American Pastoral* and *Paradise* in terms of the history of the racial politics of criticism.

4. For *Paradise* and history, see Flint, Fraile-Marcos, Gauthier, Hilfrich, Krumholz, Michael, Page, Romero, Schur ("Dream" and "Locating"), Widdowson, and Yukins.

5. For genealogy in *Paradise*, see Hilfrich, Schur ("Dream"), and Yukins.

6. Morrison has described her desire "to provide the places and spaces so that the reader can participate" in the work of creating sense in her novels ("Rootedness" 342). While she is referring to the kind of call-and-response found in African American preaching traditions and oral and oral-inspired literature, elsewhere she has described her work's elliptical nature in terms more akin to those used in discussions of difficulty in the modernist fiction she wrote her master's thesis about (and whose influence she has downplayed [McKay, "Interview" 426]). Michael Nowlin characterizes Morrison's debt to these writers as "increasingly difficult to deny" (154); see Nowlin 169–71 n. 15 for an account of the discussion of this issue.

7. On the difficulty of Morrison's work, see Morrison herself (Tate). On the difficulty of *Paradise* in particular, see Page, who likens the effect of reading the novel on many to the central image in the novel of the furrowed brow; and Aubrey, who writes about the emphasis on the novel's difficulty surrounding its presence in Oprah Winfrey's book club (including an episode of the show devoted to it); and Storace.

8. Brooke Allen thought that Pallas was the white girl, while Louis Menand claimed that Seneca was ("War").

9. Many government programs seen as assigning preference according to minority status were under attack at the time, including those concerned with education and employment such as those meant to be enforced by the Equal Employment Opportunity Commission, whose commissioner, Fred Alvarez, said in 1985, "When somebody tells me they ought to get something because they're Irish and saw signs in Boston that said IRISH NEED NOT APPLY . . . or because their ancestors were in slavery, I say, 'So what?'" (qtd. in Evan Thomas). For more on affirmative action, see Terry Anderson, also Bowen and Bok.

10. For accounts of the culture wars, see Hunter and Patterson; for contemporary arguments about multiculturalism, see Glazer and Schlesinger.

11. In support of this argument, Appiah notes that there is wider genetic between different groups in his West African village than between white and black in America.

12. For more on contemporary debates over racial identity, see Awkward, *Negotiating Difference*; Baker, "In Dubious Battle"; Appiah, "Identity, Authenticity, Survival"; and the 1987 debate in *New Literary History* between Baker, Gates, and Joyce.

13. As Appiah noted in "Post" and which has by now become a commonplace. For more on the relationship between postmodernism and postcolonial and ethnic studies, see hooks, *Postmodern Blackness*. See also Madhu Dubey's introduction to a special double issue of *Novel* on postmodernism and contemporary African American fiction.

14. For a brief, cogent account, see Brenkman, "Multiculturalism and Criticism."

15. As Michael Awkward has written, "the narrative events of *The Bluest Eye*—and particularly Pecola's schizophrenic double voicedness exhibited when she believes she has been granted 'the bluest eyes in the whole world'—portray double consciousness as a constant and, for Pecola at least, a permanently debilitating state" (58).

16. For historical dates in *Song of Solomon*, see Walker.

17. For more on Patricia Best's role in the novel, see Yukins.

18. In an interview, Morrison said the word "Paradise" should not have been capitalized because "[t]he whole point is to get paradise off its pedestal, as a place for anyone" (Peterson 204).

19. As Morrison herself characterized her efforts in *Paradise*, the aim is to "enunciate and then eclipse the racial gaze altogether" (qtd. in Schur, "Locating" 278).

20. According to a Hilton Als profile of Morrison, the manuscripts were actually destroyed not by flames but by freezing—by the water used to put out the fire.

21. Two among the many who have noted this aspect of *Our America* are Perloff and Glass; for this take on New Historicism, see Brook Thomas and Glass. See also my "It's the End of the World as We Know It."

22. Readers will hear the echo of Fukuyama here, but Michaels's use of him is complicated, as Fukuyama's triumphant declaration of the victory of capitalism or liberal democracy is not one that Michaels would himself make, given his feelings about economic inequity, which provide the real impetus behind his attack on identitarianism—it being the thing that distracts us from economic inequity.

23. Michaels anticipates this objection in a footnote in which he claims that, while he understands the end of the Cold War as "the end of or the irrelevance of or, in its purest form, the impossibility of disagreement," he does not believe "that while the Cold War was ongoing everyone was really much more interested in ideological disagreement than in

identitarian difference" or that identitarianism is unchallenged now. It is difficult to square all of this, and his statement that what he believes instead is that "the set of debates around identity and ideology" are part of the "problematic" of modernism as well as that of postmodernism (which addresses it differently) is not much help (184–85 n. l2).

24. "Plots against America: Neoliberalism and Antiracism." See also Michael Rothberg's response in that same issue of *American Literary History*.

Four. How to Tell a True Cold War Story

1. For an account of triumphalism in post-WWII American culture, see Engelhardt, *The End of Victory Culture*.

2. See Melley, Heberle, Herzog.

3. See Friedlander; LaCapra, *Representing the Holocaust*; Hartman; *Diagnostic and Statistical Manual of Mental Disorders*; Lifton, *The Nazi Doctors* and *Death in Life*.

4. For the first appearance of this argument, see Fukuyama, "The End of History?"—later expanded into *The End of History and the Last Man*.

5. For more on trauma and closure, see Berger (*After the End*), Žižek.

6. See Jeffrey Williams, "The Posttheory Generation," "The New Belletrism," "The Death of Deconstruction, the End of Theory, and Other Ominous Rumors"; Peter C. Herman, *Historicizing Theory* and *Day Late, Dollar Short*.

7. See my discussion of Michaels in chapter 3.

8. See Greenberg for work on the traumatic aspects of the events of September 11, 2001; see also the growing number of works of fiction dealing explicitly with the events and their aftermath, including Oates, Foer, McEwan, O'Neill, Walter, Updike, DeLillo.

9. By my count, thirty-six out of eighty-three total sentences in the body text of the final chapter end with a question mark (as opposed to the forty-seven ending with a period), and there are twenty-one variations on "might have," "would have," and "maybe" in a chapter of four full pages.

10. LaCapra, in *History in Transit*, calls for a similar reimagining of the way we theorize trauma, stating as his goal "a nonreductive, sociopolitically and critically inflected notion of working-through that cannot be dismissively conflated with totalization, closure, unproblematic identity, therapeutic cure, or a return to 'normality'" (11). While we share the notion that healing implies a potentially undesirable closure, my emphasis here is more specifically on the way in which the unexamined desire for

closure evident in certain conceptions of trauma relates to triumphalist narratives of our national past.

11. For Didion and narrative form, see Bloom; D'Agata; Hardwick, "In the Wasteland"; Leonard, "The Black Album"; Parrish, "After Henry Adams"; Reinert.

12. This is a central point of contention in discussions of Didion's work—whether she is throwing up her hands at her failure to find meaning or registering the difficulty of finding meaning as part of her attempt to do so—and some see her doing both. Muggli, for example, contrasts *The White Album* to *Slouching Towards Bethlehem* by saying that the earlier work "reverberates with explanation of the culture at large" (411) while the later work "is Didion's report on events that have resisted her understanding." As Muggli himself says though, that resistance is part of her subject: "'The White Album' contains events that testify to this personal and cultural breakdown" (412). And he argues that critics have relied too heavily on the notion that she is throwing up her hands, most persuasively when he states that even *The White Album* "undermines even further Didion's claim to impenetrability" (416).

Five. History Is What Heals

1. It has also, at the time of this writing, just been named a selection for Oprah's Book Club, prompting a new printing of 750,000 copies ("Oprah").

2. In *The Historical Novel*, Lukács writes, "This continuation of the historical novel, in the sense of a consciously historical conception of the present, is the great achievement of . . . Balzac. . . . Balzac passes from the portrayal of *past history* to the portrayal of the *present as history*" (81, 83).

3. One interesting take on this aspect of the novel, and more generally on the essentialism of Eugenides's portrayal of gender and sexuality, can be found in Daniel Mendelsohn's review.

Afterword

1. Last panel p. 103, accompanied by text describing the signing of a new directive concerning "the elimination of terrorism as a threat to our way of life"; top panel p. 104, in which Bush is shown saying, "See if Sadaam did this. See if he's linked in any way" (and in accompanying text is described as "wondering" if there were any connection); middle panel p. 105, Bush is pictured over map, in jacket, with general, below

panel depicting Congress and above panel showing troops in the field, implying both troops' presence as expression of people's will and Bush's status as a soldier.

2. Sontag wrote a piece for the *New Yorker* arguing for attention to American responsibility for the anger directed at it around the world in which she wrote, "Where is the acknowledgment that this was not a 'cowardly' attack on 'civilization' or 'liberty' or 'humanity' or 'the free world' but an attack on the world's self-proclaimed superpower, undertaken as a consequence of specific American alliances and actions?" Sontag ignited a firestorm of criticism for this short piece. Bill Maher's late night political talk show was cancelled in the wake of these comments on the show on September 17, 2001: "We have been the cowards, lobbing cruise missiles from 2,000 miles away. That's cowardly. Staying in the airplane when it hits the building, say what you want about it, it's not cowardly" (qtd. in Tapper).

3. As Tom Engelhardt argues in a recent essay, the similarity of the image of the towers' destruction to popular imaginings of nuclear apocalypse is significant. Pointing to the immediate references to Pearl Harbor and nuclear winter, the naming of the site "ground zero," and the discrepancy in reactions to events at that site and to those at the less apocalyptic-seeming Pentagon, Engelhardt argues that the histories constructed of that day and of what led to it would have been very different—as would events since—if unconscious fears of the nation's vulnerability had not been so played upon by the visual impact of the towers' collapse ("9/11").

4. The metaphor was produced by speechwriter Michael Gerson and was intended for a presidential speech but was leaked ahead of schedule by group members especially fond of it (Isikoff 35). It was used most prominently (prior to Bush's use in a speech a month later) by Condoleezza Rice in an interview on CNN on September 8, 2002.

5. In an interview with the *New York Times* on September 6, 2002, Card, when asked why the White House waited until after Labor Day to sell the war, famously responded, "From a marketing point of view, you don't introduce new products in August" (Bumiller).

6. In a 2006 *New York Times* survey of writers, editors, and critics which many consider flawed but not entirely invalid—A. O. Scott of the *Times* called it "a rich, if partial and unscientific, picture of the state of American literature" ("In Search")—*Underworld* ranked second on a list of the most important American novels of the previous twenty-five years.

WORKS CITED

Adair, Jordan. "Wolfe Pack." Rev. of *Hooking Up*, by Tom Wolfe. *Spectator Online* 31 Jan. 2001. 5 Apr. 2002. <http://www.spectatoronline.com/2001-01-31/artforum_books.html>.

Adorno, Theodor, and Max Horkheimer. *Dialectic of Enlightenment.* Trans. John Cumming. New York: Continuum, 1995.

Aguiar, Sarah Appleton. "'Passing On' Death: Stealing Life in Toni Morrison's *Paradise.*" *African American Review* 38.3 (Fall 2004): 513–19.

Allen, Brooke. "The Promised Land." Rev. of *Paradise*, by Toni Morrison. *New York Times* 11 Jan. 1998. <http://query.nytimes.com/gst/fullpage.html?res=9A02E7DD1F31F932A25752C0A96E958260>.

Als, Hilton. "Ghosts in the House." *New Yorker* 27 Oct. 2003: 64–72.

Althusser, Louis, and Étienne Balibar. *Reading Capital.* Trans. Ben Brewster. London: Verso, 1979.

Amis, Martin. "Survivors of the Cold War." Rev. of *Underworld*, by Don DeLillo. *New York Times* 5 Oct. 1997. July 2008. <http://www.nytimes.com/books/97/10/05/reviews/971005.05amisdt.html>.

Anastas, Benjamin. "American Friction: Philip Roth's History Lessons." *Bookforum* Oct./Nov. 2004. <http://www.bookforum.com/archive/Oct_04/anastas_oct.html>.

Anderson, Benedict. *Imagined Communities: Reflections on the Origin and Spread of Nationalism.* New York: Verso, 1991.

Anderson, Terry. *The Pursuit of Fairness: A History of Affirmative Action.* Oxford: Oxford UP, 2004.

Appiah, K. Anthony. "Identity, Authenticity, Survival: Multicultural Societies and Social Reproduction." Taylor 149–63.

———. *In My Father's House: Africa in the Philosophy of Culture.* Oxford: Oxford UP, 1992.

———. "Is the Post- in Postmodernism the Post- in Postcolonial?" *Critical Inquiry* 17 (Winter 1991): 336–57.

Appiah, K. Anthony, and Henry Louis Gates, Jr. "Editors' Introduction: Multiplying Identities." *Critical Inquiry* 18 (Summer 1992): 625.

Apuleius. *"The Transformations of Lucius"; Otherwise Known as "The Golden Ass."* Trans. Robert Graves. New York: Farrar, 1951.

Aubry, Timothy. "Beware the Furrow of the Middlebrow." *Modern Fiction Studies* 52.2 (2006): 350–73.

Auerbach, Erich. *Mimesis: The Representation of Reality in Western Literature.* Princeton: Princeton UP, 1953.

Awkward, Michael. *Inspiriting Influences: Tradition, Revision, and Afro-American Women's Novels.* New York: Columbia UP, 1989.

———. *Negotiating Difference: Race, Gender, and the Politics of Positionality.* Chicago: Chicago UP, 1995.

Baker, Houston. *Blues, Ideology, and Afro-American Literature: A Vernacular Theory.* Chicago: U of Chicago P, 1987.

———. "In Dubious Battle." *New Literary History* 18.2 (1987): 363–69.

———, ed. *Unsettling Blackness.* Spec. issue of *American Literature* 72.2 (June 2000).

Bakhtin, Mikhail. *The Dialogic Imagination: Four Essays.* Trans. Caryl Emerson and Michael Holquist. Austin: U of Texas P, 1981.

Baldwin, James. "Everybody's Protest Novel." *Notes of a Native Son.* Boston: Beacon, 1955.

Barth, John. "The Literature of Exhaustion." *Atlantic Monthly* Aug. 1967: 29–34.

———. *Lost in the Funhouse: Fiction for Print, Tape, Live Voice.* New York: Doubleday, 1968.

———. *The Sot-Weed Factor.* New York: Doubleday, 1960.

Barthes, Roland. *S/Z.* 1970. Trans. Richard Miller. New York: Hill, 1975.

Baseball. Dir. Ken Burns. PBS. 1994.

Baucom, Ian. "Globalit, Inc.; or, The Cultural Logic of Global Literary Studies." *PMLA* 116.1 (Jan. 2001): 158–72.

———. *Specters of the Atlantic: Finance Capital, Slavery, and the Philosophy of History.* Durham: Duke UP, 2005.

Bauman, Zygmunt. *Globalization: The Human Consequences.* New York: Columbia UP, 1998.

Beardsworth, Richard. "In Memorium Jacques Derrida: The Power of Reason." *Theory and Event* 8.1 (2005). 17 May 2006. <http://muse.jhu.edu/journals/theory_and_event/v008/8.1beardsworth.html>.

Benjamin, Walter. *Illuminations.* Trans. Harry Zohn. Ed. Hannah Arendt. New York: Schocken, 1968.

Berger, James. *After the End: Representations of Post-Apocalypse.* Minneapolis: U of Minnesota P, 1999.

———. "Cultural Trauma and the 'Timeless Burst': Pynchon's Revision of Nostalgia in *Vineland*." *Postmodern Culture* 5.3 (May 1995). <http://www.iath.virginia.edu/pmc/text-only/issue.595berger.595>.

Bhabha, Homi. *The Location of Culture*. London: Routledge, 1994.

Bloom, James D. "Hollywood Intellect." *Canadian Review of American Studies/Revue Canadienne d'Études Américaines* 34:3 (2004): 233–48.

Borradori, Giovanna, Jacques Derrida, and Jürgen Habermas. *Philosophy in a Time of Terror: Dialogues with Jürgen Habermas and Jacques Derrida*. Chicago: U of Chicago P, 2003.

Bouson, J. Brooks. *Quiet as It's Kept: Shame, Trauma, and Race in the Novels of Toni Morrison*. Albany: State U of New York P, 2000.

Bowen, William, and Derek Bok. *The Shape of the River: Long-Term Consequences of Considering Race in College and University Admissions*. Princeton: Princeton UP, 1998.

Boyer, Paul. *By the Bomb's Early Light: American Thought and Culture at the Dawn of the Atomic Age*. New York: Pantheon, 1985.

———. *Fallout: A Historian Reflects on America's Half-Century Encounter with Nuclear Weapons*. Columbus: Ohio State UP, 1998.

Boyer, Paul, and Eric Idsvoog. "Nuclear Menace in the Mass Culture of the Late Cold War Era and Beyond." Boyer, *Fallout* 199–225.

Boyle, T. Coraghessan. "*Mason & Dixon*, by Thomas Pynchon." *New York Times Book Review* 18 May 1997: 9.

Boynton, Robert S. "The New Intellectuals." *Atlantic Monthly* Mar. 1995: 53–66.

Brenkman, John. "Innovation: Notes on Nihilism and the Aesthetics of the Novel." *The Novel*. Ed. Franco Moretti. Vol 2, *Themes and Forms*. Princeton: Princeton UP, 2007. 808–38.

———. "Multiculturalism and Criticism." *English Inside and Out*. Ed. Susan Gubar and Jonathan Kamholtz. New York: Routledge, 1993. 87–101.

———. "Politics and Form in *Song of Solomon*." *Social Text* 39 (1994): 57–82.

Brooks, Peter. *Reading for the Plot: Design and Intention in Narrative*. New York: Vintage, 1984.

Buchanan, Patrick. Speech. 1992 Republican National Convention. 17 Aug. 1992. *Internet Brigade*. 5 Apr. 2001. <http://www.buchanan.org/pa-92-0817-rnc.html>.

Bumiller, Elisabeth. "Traces of Terror: The Strategy; Bush Aides Set Strategy to Sell Policy on Iraq." *New York Times* 7 Sept. 2002. 21 July 2008. <http://query.nytimes.com/gst/fullpage.html?res=9C07E6D7103 EF934A3575AC0A9649C8B63>.

Carlton, Evan. "Joan Didion's Dreampolitics of the Self." *The Critical Response to Joan Didion*. Ed. Sharon Felton. Westport: Greenwood, 1994. 34–90.

Caruth, Cathy, ed. *Psychoanalysis, Culture, and Trauma*. Spec. issue of *American Imago* 1.4 (1991).

———, ed. *Trauma: Explorations in Memory*. Baltimore: Johns Hopkins UP, 1995.

———. *Unclaimed Experience: Trauma, Narrative, and History*. Baltimore: Johns Hopkins UP, 1996.

Charles, Ron. "There Goes the Neighborhood." Rev. of *The Fortress of Solitude*, by Jonathan Lethem. *Christian Science Monitor* 11 Sept. 2003. <http://www.csmonitor.com/2003/0911/p15s01-bogn.html>.

Civil War. Dir. Ken Burns. PBS. 1990.

CNN: Cold War. 12 Feb. 2002. <http://www.cnn.com/SPECIALS/cold.war/guides/about.series/>.

Cohen, Samuel. "It's the End of the World as We Know It." Rev. of *The Shape of the Signifier*, by Walter Benn Michaels. *Twentieth-Century Literature* 51.1 (Spring 2005): 98–104.

Cooper, Alan. *Philip Roth and the Jews*. Albany: State U of New York P, 1996.

Cowart, David. "Pynchon and the Sixties." *Critique* 41.1 (Fall 1999): 3–12.

———. *Thomas Pynchon: The Art of Allusion*. Carbondale: Southern Illinois UP, 1980.

Cumings, Bruce. "Time of Illusion: Post–Cold War Visions of the World." Schrecker, *Cold War* 71–99.

D'Agata, John. "Joan Didion's Formal Experience of Confusion." *Believer* Oct. 2003. <http://www.believermag.com/issues/200310/?read=article_dagata>.

Dalsgard, Katrine. "The One All-Black Town Worth the Pain: (African) American Exceptionalism, Historical Narration, and the Critique of Nationhood in Toni Morrison's *Paradise*." *African American Review* 35.1 (Spring 2001): 233–48.

DeFoe, Daniel. *The Fortunes and Misfortunes of the Famous Moll Flanders*. London: Penguin, 1989.

———. *The Life and Adventures of Robinson Crusoe*. London: Penguin, 1985.

DeLillo, Don. "Everything under the Bomb." Interview with Richard Williams. *Guardian* [London] 10 Jan. 1998. 17 July 2008. <http://www.guardian.co.uk/books/1998/jan/10/fiction.dondelillo>.

———. *Falling Man*. New York: Scribner, 2007.

———. *Mao II*. New York: Penguin, 1990.

———. *Underworld*. New York: Scribner's, 1997.

———. *White Noise*. New York: Viking, 1985.

DeMott, Benjamin. "Whitewash as Public Service: How *The 9/11 Commission Report* Defrauds the Nation." *Harper's Magazine* Oct. 2004: 35–45.

Derrida, Jacques. *Negotiations: Interventions and Interviews 1971–2001*. Ed. and trans. Elizabeth Rottenberg. Stanford: Stanford UP, 2002.

———. *Of Grammatology*. Trans. Gayatri Chakravorty Spivak. Baltimore: Johns Hopkins UP, 1976.

———. *Writing and Difference*. Trans. Alan Bass. Chicago: U of Chicago P, 1978.

Diagnostic and Statistical Manual of Mental Disorders. 3rd ed. Washington, DC: American Psychiatric Association, 1980.

Dickstein, Morris. *Leopards in the Temple*. Cambridge: Harvard UP, 2002.

———. *A Mirror in the Roadway: Literature and the Real World*. Princeton: Princeton UP, 2005.

Diderot, Denis. *Jacques the Fatalist and His Master*. Trans. Michael Henry. London: Penguin, 1986.

Didion, Joan. "Cheney: The Fatal Touch." *New York Review of Books* 5 Oct. 2006. <http://www.nybooks.com/articles/19376>.

———. *Democracy*. New York: Simon, 1984.

———. *Fixed Ideas: America Since 9/11*. New York: Random, 2003.

———. "Fixed Opinions, or The Hinge of History." *New York Review of Books* 16 Jan. 2003. <http://www.nybooks.com/articles/15984>.

———. *The Last Thing He Wanted*. New York: Knopf, 1996.

———. *Play It as It Lays*. New York: Farrar, 1970.

———. *Run, River*. New York: Obolensky, 1963.

———. *Slouching Towards Bethlehem*. New York: Farrar, 1968.

———. *The White Album*. New York: Simon, 1979.

Dubey, Madhu. "Contemporary African American Fiction and the Politics of Postmodernism." *Novel: A Forum on Fiction* 35.2/3 (2002): 151–68.

DuBois, W. E. B. *The Souls of Black Folk*. 1903. New York: Penguin, 1995.

Dudziak, Mary L., ed. *September 11 in History: A Watershed Moment?* Durham: Duke UP, 2003.

Duyfhuizen, Bernard. Rev. of *Mason & Dixon*, by Thomas Pynchon. *News and Observer* [Raleigh] 4 May 1997: G4.

Edwards, Brent Hayes. *The Practice of Diaspora: Literature, Translation, and the Rise of Black Internationalism*. Cambridge: Harvard UP, 2003.

Elias, Amy J. *Sublime Desire: History and Post-1960s Fiction*. Baltimore: Johns Hopkins UP, 2001.

Ellison, Ralph. *Going to the Territory*. New York: Random, 1986.

———. *Shadow and Act*. 1964. New York: QPB, 1994.

Engelhardt, Tom. *The End of Victory Culture: Cold War America and the Disillusioning of a Generation*. New York: Basic, 1995.

———. "9/11 in a Movie-Made World." *Nation* 25 Sept. 2006: 15–21.

———. "The Victors and the Vanquished." *History Wars: The Enola Gay and Other Battles for the American Past*. Ed. Tom Engelhardt and Edward T. Linenthal. New York: Holt, 1996. 210–49.

Eugenides, Jeffrey. Interview with Bram van Moorhem. *3:AM Magazine* 2003. <http://www.3ammagazine.com/litarchives/2003/sep/interview_jeffrey_eugenides.html>.

———. *Middlesex*. New York: Picador, 2002.

Felman, Shoshana, and Dori Laub, eds. *Testimony: Crises of Witnessing in Literature, Psychoanalysis, and History*. New York: Routledge, 1992.

Fiedler, Leslie A. "The New Mutants." *Partisan Review* 32.4 (1965): 505–25.

Flint, Holly. "Toni Morrison's *Paradise*: Black Cultural Citizenship in the American Empire." *American Literature: A Journal of Literary History, Criticism, and Bibliography* 78.3 (Sept. 2006): 585–612.

Foer, Jonathan Safran. *Extremely Loud and Incredibly Close*. Boston: Houghton, 2005.

Foley, Barbara. *Telling the Truth: The Theory and Practice of Documentary Fiction*. Ithaca: Cornell UP, 1986.

Foucault, Michel. *The Archaeology of Knowledge and the Discourse on Language*. Trans. A. M. Sheridan Smith. New York: Pantheon, 1972.

Fraile-Marcos, Ana María. "Hybridizing the 'City upon a Hill' in Toni Morrison's *Paradise*." *MELUS* 28.4 (Winter 2003): 3–33.

Freud, Sigmund. *The Standard Edition of the Complete Psychological Works of Sigmund Freud*. Trans. James Strachey. 24 vols. London: Hogarth, 1953–74.

Friedlander, Saul. *Memory, History, and the Extermination of the Jews in Europe*. Bloomington: Indiana UP, 1993.

Fukuyama, Francis. "The End of History?" *National Interest* (Summer 1989): 3–18.

———. *The End of History and the Last Man*. New York: Basic, 1992.

Gaddis, John Lewis. "The Cold War, the Long Peace, and the Future." Hogan 21–38.

———. "Setting Right a Dangerous World." *Chronicle of Higher Education* 11 Jan. 2002. <http://chronicle.com/free/v48/i18/18b00701.htm>.

Gardner, John. *On Moral Fiction*. New York: Basic, 1978.

Garthoff, Raymond. "Why Did the Cold War Arise, and Why Did It End?" Hogan 127–36.

Gass, William H. *Fiction and the Figures of Life*. New York: Knopf, 1970.

Gates, Henry Louis, Jr. "Blackness without Blood." Mills 109–29.

———. "'What's Love Got to Do with It?': Critical Theory, Integrity, and the Black Idiom." *New Literary History* 18.2 (1987): 345–62.

Gauthier, Marni. "The Other Side of Paradise: Toni Morrison's (Un)Making of Mythic History." *African American Review* 39.3 (Fall 2005): 395–414.

Genette, Gérard. *Narrative Discourse: An Essay in Method*. Trans. Jane E. Lewin. Ithaca: Cornell UP, 1980.

Giles, Paul. *Virtual Americas: Transnational Fictions and the Transatlantic Imaginary*. Durham, Duke UP, 2002.

Gilroy, Paul. *The Black Atlantic: Modernity and Double Consciousness*. Cambridge: Harvard UP, 1993.

Gitlin, Todd. *The Twilight of Common Dreams: Why America Is Wracked by Culture Wars*. New York: Metropolitan, 1995.

Glass, Loren. "The End of Culture: Reviewing Walter Benn Michaels's *Our America: Nativism, Modernism, and Pluralism*." *Modern Language Studies* 26.2–3 (Spring/Summer 1996): 1–17.

Glazer, Nathan. *We Are All Multiculturalists Now*. Cambridge: Harvard UP, 1997.

Goldmann, Lucien. *The Hidden God: A Study of Tragic Vision in the Pensées of Pascal and the Tragedies of Racine*. Trans. P. Thody. New York: Humanities, 1964.

———. *Towards a Sociology of the Novel*. Trans. Alan Sheridan. London: Tavistock, 1975.

Gordon, Andrew. "The Critique of Utopia in Philip Roth's *The Counterlife* and *American Pastoral*." Halio and Siegel 151–59.

Gray, John. *False Dawn: The Delusions of Global Capitalism*. London: Granta, 1998.

Greenberg, Judith, ed. *Trauma at Home: After 9/11*. Lincoln: U of Nebraska P, 2003.

Greenberg, Robert M. "Transgression in the Fiction of Philip Roth." *Twentieth-Century Literature* 43 (1997): 487–506.

Habermas, Jürgen. "Modernity: An Unfinished Project." *Habermas and the Unfinished Project of Modernity: Critical Essays on "The Philosophical Discourse of Modernity."* Ed. Maurizio Passerin d'Entrèves and Seyla Benhabib. Cambridge: MIT P, 1997.

Haley, Alex. *Roots*. New York: Doubleday, 1976.

Halio, Jay L., and Ben Siegel, eds. *Turning Up the Flame: Philip Roth's Later Novels*. Newark: U of Delaware P, 2005.

Hardt, Michael, and Antonio Negri. *Empire*. Cambridge: Harvard UP, 2000.

Hardwick, Elizabeth. "In the Wasteland." *New York Review of Books* 31 Oct. 1996. <http://www.nybooks.com/articles/1368>.

———. "Paradise Lost." Rev. of *American Pastoral*. *New York Review of Books* 12 June 1997: 12–14. <http://www.nybooks.com/articles/1368>.

Harris, Middleton A. *The Black Book*. New York: Random, 1974.

Hartman, Geoffrey. *The Longest Shadow: In the Aftermath of the Holocaust*. Bloomington: Indiana UP, 1996.

Hassan, Ihab. "The Dismemberment of Orpheus." *American Scholar* 32 (1963): 463–84.

Heberle, Mark A. *A Trauma Artist: Tim O'Brien and the Fiction of Vietnam*. Iowa City: U of Iowa P, 2001.

Herman, Judith. *Trauma and Recovery*. New York: Basic, 1992.

Herman, Peter C., ed. *Day Late, Dollar Short: The Next Generation and the New Academy*. Albany: State U of New York P, 2000.

———, ed. *Historicizing Theory*. Albany: State U of New York P, 2004.

Herzog, Tobey C. "Tim O'Brien's 'True Lies' (?)." *Modern Fiction Studies* 46.4 (2000): 893–916.

Hilfrich, Carola. "Anti-Exodus: Countermemory, Gender, Race, and Everyday Life in Toni Morrison's *Paradise*." *Modern Fiction Studies* 52.2 (2006): 321–49.

Hogan, Michael J., ed. *The End of the Cold War: Its Meanings and Implications*. Cambridge: Cambridge UP, 1992.

Homer. *The Odyssey*. Trans. Robert Fagles. New York: Penguin, 1996.

hooks, bell. "Postmodern Blackness." *Postmodern Culture: An Electronic Journal of Interdisciplinary Criticism* 1.1 (Sept. 1990). <http://www.iath.Virginia.edu/pmc/text-only/issue.990/hooks.990>.

Howe, Irving. "Philip Roth Reconsidered." *Commentary* (Dec. 1972): 69–77.

Howells, William Dean. *The Rise of Silas Lapham*. Ed. Don L. Cook. New York: Norton, 1982.

Hunter, James Davison. *Culture Wars: The Struggle to Define America*. New York: Basic, 1991.

Huntington, Samuel P. *The Clash of Civilizations and the Remaking of World Order*. New York: Simon, 1996.

Hutcheon, Linda. *A Poetics of Postmodernism: History, Theory, Fiction*. New York: Routledge, 1988.

Isikoff, Michael, and David Corn. *Hubris: The Inside Story of Spin, Scandal, and the Selling of the Iraq War.* New York: Crown, 2006.

Jackson, Tony. Archived e-mail discussion list post. 29 July 2005. <http://www2.cddc.vt.edu/ spoon-archives/postcolonial.archive/ postco_1995/postco_Jun.95>.

Jacobson, Sid, and Ernie Colón. *The 9/11 Report: A Graphic Adaptation.* New York: Hill, 2006.

Jameson, Fredric. "Periodizing the 60s." Sayres et al. 178–209.

———. *The Political Unconscious: Narrative as a Socially Symbolic Act.* Ithaca: Cornell UP, 1981.

———. "Postmodernism and Consumer Society." *The Anti-Aesthetic: Essays on Postmodern Culture.* Ed. Hall Foster. Port Townsend, WA: Bay Press, 1983. 111–25.

———. *Postmodernism: or, The Cultural Logic of Late Capitalism.* Durham: Duke UP, 1991.

Jameson, Fredric, and Masao Miyoshi, eds. *The Cultures of Globalization.* Durham: Duke UP, 1998.

Jazz. Dir. Ken Burns. PBS. 2001.

Joyce, Joyce A. "The Black Canon: Reconstructing Black American Literary Criticism." *New Literary History* 18.2 (1987): 335–44.

———. "'Who the Cap Fit': Unconsciousness and Unconscionableness in the Criticism of Houston A. Baker, Jr., and Henry Louis Gates, Jr." *New Literary History* 18.2 (1987): 371–84.

Kant, Immanuel. *Political Writings.* Trans. H. B. Nisbet. Ed. Hans Reiss. 2nd enl. ed. Cambridge: Cambridge UP, 1991.

Kaplan, Amy. "Homeland Insecurities: Transformations of Language and Space." Dudziak 55–69.

Kaplan, Robert. "Indian Country." *Wall Street Journal* 25 Sept. 2004. 5 Apr. 2006. <http://www.opinionjournal.com/extra/?id110005673>.

Kazin, Alfred. *Bright Book of Life: American Novelists and Storytellers from Hemingway to Mailer.* 1973. Notre Dame: U of Notre Dame P, 1980.

Kellner, Douglas. "9/11, Spectacles of Terror, and Media Manipulation: A Critique of Jihadist and Bush Media Politics." *Critical Discourse Studies* 1.1 (2004): 41–64.

Kennan, George. "Long Telegram." *National Security Archive.* <http:// www.gwu.edu/~nsarchiv/coldwar/documents/episode-1/kennan.htm>.

———. "The Sources of Soviet Conduct." *Foreign Affairs* 25 (July 1947): 575–76.

Kermode, Frank. *The Sense of an Ending: Studies in the Theory of Fiction: With a New Epilogue.* London: Oxford UP, 2000.

Knight, Peter. "Everything Is Connected: Underworld's Secret History of Paranoia." *Modern Fiction Studies* 45.3 (1999): 811–36.

Koppel, Ted. "Coming Home: Invisible Casualties." *Nightline* 16 Dec. 2004.

Krumholz, Linda J. "Reading and Insight in Toni Morrison's *Paradise*." *African American Review* 36.1 (Spring 2002): 21–34.

Kundera, Milan. *The Art of the Novel*. Trans. Linda Asher. New York: Harper, 1988.

Kurth, Peter. "The Dreamer of Brooklyn." Rev. of *The Fortress of Solitude*, by Jonathan Lethem. *Salon* 12 Sept. 2003. <http://dir.salon.com/story/books/feature/2003/09/12/lethem/index.html>.

Lacan, Jacques. *The Language of the Self: The Function of Language in Psychoanalysis*. Trans. Anthony Wilden. Baltimore: Johns Hopkins UP, 1981.

LaCapra, Dominick. *History and Memory after Auschwitz*. Ithaca: Cornell UP, 1998.

———. *History in Transit: Experience, Identity, Critical Theory*. Ithaca: Cornell UP, 2004.

———. *Representing the Holocaust: History, Theory, Trauma*. Ithaca: Cornell UP, 1994.

———. *Rethinking Intellectual History: Texts, Contexts, Language*. Ithaca: Cornell UP, 1983.

LeGoff, Jacques. *History and Memory*. Trans. Steven Rendall. Ed. Elizabeth Claman. New York: Columbia UP, 1992.

Lentricchia, Frank, ed. *Introducing Don DeLillo*. Durham: Duke UP, 1991.

Leonard, John. "The Black Album." *New York Review of Books* 20 Oct. 2005. <http://www.nybooks.com/articles/18352>.

———. "Crazy Age of Reason." *Nation* 12 May 1997: 65–68.

———. "Welcome to New Dork." *New York Review of Books* 7 Apr. 2005. 16 June 2006. <http://www.nybooks.com/articles/17897>.

Lethem, Jonathan. *The Fortress of Solitude*. New York: Doubleday, 2003.

———. "Out of Brooklyn." Interview with Matt Dellinger. *New Yorker* 28 July 2003. <http://www.newyorker.com/archive/2003/07/28/030728on_onlineonly01>.

Lévi-Strauss, Claude. *Structural Anthropology*. Trans. Claire Jacobson and Brooke Grundfest Schoepf. New York: Basic, 1963.

Lifton, Robert Jay. *Death in Life: Survivors of Hiroshima*. New York: Random, 1968.

———. *The Nazi Doctors: Medical Killing and the Psychology of Genocide*. New York: Basic, 1986.

Lifton, Robert Jay, and Greg Mitchell. *Hiroshima in America: A Half Century of Denial*. New York: Harper, 1996.

Linenthal, Edward T., and Tom Engelhardt, eds. *History Wars: The Enola Gay and Other Battles for the American Past*. New York: Holt, 1996.

Locke, Richard. "One of the Longest, Most Difficult, Most Ambitious Novels in Years." *New York Times Book Review* 11 Mar. 1973: 1–2+.

Lukács, Georg. *The Historical Novel*. Trans. Hannah Mitchell and Stanley Mitchell. Lincoln: U of Nebraska P, 1962.

———. *The Theory of the Novel*. Trans. Anna Bostock. Cambridge: MIT P, 1971.

Lyotard, Jean-François. *The Postmodern Condition: A Report on Knowledge*. Trans. Geoff Bennington and Brian Massumi. Minneapolis: U of Minnesota P, 1984.

Mailer, Norman. *The Armies of the Night: History as a Novel, The Novel as History*. New York: New American Library, 1968.

May, Elaine Tyler. "Echoes of the Cold War: The Aftermath of September 11." Dudziak 35–54.

McEwan, Ian. *Saturday*. New York: Talese, 2005.

McHale, Brian. *Postmodernist Fiction*. New York: Methuen, 1987.

McKay, Nellie Y. "An Interview with Toni Morrison." *Contemporary Literature* 24.4 (Winter, 1983): 413–29.

———. "Introduction." *Toni Morrison's "Beloved": A Casebook*. Ed. William L. Andrews and Nellie Y. McKay. New York: Oxford UP, 1999. 3–19.

McKeon, Michael. *The Origins of the English Novel, 1600–1740*. Baltimore: Johns Hopkins UP, 1987.

Melley, Timothy. "Postmodern Amnesia: Trauma and Forgetting in Tim O'Brien's *In the Lake of the Woods*." *Contemporary Literature* 44.1 (2003): 106–31.

Menand, Louis. "Entropology." Rev. of *Mason & Dixon*, by Thomas Pynchon. *New York Review of Books* 12 June 1997: 22–25.

———. "In a Strange Land." Rev. of *Hooking Up*, by Tom Wolfe. *New Yorker* 6 Nov. 2000: 94–97.

———. "The War between Men and Women." Rev. of *Pastoral*, by Toni Morrison. *New Yorker* 12 Jan. 1998: 78–82.

Mendelsohn, Daniel. "Mighty Hermaphrodite." Rev. of *Middlesex*, by Jeffrey Eugenides. *New York Review of Books* 7 Nov. 2002. 29 July 2005. <http://www.nybooks.com/articles/15794>.

Michael, Magali Cornier. "Re-Imagining Agency: Toni Morrison's *Paradise*." *African American Review* 36.4 (Winter 2002): 643–61.

Michaels, Walter Benn. *Our America: Nativism, Modernism, Pluralism.* Durham: Duke UP, 1995.

———. "Plots against America: Neoliberalism and Antiracism." *American Literary History* 18.2 (2006): 288–302.

———. *The Shape of the Signifier: 1967 to the End of History.* Princeton: Princeton UP, 2004.

Miller, Stephen Paul. *The Seventies Now: Culture as Surveillance.* Durham: Duke UP, 1999.

Mills, Nicolaus, ed. *Culture in an Age of Money: The Legacy of the 1980s in America.* Chicago: Dee, 1990.

Moody, Rick. "Surveyors of the Enlightenment." *Atlantic* July 1997. <http://www.atlantic.com/97jul/pynchon.htm>.

Morrison, Toni. *Beloved.* 1987. New York: Plume, 1988.

———. *The Bluest Eye.* 1970. New York: Penguin, 1993.

———. Interview with Charlie Rose. *Charlie Rose.* PBS. 20 Jan. 1998.

———. *Jazz.* New York: Knopf, 1992.

———. "On 'The Radiance of the King.'" *New York Review of Books* 9 Aug. 2001: 18–20.

———. *Paradise.* New York: Knopf, 1998.

———. *Playing in the Dark.* Cambridge: Harvard UP, 1992.

———. *Race-ing Justice, En-gendering Power: Essays on Anita Hill, Clarence Thomas, and the Construction of Social Reality.* New York: Pantheon, 1992.

———. "Rootedness: The Ancestor as Foundation." *Black Women Writers: A Critical Evaluation.* Ed. Mari Evans. New York: Anchor, 1984.

———. *Sula.* 1974. New York: Knopf, 1993.

———. *Song of Solomon.* 1977. New York: Knopf, 1978.

———. *Tar Baby.* 1981. Plume, 1982.

———. "What the Black Woman Thinks about Women's Lib." *New York Times Magazine* 22 Aug. 1971: 14–15+.

Morrison, Toni, and Claudia Brodsky Lacour, eds. *Birth of a Nation'hood: Gaze, Script, and Spectacle in the O. J. Simpson Case.* New York: Pantheon, 1996.

Muggli, Mark Z. "The Poetics of Joan Didion's Journalism." *American Literature* 59.3 (1987): 402–21.

Mxyzptlk, Mr. "Great Expectations." *Suck* 28 July 1997. <http://www.suck.com/daily/97/07/28/daily.html>.

Nadel, Alan. *Containment Culture: American Narratives, Postmodernism, and the Atomic Age.* Durham: Duke UP, 1995.

National Commission on Terrorist Attacks. *The 9/11 Commission Report: Final Report of the National Commission on Terrorist Attacks upon the United States.* New York: Norton, 2004.

Noon, David. "The Triumph of Death: National Security and Imperial Erasures in Don DeLillo's *Underworld.*" *Canadian Review of American Studies* 37.1 (2007): 83–110.

Norris, Frank. *McTeague.* New York: Vintage, 1990.

Nowlin, Michael. "Toni Morrison's *Jazz* and the Racial Dreams of the American Writer." *American Literature* 71.1 (1999): 151–74.

Oates, Joyce Carol. "The Mutants." *I Am No One You Know.* New York: Ecco, 2004. 218–88.

O'Brien, Tim. *Going After Cacciato.* New York: Doubleday, 1978.

———. *In the Lake of the Woods.* Boston: Houghton, 1994.

———. *The Things They Carried.* Boston: Houghton, 1990.

O'Neill, Joseph. *Netherland.* New York: Pantheon, 2008.

"Oprah Taps Eugenides." *Publishers' Weekly* 5 June 2007. 17 June 2007. <http://www.publishersweekly.com/article/CA6448998.html>.

O'Rourke, Meghan. "Jonathan Lethem's *The Fortress of Solitude.*" *Slate* 7 October 2003. <http://www.slate.com/id/2089295/entry/2089453/>.

Page, Philip. "Furrowing All the Brows: Interpretation and the Transcendent in Toni Morrison's *Paradise.*" *African American Review* 35.4 (2001): 637–49.

Parrish, Timothy. "After Henry Adams: Rewriting History in Joan Didion's *Democracy.*" *Critique: Studies in Contemporary Fiction* 47.2 (2006): 167–84.

———. "The End of Identity: Philip Roth's Jewish *American Pastoral.*" Halio and Siegel 131–50.

———. *From the Civil War to the Apocalypse: Postmodern History and American Fiction.* Amherst: U Massachussets P, 2008.

Patterson, James T. *Grand Expectations: The United States, 1945–1975.* New York: Oxford UP, 1996.

Pearl Harbor. Dir. Michael Bay. Touchstone, 2001.

Perloff, Marjorie. "Modernism without Modernists: A Response to Walter Benn Michaels." *Modernism/Modernity* 3.3 (1996): 99–105.

Peterson, Nancy J. *Against Amnesia: Contemporary Women Writers and the Crises of Historical Memory.* Philadelphia: U of Pennsylvania P, 2001.

Podhoretz, Norman. "The Adventures of Philip Roth." *Commentary* Oct. 1998: 25–36.

Posnock, Ross. *Color and Culture: Black Writers and the Making of the Modern Intellectual.* Cambridge: Harvard UP, 1998.

———. *Philip Roth's Rude Truth: The Art of Immaturity*. Princeton: Princeton UP, 2006.

Pynchon, Thomas. *The Crying of Lot 49*. New York: Harper, 1966.

———. *Gravity's Rainbow*. New York: Penguin, 1973.

———. "A Journey into the Mind of Watts." *New York Times Magazine* 12 June 1966: 34–35+.

———. *Mason & Dixon*. New York: Holt, 1997.

———. *V*. New York: Harper, 1963.

———. *Vineland*. New York: Penguin, 1990.

Reinert, Thomas. "Joan Didion and Political Irony." *Raritan* 15.3 (1996): 122–36.

Ricciardi, Alessia. "Lightness and Gravity: Calvino, Pynchon, and Postmodernity." *MLN* 114 (1999): 1062–77.

Richardson, Samuel. *Pamela; or, Virtue Rewarded*. London: Penguin, 1985.

Ricoeur, Paul. *History and Truth*. Trans. Charles A. Kelbley. Evanston: Northwestern UP, 1965.

Robin, Corey. "Remembrance of Empires Past: 9/11 and the End of the Cold War." Schrecker, *Cold War* 274–97.

Romero, Channette: "Creating the Beloved Community: Religion, Race, and Nation in Toni Morrison's *Paradise*." *African American Review* 39.3 (Fall 2005): 415–30.

Rorty, Richard. *Achieving Our Country: Leftist Thought in Twentieth-Century America*. Cambridge: Harvard UP, 1998.

Roth, Philip. *American Pastoral*. Boston: Houghton, 1997.

———. *The Anatomy Lesson*. New York: Farrar, 1983.

———. *The Counterlife*. 1986. New York: Penguin, 1988.

———. *The Dying Animal*. Boston: Houghton, 2001.

———. *The Facts*. 1988. New York: Penguin, 1989.

———. *The Ghost Writer*. New York: Farrar, 1979.

———. *Goodbye, Columbus*. 1959. New York: Bantam, 1968.

———. *The Human Stain*. Boston: Houghton, 2000.

———. *I Married a Communist*. Boston: Houghton, 1998.

———. Interview with Jean-Louis Turlin. *Independent* 15 Oct. 2002. 21 Oct. 2002. <http://independent.co.news.uk/people/profiles/story .jsp?story=342912>.

———. *Letting Go*. 1962. New York: Touchstone, 1991.

———. *Patrimony: A True Story*. New York: Simon, 1991.

———. *The Plot against America*. Boston: Houghton, 2001.

———. *Portnoy's Complaint*. 1969. New York: Bantam, 1981.

———. *Reading Myself and Others*. 1975. New York: Penguin, 1985.

———. *Sabbath's Theater.* Boston: Houghton, 1995.

———. *Shop Talk: A Writer and His Colleagues and Their Work.* Boston: Houghton, 2001.

———. *Zuckerman Bound.* New York: Farrar, 1985.

———. *Zuckerman Unbound.* London: Cape, 1981.

Rothberg, Michael. "Against Zero-Sum Logic: A Response to Walter Benn Michaels." *American Literary History* 18.2 (Summer 2006): 303–11.

Rowlandson, Mary. *The Sovereignty and Goodness of God.* Ed. Neal Salisbury. Boston: Bedford, 1997.

Royal, Derek Parker. "Fictional Realms of Possibility: Reimagining the Ethnic Subject in Philip Roth's *American Pastoral.*" *Studies in American Jewish Literature* 20 (2001): 1–16.

———. "Plotting the Frames of Subjectivity: Identity, Death, and Narrative in Philip Roth's *The Human Stain.*" *Contemporary Literature* 47.1 (2006): 114–40.

Rubin-Dorsky, Jeffrey. "Honor Thy Father." *Raritan* 11 (1992): 137–45.

Safer, Elaine B. *Mocking the Age: The Later Novels of Philip Roth.* Albany: State U of New York P, 2006.

Sanger, David. "War Figures Honored with Medal of Freedom." *New York Times* 15 Dec. 2004: sec. A.

Saving Private Ryan. Dir. Steven Spielberg. Dreamworks, 1998.

Sayres, Sohnya, Anders Stephanson, Stanley Aronowitz, and Fredric Jameson, eds. *The 60s without Apology.* Minneapolis: U of Minnesota P, 1984.

Schaub, Thomas Hill. *American Fiction in the Cold War.* Madison: U of Wisconsin P, 1991.

Schivelbusch, Wolfgang. *The Culture of Defeat: On National Trauma, Mourning, and Recovery.* New York: Metropolitan, 2003.

Schlesinger, Arthur. *The Disuniting of America: Reflections on a Multicultural Society.* Rev. ed. New York: Norton, 1998.

Schrecker, Ellen. "Cold War Triumphalism and the Real Cold War." Schrecker 1–24.

———, ed. *Cold War Triumphalism: The Misuse of History after the Fall of Communism.* New York: New Press, 2004.

Schur, Richard. "Dream or Nightmare? Roth, Morrison, and America." *Philip Roth Studies* 1.1 (2005): 19–36.

———. "Locating *Paradise* in the Post–Civil Rights Era: Toni Morrison and Critical Race Theory." *Contemporary Literature* 45.2 (2004): 276–99.

Schwartz, Herman. "Civil Rights and the Reagan Court." Mills 130–41.

Scott, A. O. "In Search of the Best." *New York Times* 21 May 2006. <http://www.nytimes.com/2006/05/21/books/review/scott-essay.html>.

———. "When Dylan Met Mingus." Rev. of *The Fortress of Solitude*. *New York Times* 21 Sept. 2003. http://query.nytimes.com/gst/fullpage.html?res=950DE1D6103BF932A1575AC0A9659C8B63>.

Shane, Scott. "A Deluge of Troubled Soldiers Is in the Offing, Experts Predict." *New York Times* 16 Dec. 2004: A1.

Shechner, Mark. *Up Society's Ass, Copper: Rereading Philip Roth*. Madison: U of Wisconsin P, 2003.

Sherry, Michael S. "Patriotic Orthodoxy and American Decline." Linenthal and Engelhardt 97–114.

Shklovsky, Viktor. *Theory of Prose*. Chicago: Dalkey, 1991.

Shostak, Debra. *Philip Roth—Countertexts, Counterlives*. Columbia: U of South Carolina P, 2004.

Sontag, Susan. "Talk of the Town." *New Yorker* 24 Sept. 2001: 32.

Spanos, William V. "The Detective and the Boundary: Some Notes on the Postmodern Literary Imagination." *Boundary* 2 1.1 (Fall 1972): 147–68.

Spiegelman, Art. *In the Shadow of No Towers*. New York: Pantheon, 2004.

Stave, Shirley A. "The Master's Tools: Morrison's *Paradise* and the Problem of Christianity." *Toni Morrison and the Bible: Contested Intertextualities*. New York: Lang, 2006. 215–31.

Stendhal. *Red and Black*. Trans. and ed. Robert M. Adams. New York: Norton, 1969.

Sterne, Laurence. *The Life and Opinions of Tristram Shandy, Gentleman*. London: Allen, 1985.

Stiglitz, Joseph E. *Globalization and Its Discontents*. New York: Norton, 2002.

Storace, Patricia. "The Scripture of Utopia." *New York Review of Books* 11 June 1998. <http://www.nybooks.com/articles/831>.

Tager, Michael. "The Political Vision of Joan Didion's *Democracy*." *Critique* 31.3 (1990): 173–84.

Tanenbaum, Laura. "Reading Roth's Sixties." *Studies in American Jewish Literature* 23 (2004): 41–54.

Tanner, Tony. *The American Mystery: American Literature from Emerson to DeLillo*. Cambridge: Cambridge UP, 2000.

Tapper, Jake. "The Salon Interview: Bill Maher." *Salon.com* 11 Dec. 2002. <http://archive.salon.com/people/interview/2002/12/11/maher/index.html>.

Tate, Claudia, ed. *Black Women Writers at Work*. New York: Continuum, 1983.

Taylor, Charles. *Multiculturalism: Examining the Politics of Recognition*. Ed. Amy Gutmann. Princeton: Princeton UP, 1994.

Terry, Jennifer: "A New World Religion? Creolisation and Candomblé in Toni Morrison's *Paradise*." *Toni Morrison and the Bible: Contested Intertextualities*. Ed. Shirley A. Stave. New York: Lang, 2006. 192–214.

The Thin Red Line. Dir. Terence Malick. 20th Century Fox, 1998.

Thomas, Brook. "Walter Benn Michaels and the New Historicism: Where's the Difference?" *Boundary 2* 18.1 (Spring 1991): 18–59.

Thomas, Evan, Carolyn Lesh, and Melissa Ludtke. "Assault on Affirmative Action." *Time* 25 Feb. 1985. <http://www.time.com/time/magazine/article/0,9171,961192-2,00.html>.

Thwaites, Tony. "Facing Pages: On Response, a Response to Steven Helmling." *Postmodern Culture* 6.1 (1995). 17 May 2006. <http://proxy .mul.missouri.edu:2200/ journals/postmodern_culture/v006/6 .1thwaites.html>.

Trilling, Diana. Rev. of *My Father and Myself*, by J. R. Ackerley, and *Portnoy's Complaint*, by Philip Roth. *Harper's* Aug. 1969: 90+.

Trumpener, Katie. *Bardic Nationalism: The Romantic Novel and the British Empire*. Princeton: Princeton UP, 1997.

Updike, John. *Rabbit at Rest*. New York: Knopf, 1990.

———. *Terrorist*. New York: Knopf, 2006.

Voltaire. *Candide, or Optimism: A Fresh Translation, Backgrounds, Criticism*. Trans. and ed. Robert M. Adams. 2nd ed. New York: Norton, 1991.

Walker, Melissa. *Black Women's Novels in the Wake of the Civil Rights Movement, 1966–1989*. New Haven: Yale UP, 1991.

The Wallflowers. *Bringing Down the Horse*. Interscope Records, 1996.

Walter, Jess. *The Zero*. New York: Harper, 2006.

Watt, Ian. *The Rise of the Novel: Studies in DeFoe, Richardson, and Fielding*. Middlesex: Penguin, 1957.

Weber, Max. *The Protestant Ethic and the Spirit of Capitalism*. Trans. Talcott Parsons. New York: Scribner's, 1976.

Weiner, Tim, and Barbara Crossette. "George F. Kennan Dies at 101." *New York Times* 18 Mar. 2005. <http://select.nytimes.com/search/restricted/article?res=F20911FE3A580C7B8DDDAA0894DD404482>.

"What Is the Best Work of American Fiction of the Last 25 Years?" *New York Times* 21 May 2006. <http://nytimes.com/2006/05/21/books/fiction-25-years.html>.

White, Hayden. *Metahistory: The Historical Imagination in Nineteenth-Century Europe*. Baltimore: Johns Hopkins UP, 1975.

———. *Tropics of Discourse: Essays in Cultural Criticism*. Baltimore: Johns Hopkins UP, 1986.

Widdowson, Peter. "The American Dream Refashioned: History, Politics, and Gender in Toni Morrison's *Paradise*." *Journal of American Studies* 35 (2001): 2+.

Williams, Jeffrey. "The Death of Deconstruction, the End of Theory, and Other Ominous Rumors." *Narrative* 4 (1996): 17–35.

———. "The New Belletrism." *Style* (Fall 1999): 414–42.

———. "The Posttheory Generation." Herman, *Day Late* 25–44.

Willis, Susan. *Portents of the Real: A Primer for Post-9/11 America*. London: Verso, 2005.

Wittgenstein, Ludwig. *Tractatus Logico-Philosophicus*. Trans. David Pears and Brian McGuinness. London: Routledge, 2001.

Wolfe, Tom. *Hooking Up*. New York: Farrar, 2000.

———. *A Man in Full*. New York: Farrar, 1998.

———. "Stalking the Billion-Footed Beast." *Harper's Magazine* Nov. 1989: 45–56.

Wolfe, Tom, and E. W. Johnson, eds. *The New Journalism*. New York: Harper, 1973.

Wood, Michael. "Pynchon's *Mason & Dixon*." *Raritan* 17.4 (Spring 1998): 120–30.

Woolf, Virginia. *To the Lighthouse*. 1927. San Diego: Harcourt, 1981.

Wright, Richard. "How Bigger Was Born." *Native Son*. New York: Harper, 1993.

———. *Uncle Tom's Children*. 1938. New York: Harper, 1969.

Young, Marilyn B. "Ground Zero: Enduring War." Dudziak 10–34.

Yukins, Elizabeth. "Bastard Daughters and the Possession of History in *Corregidora* and *Paradise*." *Signs* 28.1 (Fall 2002): 221–47.

Žižek, Slavoj. *The Sublime Object of Ideology*. London: Verso, 1989.

INDEX

Clinton, William Jefferson, 11, 12
closure: collapse of Soviet union
as, 122; false, 137, 160, 185; historical, 132, 150–51, 170, 184, 187;
narrative, 123–24, 128, 134–38,
140, 147, 149, 160–61, 172–73, 183,
195; and theory, 158–59, 166–67,
187; and trauma, 130, 161, 170–73,
186
Cold War, 4–11, 29, 54, 165, 196–97,
199; after, 27, 54, 57, 94, 161, 191–
92, 198; and democracy, 145; as
end of 1990s, 4; end of, 1, 3, 4,
7–12, 28, 34, 54, 63, 117–18, 123,
131–32, 143, 157–58, 172–73, 187,
191–92, 195, 199, 201; foreign
policy during, 121–23, 129–30,
150–53; and rise of New Criticism, 131
Colón, Ernie, 192–93
conservatism, 11, 63, 82
conspiracy, 49, 51–52, 54, 139, 145,
151
containment, 19, 117, 121–22, 151
contingency, 158–59, 168, 170–73,
181–86, 195
Contract with America, 150
Cooke, Sam, 176
Crow, Jim, 46
Crying of Lot 48 (Pynchon), 48,
52, 53
Cuban missile crisis, 5, 191, 197
culture wars, 9, 12, 94, 99, 117–18,
157

"Declarations of Independence"
(Derrida), 167
DeFoe, Daniel, 25
DeLillo, Don, 17, 137, 153, 191–202
democracy, 7, 56, 145, 150, 152, 158
Democracy (Didion), 143–47, 149

DeMott, Benjamin, 193
Derrida, Jacques, 19, 166–67,
182–83, 186
Dialectic of Enlightenment
(Adorno and Horkheimer), 37
Dickstein, Morris, 72, 89, 131
Diderot, Denis, 25, 36
Didion, Joan, 3, 138–53
Dreiser, Theodore, 24
Duyfhuizen, Bernard, 57
Dylan, Bob, 10, 174
Dylan, Jakob, 10

Eden, 87, 94; America as new, 15,
39, 41, 45, 50, 64, 71
Eisenhower, Dwight D., 197
Elias, Amy, 22–23, 26
Eliot, T. S., 141
Ellis, Bret Easton, 116
empire, 56–57, 186
emplotment, 22
Enlightenment, 14, 31, 34, 36–39,
43–44, 48, 50, 53, 55
Enola Gay, 9
entropy, 50–51
essentialism, 96, 100, 115
Eugenides, Jeffrey, 4, 15, 159–73,
186, 187
exceptionalism, 13, 15, 28, 55

fabula, 147, 149, 198, 200
Facts (Roth), 78, 80
Felman, Shoshana, 129
Fiedler, Leslie, 16, 158
Fixed Ideas (Didion), 152
Flaubert, Gustave, 67, 79, 88
Foley, Barbara, 21
Fortress of Solitude (Lethem), 4
Foucault, Michel, 21, 22
Frankfurt School, 19, 37
Franks, Tommy, 124

French Revolution, 37
Freud, Sigmund, 128, 132, 161, 202
Friedlander, Saul, 129
From the Civil War to the Apocalypse (Parrish), 27
Fukuyama, Francis, 4, 7, 27, 28, 130
future anterior, 166–68, 201

Gaddis, John Lewis, 5, 121
Gass, William, 25
Gates, Henry Louis, Jr., 99–100
Gaye, Marvin, 175
genealogy, 24, 95–96, 106–08, 115, 118, 162
Genette, Gérard, 19
Ghost Writer (Roth), 80
Gingrich, Newt, 12
Gitlin, Todd, 9
globalization, 13, 56
Goldmann, Lucien, 19, 24
Goodwin, Doris Kearns, 10
Gordon, Andrew, 82
grands recits, 20
Gravity's Rainbow (Pynchon), 1, 35, 38, 48, 51, 53
great migration, 95, 106
Guercino, 86
Gulf War, 4, 9, 129, 132

Habermas, Jürgen, 31
Haditha, 134
Haley, Alex, 107
Hardwick, Elizabeth, 143, 149
Harris, Middleton A., 105
Hartman, Geoffrey, 128
Hassan, Ihab, 16, 158
Hawkes, John, 17
Hawthorne, Nathaniel, 24
Herman, Judith, 129
Herman, Peter, 131

Hill, Anita, 11, 99
Hiroshima, 9, 10, 17, 194
historical narrative, 4, 29, 63, 123, 134, 149, 161, 172, 187, 196, 202
historical novel, 14–15, 21–23, 26, 63, 96, 108, 159, 163, 171
historical trauma, 129–31, 159, 170
historicism, 4, 131
historiographic metafiction, 3, 21, 22, 171
history, 10, 14, 22, 24, 27, 39, 50–54, 56, 75, 83, 91, 94–96, 99, 117, 126, 131–32, 159, 161, 165, 171, 184, 186, 199; African American, 93, 106–07; American, 6–7, 9, 11–13, 15, 27–29, 40–41, 46, 48, 50, 53, 54, 57, 63, 64, 71, 84, 94, 106, 115, 122, 127, 129, 135, 137, 138, 151, 157, 165, 191–92; ampersandic, 56; of civil rights, 107; of criticism and theory, 18–19, 21–22, 131–32; disappearance of a sense of, 20–21; end of, 1, 3, 4, 7, 28–29, 116, 129–31, 150, 173, 192; of foreign policy, 121–22, 152; intellectual, 101; knowledge of, 2, 22–23, 26, 116, 137; literary, 16, 23–24, 53, 93, 171, 187; models of, 14, 137–38, 191; narrative construction of, 3, 123, 159, 166, 170–72, 181, 196, 201; national, 13–14, 163, 181; "new," 22; of the novel, 15, 25–26; of race relations, 98; social, 16, 22, 25; study of, 13, 21–22
History in Transit (LaCapra), 161
Holzer, Jenny, 155
Horkheimer, Max, 37
Howe, Irving, 79
Howells, William Dean, 72
Huntington, Samuel, 28, 130, 134

Vonnegut, Kurt, 17

Wallflowers, 10
Watergate, 17, 86–87, 165
Weber, Max, 37
White, Hayden, 22
White Album (Didion), 119, 141–43
White House Iraq Group, 192, 194–95
White Noise (DeLillo), 201
Wittgenstein, Ludwig, 31, 51
Wolfe, Tom, 17–18

women's movement, 11
Wood, Michael, 45, 49, 54
World Trade Center, 3, 194
World Trade Organization, 12
World War II, 71, 129, 151

Yeats, William Butler, 104
Y2K, 184

Zuckerman Bound (Roth), 81
Zuckerman Unbound (Roth), 80–81